Please return to:

University Relations

HROD Library

Praise for *The Firefly Effect*

"Who knew that learning about fireflies could shed so much light on the creativity inherent in all of us and the importance of unleashing that creativity in every team member to drive maximum team and organizational success! I found *The Firefly Effect* to be a great how-to handbook focused on inspirational and collaborative leadership. The wealth of practical, tried-and-true methods, as well as new ideas, suggestions, techniques and tools shared by Kimberly can be used to help leaders at all levels (even those who don't yet see themselves as leaders). They can leverage the creativity in themselves and others to achieve new heights of innovation, more effective team relationships and interactions, and increased business and personal performance. This book is a must read for anyone interested in 'becoming the change we want to see'."

—Denise L. Billups
Director, Sales Learning
IBM Corporation

"At a time when everyone is looking for an extra something to win in the market, *The Firefly Effect* provides that practical spark that teams need. Kimberly's passion and practicality come through in a highly usable guide to creating effective teams."

—Timothy E. Sullivan
Corporate Executive Vice President & Chief Information Officer
SunTrust Banks, Inc.

"*The Firefly Effect* is a must-read for anyone who manages teams or is a member of one. Author Kimberly Douglas literally shines a light on the importance of appreciating differences, recognizing accountability, and embracing conflict as a force for change. Implementing the techniques in this book will allow any business—big or small—to thrive."

—Laura Grams
Director, CDO Global Learning Solutions
Cisco Systems

"*The Firefly Effect* uses the childhood memories so many of us share of playing with friends to do something we thought was amazing as a metaphor to empower leaders to build, and be a part of, more collaborative, creative, and successful teams. Douglas draws on her experiences, successes, and challenges working with a great variety of organizations to make this book a practical and realistic guide for leaders to identify and use the strengths of team members to catalyze and inspire them to achieve their strategic goals."

—Kelly Caffarelli
President
The Home Depot Foundation

"The author doesn't just define management theories but instead uses relevant and interesting personal and professional experiences to highlight and inform the reader of the key points on how to lead a team. The section on the 'new' role of the team leader was particularly interesting and would be useful for any team leader in increasing the creativity and ultimately the results of a team. This book is very entertaining while also providing great advice·of how to be an effective leader."

—Bill Delahanty
Senior Vice President, Human Resources
ING

"I've had first-hand experience with Kimberly and her approach to building teams and inspiring creativity. This book builds a strong business case for establishing trust and leveraging creative abrasion. Kimberly speaks directly to you whether you are the team leader or team member. She understands that high performing teams deliver results! You'll need a highlighter!"

—Jill Wilson
Group Vice President, Human Resources
Macy's

"Kimberly Douglas' book is concerned with developing teams of enthusiastic, collaborative, and creative problem solvers in the workplace. Easy to read, informative, and exceedingly charming, Ms. Douglas opens most of the book's 21 chapters (6 sections) with a firefly story. She uses the natural history of this exceptional insect to preface her 'stories' about (ordinary) creativity and cooperativeness in the workplace, and other subjects as well. Transport yourself to your childhood; picture yourself in a field at night with net, flashlight, and collecting jar. You first have to figure out how to do it. Then, you work with your friends to capture these flying insects. The firefly field itself speaks to cooperativeness. The field contains flying males and landed females cooperating in a mating flash code. In a few North American species, the flying and flashing of 1000s of males occurs at the same (milliseconds) time. This cooperative flashing keeps the males from confusing the female, for they maintain the species code through their synchrony. Or, move to Southeast Asia, where the male fireflies are stationary. The synchrony is timed precisely. But, there is no conductor, no leader. This is a self-assembling array in which everyone stimulates everyone else as the males all adopt the same rhythm. Kimberly Douglas' book will thrill you with the fun and creativity of fireflies in your childhood and help you to transport that creative energy into the workplace."

—Dr. Jonathan Copeland
Professor of Biology
Georgia Southern University

"A must read for all human resources generalists, organizational effectiveness and talent management professionals, executive coaches, and leaders wanting to enhance the productivity of their workforce."

—Mary T. Steele
Director, Executive Compensation
Delta Air Lines, Inc.

"If you know your team needs a jolt of creativity, but you don't think of yourself as a creative leader—The Firefly Effect is a must read! Kimberly Douglas uses a story we all know—catching fireflies to light up a summer evening—to remind us how to 'fire up' our team's energy and problem solving skills. Kimberly Douglas is right—we all have synchronous fireflies in our own backyard—we just need to look for them!"

—Nancy Vepraskas
Vice President, Human Resources
Genuine Parts Company

"True to its title, Douglas leverages creativity in this insightful guide that will appeal to both left and right-brain thinkers. Leaders everywhere will welcome this new approach that taps into innate human behavior to assist them in gaining greater productivity from their teams. A well-written, practical and imagery-laden reference for anyone who's ever sought non-traditional, yet intuitive ways to release the logjam of blocked team thinking."

—Dianne Bernez
Senior Vice President, Corporate Communications
Equifax Inc.

"A management team as a whole is usually smarter than any one member thinking and acting individually. Enabling individual contributions of creativity, while at the same time ensuring the team's 'creation' is delivered on time, within scope, and able to be executed, can be a difficult task for a leader. The Firefly Effect is a practical and entertaining guide for leaders to do just that."

—Rob Schreiner, MD, FACP
Executive Medical Director, The Southeast Permanente Medical Group
Kaiser Permanente Georgia

"Seeds of creativity exist everywhere, but they need a nurturing environment to grow; using the principles outlined by Kimberly in The Firefly Effect can help ignite innovation in just about any team."

—Chris Powell
Executive Vice President, Human Resources
Scripps Networks, home of HGTV, Food Network, DIY Network, Fine Living Network and Great American Country (GAC)

The Firefly Effect

The Firefly Effect

Build Teams That
CAPTURE CREATIVITY
and
CATAPULT RESULTS

KIMBERLY DOUGLAS

WILEY

JOHN WILEY & SONS, INC.

Published by John Wiley & Sons, Inc., Hoboken, New Jersey.
Published simultaneously in Canada.

Wiley and the Wiley logo are trademarks or registered trademarks of John Wiley &
Sons, Inc. and/or its affiliates in the United States/or other countries, and may
not be used without written permission. HBDI, Herrmann Brain Dominance
Instrument, and Whole Brain are trademarks or registered trademarks of
Herrmann International and may not be used without written permission. All
other trademarks are the property of their respective owners. John Wiley & Sons,
Inc. is not associated with any product or vendor mentioned in the book.

No part of this publication may be reproduced, stored in a retrieval system, or
transmitted in any form or by any means, electronic, mechanical, photocopying,
recording, scanning, or otherwise, except as permitted under Section 107 or 108
of the 1976 United States Copyright Act, without either the prior written
permission of the Publisher, or authorization through payment of the appropriate
per-copy fee to the Copyright Clearance Center, Inc., 222 Rosewood Drive,
Danvers, MA 01923, (978) 750-8400, fax (978) 646-8600, or on the web at www
.copyright.com. Requests to the Publisher for permission should be addressed
to the Permissions Department, John Wiley & Sons, Inc., 111 River Street,
Hoboken, NJ 07030, (201) 748-6011, fax (201) 748-6008, or online at
http://www.wiley.com/go/permissions.

Limit of Liability/Disclaimer of Warranty: While the publisher and author have
used their best efforts in preparing this book, they make no representations or
warranties with respect to the accuracy or completeness of the contents of this
book and specifically disclaim any implied warranties of merchantability or
fitness for a particular purpose. No warranty may be created or extended by sales
representatives or written sales materials. The advice and strategies contained
herein may not be suitable for your situation. You should consult with a
professional where appropriate. Neither the publisher nor author shall be liable
for any loss of profit or any other commercial damages, including but not limited
to special, incidental, consequential, or other damages.

For general information on our other products and services or for technical
support, please contact our Customer Care Department within the United States
at (800) 762-2974, outside the United States at (317) 572-3993 or fax (317) 572-
4002.

Wiley also publishes its books in a variety of electronic formats. Some content that
appears in print may not be available in electronic books. For more information
about Wiley products, visit our web site at www.wiley.com.

Library of Congress Cataloging-in-Publication Data:

Douglas, Kimberly, 1958-
    The firefly effect : build teams that capture creativity and catapult
results / by Kimberly Douglas.
        p. cm.
    ISBN 978-0-470-43832-9 (cloth)
    1. Teams in the workplace. 2. Leadership. 3. Creative ability in business.
I. Title.
    HD66.D675 2009
    658.4'022–dc22
                                                                2008054903

Printed in the United States of America

10 9 8 7 6 5 4 3 2 1

Contents

Acknowledgments

I will always be amazed by and very grateful to those wonderful individuals I have had the pleasure of working with throughout the years, who sparked my creative urge to take this journey . . . and the many who helped my vision of *The Firefly Effect* to become a reality. On this path I encountered . . .

- The wonderful individuals for whom I have such respect and gratitude, who blur the line between client and colleague—Bo Adams, Kelly Caffarelli, Tom Darrow, Halle Holland, Henrietta King, Kathy O'Hara, Janet Parker, Rob Payne, Haven Riviere, Rob Schreiner, Brad Shaw, Elizabeth Spence, Nancy Vepraskas, Fred Wacker, and Ed Wolff.
- Amazing thought leaders who shared their provocative insights, and I hope made me a better resource to my clients. I personally thank you . . . Marshall Goldsmith, Pat Lencioni, Don Clifton, and Marcus Buckingham.
- The many people who were there when this book was just the flicker of an idea—Jennifer Kahnweiler, who first encouraged me to believe I had a book in me . . . Sam Horn, without whom the concept and the title would never have been . . . Marilynn Mobley, for her engaging and brilliant mind.

- Matt Holt, my publisher, who together with my editor, Shannon Vargo, first saw the potential of *The Firefly Effect*, and to Christine Moore and the rest of the dedicated team of professionals at Wiley, who incredibly grasped the creative magical metaphor of the fireflies and what they could signify to a whole business community trying to improve their teams' capacity and capability.

- My many colleagues in SHRM and NSA, who have so freely shared their knowledge and expertise with me.

- My parents, Jeanne and Shelby Clark, and the rest of the members of our close-knit family (Debbie, Barbara, Bob, Van, Melanie, and Dorothy), who received (lived through!) regular updates on my book's progress, always encouraging me that this was possible and that I really could do it.

- The rest of my extended family, with whom I first experienced the joy and fascination of coming together to chase fireflies which led to my passion for bringing teams together in the true spirit of collaboration and creativity.

And above all, I wish to thank my husband, D.K., who responded with an emphatic and loving "yes" when I asked if he thought I should write this book . . . and then worked side-by-side with me to make it an accomplishment of which I could be proud. Both you and our beautiful firefly of a daughter, Madison, encouraged, supported, and uplifted me. You fended for yourselves on more occasions than I would like to remember . . . all so that I could fulfill this dream. I can never thank you enough, yet I will spend the rest of our years together trying.

Part I

Rediscover Your Creative Spark

Chapter One

What Is the Firefly Effect?

Do you remember . . .

> *. . . the magic of a childhood summer evening?*
> *. . . catching fireflies with your friends?*
> *. . . watching in awe as they lit up the night?*

The Firefly Effect will change how you discover and apply creativity within your team to get results. A lone firefly—like the lone genius—does not ignite the imagination of others. It takes the brilliant light of many, and the creative effort of the entire team, to truly spark innovation with impact. You will learn about proven tools and techniques that have already generated qualitative and quantitative results for hundreds of teams in such companies as Coca-Cola, Home Depot, and AT&T. The use of the "firefly hunt" metaphor—as well as facts about these fascinating creatures—along with actual client examples will make the process easy to understand, to remember, and to achieve.

So what exactly *is* the Firefly Effect? Well, it is the behavior on display anytime you see children chase fireflies. You might notice that:

- Few children chase fireflies alone. The excitement comes from the sharing of effort and results with others.
- Everyone is clear on what the goal is—to catch fireflies—and enthusiasm remains high, because their target is so well understood and so simple.
- Each individual knows his or her task. No one needs—or wants—a dictating leader.
- Children do not criticize one another on a good firefly hunt. Everyone is clearly giving his or her best effort.
- The group eagerly seeks out new and better ways to get to realize a successful result.
- In the end, there is joy in what they accomplished together.

This, in essence, is the Firefly Effect. It is first about *the individual*—how every one of us can rediscover our unique and creative talents and best apply these to enhance the group's experience. Second, it is about *the leader*—how to be an almost invisible role model for inspiring others to do their best work. Third, it is about *the team*—using their individual talents collectively to focus on the critical business challenges and opportunities, instead of focusing their attention inward on petty personal differences. Finally, it is about *the organization*—having achieved powerful results as one team, then becoming a spark for the change that's needed in other parts of the company so that you're all ultimately working with a one-team mind-set.

Before we go further, I should clarify what I mean by creativity, and the scope of what we are undertaking here. My office is filled with books I have read on developing wacky, brainstorming prompts and driving organizational creativity. While many of these contain great tips and tools for discovering new product ideas—and I have used them with marketing teams for that very purpose—regular business teams focus most often on finding effective ways to capitalize on business opportunities and solve tough challenges. I am not trying to incite a creativity revolution across entire companies. I merely want to provide tools that can help guide you down a path that will dramatically improve your team's effectiveness.

Your time is valuable and limited. If you lead teams, my promise to you is that reading this book will be worth your while. I know that this is a bold promise; yet I choose to make it, because I have written the book with you in mind. Team leaders—along with aspiring team leaders and ambitious team members—will find new insights and approaches that will make you even more effective in your role. Your entire team will benefit from reading this book and together applying what you learn.

To quote Samuel Johnson, "People need to be reminded more often than they need to be instructed." My hope is to remind you, in meaningful and memorable ways, of those unique differences that truly distinguish the very best aspects of powerful teams. These things are not hard to understand, but will require the group members' commitment to stay on track. I have shown teams that once they take that first step and thereby experience—and celebrate—their early successes, a magical transformation occurs. And the momentum of their collective results sparks new levels of team effectiveness.

Each chapter will be brief and to the point, while also being fun, entertaining, and memorable through the use of firefly analogies and stories designed to create a flash of "Aha!" My goal is to create a handy field guide that can be used and referred to repeatedly. Here is a partial listing of topics to be covered:

- What to do when the fireflies don't show up (or when creativity dries up).
- How to know when it's time to find a new meadow (or a new approach, place, or process).
- What to do if the leader is keeping too tight a lid on the jar (and team innovation is gasping for air).
- How to get inventive when it rains on your firefly hunt (or parade of ideas).

- What happens when everyone is too busy to join in (and group problems remain unresolved).
- How synchronizing makes everyone's light brighter (and how to tap into the power of synergized effort).

You can create the Firefly Effect in your team, group, or organization; and I will show you how to go about doing so. The first step on this path is to "Rediscover Your Creative Spark" (Part I). You have creative power within you, and the steps in this book will help you tap into it. You will find it in yourself to be alive and driven to do a great job.

Our journey continues with an exploration of the two critical roles of leadership. "Creating the Right Environment" (Part II) considers the new direction and calling for leaders to create a fertile environment for breakthrough creativity and business results. An appreciation of the unique talents and perspectives of each member, along with an unshakable foundation of trust are critical elements of team development. Once this groundwork is laid, conflict takes on a completely new meaning when viewed constructively as creative abrasion that leads to incredible breakthroughs.

Your team is undoubtedly comprised of a group of individuals who likely have very different personalities, talents, experiences, and points of view. How do very diverse people capitalize on their strengths? By "Targeting Team Energy" (Part III), all members of a team will have—despite their differences—a clear, common picture of the road on which they are traveling, the important mile markers, and guardrails for how we will work together.

Your team will truly be "Firing on All Cylinders" (Part IV) when you gain an insider's perspective on the secrets of powerful collaboration, including how to maximize your time together, reach decisions based on each person's candid input, and to hold each other accountable for honoring commitments.

Creativity really occurs when the fieldwork completed in the first four sections leads to "Sparking Creativity" (Part V). This section shows exactly how to do this, with creativity boosters, fixes for when the fireflies (aka creativity) don't show up, and dealing with colliding team purposes.

The grand finale is a light show beyond compare—the magical synchronicity of thousands of fireflies. "Sync—The Magic" (Part VI) will renew your belief in the possible, and will show you that by experimenting with what you have learned, you can individually shine like never before. You will see how your role as leader is more empowering and fulfilling than you could ever have imagined, and the team and the organization as a whole will reach new heights of breakthrough performance.

My memory of chasing fireflies—of gathering them and having fun with those close to me as we all strove to achieve a common purpose—was so powerful for me that I chose to name my company after it: FireFly Facilitation. I have spent the past 10 years pursuing my passion by working with leaders to help them build more successful teams. *The Firefly Effect* is my way of sharing what I have taught and learned throughout the process. Now—let's begin a new chapter about being part of a highly effective team!

Chapter Two

The Individual—Creativity Found Again

Limitations live only in our minds. But if we use our imaginations, our possibilities become limitless.
—Jamie Paolinetti

Everyone has the ability to be creative—if you broaden your concept of what creativity means, and if you know how to tap into it. My experience with hundreds of groups leads me to be able to say, with confidence, that at their core, great teams are comprised of creative, committed individuals who are using their best efforts to reach a common goal. In fact, teams that solve problems and tackle challenges together have a special bond that's not often found in other groups. And they don't see these challenges as drudgery or something outside the scope of their work; they view it as the excitement and fun of being a part of a team.

Think of the members of the team of which you are currently a member or a leader. Would *creative* and *committed* be the words you would use to describe each one of them? If not, how do you get them—or yourself—to acknowledge and willingly apply their original talents to the success of the group? Let's begin by rethinking the very word creative.

We tend to hold grandiose views of creativity—why is this? Most likely because there are so many myths and misconceptions associated with this word. First of all, many of us think of creativity as being dichotomous—something you either have or you don't, like blue eyes, brown hair, or left- and right-handedness. It is, most believe people, a trait with which you are born—or not.

Second, many consider being creative to be something *you do* versus something *you are*. This mind-set lends itself to fairly harsh judgment of our own creativity that is based on the value of output versus the ingenuity of the thinking. The emphasis on the left-brain side of creativity—the measurable side—has a tendency to shut down or silence our view of ourselves as creative. Because the notion that most of us are "naturally creative" doesn't seem logical to us, it just doesn't agree with our self-image.

A third myth that hinders creativity is that of the lone creative genius, á la Thomas Edison. The negative impact this inflicts upon the teams can be counterproductive. Often when one or two individuals on the team are held up to be the creative ones, the remaining members shrink back to the sidelines, waiting to hear what's been decided. They believe that their job is to simply implement the ideas, not contribute in their formation. These groups will never know what was lost by not engaging the creative energy of everyone on the team. Even Thomas Edison's greatest strength came from using an entire team of people to help generate his many inventions. He would be the first to acknowledge (and did!) that "Genius is one percent inspiration, and ninety-nine percent perspiration"—presumably that of others as well as his own.

Each of us has some creative abilities and contributions to make. And yet if I were to ask you about yours, in all likelihood you would deny—or at least downplay—these talents. Ask a preschooler this same question, and they can't wait to proudly show you their latest creations. For many people, passage into adulthood has dimmed their creative aspirations. In fact, even though all fireflies glow when they are first born, some actually lose that ability when they become adults. How amazingly similar to what happens to so many individuals.

Do you remember how enjoyable it was to discover new things when you were younger? This childlike mentality is often replaced with more adult-centered thinking, such as knowing the right answer, and convincing others that we are correct. Creativity—both individual and team—evaporates.

As a member of the senior leadership team for a mortgage company I worked with, Mary liked being respected, and yes, even somewhat feared. During a recent team development session, I led the group through a card exercise based on the work of Ned Herrmann. (I'll expand upon the Herrmann Whole Brain® model and assessment tool in a later chapter.) Each person was asked to choose three cards (with words and descriptions) most like them, and one card least like them. "Well, I know which of these cards is least like me!" she exclaimed as she quickly moved to pick up the "Creative" card before one of her teammates could.

As I had done in this same situation with so many others, I asked her to read the description below the words "It only says that you are able to make unique connections—you don't have to say you are creative in the artistic sense of the word." "Nope, this is least like me—no question about it," she nodded vigorously as she stepped away from the table. It proved yet again that our sense of being uncreative is so strong that it often blinds us to what we have the potential to be.

Knowing all of this, how do you begin the process of rediscovering your unique creative abilities? Galileo said "You cannot teach a man anything; you can only help him find it within himself." I believe leaders can play an incredibly powerful role here. They can encourage those on their teams to embrace a new mind-set about what we mean by the very word creative, which Webster's New World Dictionary defines as "creating or able to create." There is so much potential freedom within this simple definition, and yet the emphasis on the word *able* still makes it sound like a skill that you may or may not have.

What if we were to replace the dichotomous view of creativity—where you have it or don't have it—with one that instead represents a continuum? On one end of the spectrum might be a piece of art recognized as being suitable for hanging in the Louvre next to the Mona Lisa. On the other end could be something as useful and common as a delicious meal whipped up from leftovers, the reorganization of a closet for greater capacity and efficiency, or the discovery of yet another inventive use for duct tape. Certainly all of us can see ourselves as being included somewhere along this broad spectrum. Unfortunately, as adults, we don't think of these relatively simple tasks as worthy of being called creative.

So what will it take to convince you that you are creative? Let's take a look at it through the eyes of youth. When I asked my 13-year-old daughter, Madison, how she would define creative (after remarking to me in typical teen fashion that my question was "random"), she replied off the top of her head: "To be original. To do something that no one else would think of."

Wow—the power in that definition. Every one of us is—by the very nature of our DNA—original, and thus unique, each having a different view of the world brought about by our genetic makeup and our own life experiences. In fact, you could say that we each bring something new and different to the group.

The explosion of books and online assessment tools to help people evaluate their strengths is proof that many have a desire to discover their unique talents. Let's explore finding yours right now. Take a mental trip back in time and remember when you did something that made you feel creative. What did that look like? How did you feel? What came easily to you? What could you do well that others couldn't? I saw early signs of my own ability to facilitate as early as 10 years old, when I enlisted the kids in our neighborhood to perform in the plays I created and directed in our garage. My husband shared with me that he was most creative in the sandbox, building miniature cities with Matchbox cars and plastic soldiers. And as an adult, he became an entrepreneur—building businesses with multiple locations and real people.

Recall those times where you did something well that elicited praise from colleagues, friends, parents, or even a stranger. It could be as simple as hearing a comment from a passerby while you were fishing on how far out you were able to cast the line. It could be that you were the best at finding imaginative ways to have fun with other people's discarded items; making houses, sleds, you name it, out of empty appliance boxes. Or you were always the last one to be found at hide-and-seek because of your uncanny ability to find the best spot.

Now fast forward into your adulthood. Think of a project or an activity when you were in the zone, when you didn't notice time passing or care how long it would take. Your energy and motivation grew as you got closer to achieving your goal. What were you doing? Where were you? Was anyone else there? What was the goal you were working toward?

Although you have likely experienced numerous occasions when you have felt lost in the moment like this, you probably just found it difficult to recall perhaps even one. If so, based on what I've observed, you're in the majority. The current focus for much of our lives is on improving our weakest areas. Would you have responded faster if I had asked you what you needed to work on to be a better person, spouse, employee, or citizen of the world?

There is a familiar recruiting slogan for the Army—"Be all you can be." I agree with that phrase, depending on whether you put the emphasis on the word *all* or the word *you*. One should not strive for *all*; this implies that we should always be pushing ourselves to get better, to work harder, and to struggle more. Instead, the emphasis should be on *you*— reinforcing the fact that we are each unique individuals with distinctive strengths and talents. If that's the case, then people can discover and tap into the abilities at which they are especially strong. Yes, you may need to mitigate extreme weaknesses that might keep you from being able to function, but spend more time on your strengths. This is where you'll find your greatest energy and motivation, and it will come to you easier.

In many of the team effectiveness sessions I lead, this question is often raised: Should people focus on their strengths or should they try to be well-rounded, Renaissance people who always strive to be best at everything? In particular, I have seen this long-standing controversy among the leaders with whom I work. The stance that a leader takes usually tells me a lot about them and their view of the inherent worth of others.

Recently, a senior leader at a retailer asked me which of these I thought was a better approach. I asked him to share his viewpoint with me (since this was obviously one of those situations where he already had an opinion when he asked me the question). "Well, I think you should first identify and reinforce what people are good at, instead of always focusing on their weaknesses to be overcome. Only then can you help them to improve in those other areas," Bob shared with me. I think that this positive affirmation of his members' strengths contributed significantly to the continued success of his team.

You might be thinking, "Sure, I've got some strengths; but does that make me creative?" One guaranteed path to discovering your unique creativity is using your inherent strengths to light the way. The creative aspect comes into play when you decide to apply those strengths to the situation, goal, or opportunity before you. Sometimes we need a stimulating event to change our view of what it means to be creative; I know, because it happened to me.

Even though I'm always encouraging others to view themselves as creative, I hadn't been challenged to do the same for myself; and then a business colleague and author strongly suggested I write this book. My first reaction was to disregard her comment, because I didn't see myself as being creative in that way—that is, as a professional writer. And then I recalled my college and graduate school days and thought, hey, wait a minute, I have written things that were published in professional journals. Maybe this wasn't such a leap after all. So this spark of an idea began to take hold of me. Even I myself serve as an example of how often we turn a deaf ear (or a blind eye) to the cues that surround us.

The important thing to learn from all of this is that *everyone* has a creative spark within them. It can be a powerfully motivating force for you individually and an invaluable asset to the team if you have the confidence to tap into it and let it shine. So, what cue or spark of creativity have you pushed aside? Some questions that might help you discover this are: What do you like to do away from the office? What captures your interest when reading, traveling, or working? If you're like me—as I suspect you might be—then nothing needs to change except your mind-set and your belief in your own creative potential. Pay more attention to what you are paying attention to.

You never know where your particular creative spark will come from . . . or where it will lead. I was having lunch with Lisa, a wonderful friend and colleague. In the course of our meal, she admitted to me that, as a guilty pleasure and escape from a very hectic work schedule, she reads romance novels

and inspirational stories just before bed. One story in particular captured her imagination—*Twenty Wishes* by Debbie
Macomber—about four widows who write down their wishes,
and then begin to follow the path to their fulfillment. She
decides that this sounds like just what she and her small
circle of friends who meet monthly for dinner need to do.

Lisa's own path takes her in a direction she hadn't imagined. One of her wishes is to write a book. The very next day
she receives a notice about a writer's workshop at a nearby
university, which she decides to attend. Weeks later, she
receives an e-mail from me telling about the book I am writing.
She is becoming more and more excited—and more open to
this idea that a book could be in her future. This becomes the
subject of the rest of our lunch—what the book is that she has
in her. What is the creative spark in you just waiting to be
ignited into a full flame? Are you turning toward or away from
these whispers that you might be hearing? Take a chance.
Accept the fact that you have creativity within you, and there
is no telling where you will go if you free yourself to follow that
possibility, no matter where it takes you.

Once you acknowledge that everybody, including yourself, has some natural creativity, then you will begin to act on
it. The theory of cognitive dissonance states that the mind
can't hold two divergent pictures at the same time. It will try to
close the gap. You need only believe in the picture that says
you are creative, and you will begin to work toward making
that perception reality.

An effective team is composed of individuals who recognize their own creative talents. If you change your view of the
word creative from a quality that is inherent (or not!) and
unattainable to one that's more commonplace, and naturally
present in each of us, then you, too can rediscover your
creativity. Think back to your childhood and remember the
things that you were able to do better than others, that came
easily to you. This is the root of your creativity, and your
current world is fertile ground for you to begin to explore it if
you simply expand your awareness of the cues that surround
you. The bottom line is that you control your creativity; but
only *after* you recognize it within yourself. Rediscover your
spark because, as a team leader, you want to light up your own
creativity so that others will do the same.

Part II

The Leader's Role—Creating the Right Environment

Chapter Three

The New Role of Leadership

The leaders who work most effectively . . . never say "I." And that's not because they have trained themselves not to say "I." They don't think "I." They think "we"; they think "team." They understand their job to be to make the team function. They accept responsibility and don't sidestep it, but "we" gets the credit. This is what creates trust, what enables you to get the task done.

—Peter Drucker

Chapter 2 showed you how a shift in mind-set for what—and *who*—is creative can lead to an entirely new understanding of the word and of ourselves as creative beings. Now consider our notions about another vaguely defined term: *leadership*. As we did with creativity, we need to engage in new thinking about what constitutes an effective team—and a great team leader. As a country begins to make a transition from one founded on making the best use of the agricultural resources to one that focuses on capitalizing on its human resources, we see a related transition occur in an emphasis on a new role for leadership. Best-selling author Daniel Pink (*A Whole New Mind*) outlines this dramatic shift in America from the Agricultural Age, to the Industrial Age, to the Information Age, and now to the emerging *Conceptual* Age. And this transition is not just occurring in the United States, as evidenced by the theme of the 2008 World Economic Forum in Davos—collaborative innovation. The focus in many parts of the developed world is moving toward such skills and talents as creativity, empathy, intuition, and the ability to link seemingly unrelated objects and events into something new and different. This emphasis on those elements traditionally thought of as right-brained has been newly recognized as absolutely essential for the leader of the future.

There are other signs that there are new expectations in terms of leadership that are emerging in corporate America. In 2004–2005, the Center for Creative Leadership surveyed 118 executives and middle managers to compile "The State of Teams" report. This report found that 91 percent of respondents think that teams are central to the organization's success; that 87 percent consider collaboration with other teams to be essential to achieving goals; and that 80 percent believe that leaders needed help building strong teams, and keeping them on track toward exceeding expectations.

A survey cited in *BusinessWeek*'s April 28, 2008, issue noted an interesting shift that's under way. Across the entire surveyed population, only 30 percent said they were motivated to collaborate to accomplish a specific task, while 46 percent cited learning from others as motivation for collaborating. Women responded that they liked working together to learn from others only slightly more often than men (51 percent versus 40 percent). However, when you break the data down by age range, a fascinating pattern emerges. Of 18-to-24-year-olds, 60 percent said that they liked working together to learn from others, versus 44 percent of 25-to-64-year-olds and only 28 percent of those over the age of 65. It therefore appears that new entrants to the workforce are increasingly expecting to work as part of a team that proactively shares knowledge and skills among its members.

One anecdotal piece of evidence: For the last four years I have conducted workshops for the new management associates of a financial institution to teach them how to work together effectively in a team setting as they collaborate to successfully complete their group projects. For most of them, this is not a new concept, but rather carrying over into the corporate world what many of them have been doing since their college days. As any parent of today will attest, the roots of this shift to teamwork is even starting as young as kinder-garten, when they discuss and reach agreement on how they will behave toward each other. Believe me, many of the teams I work with could take guidance from the no hitting and no biting rules. Even if the adult misbehaviors are through their words, the hurt and pain can be just as real.

Leading authority on Emotional Intelligence (EQ) Daniel Goleman is quoted as saying that "Sensitivity to emotional states (one's own and others') and effective relationship skills are the critical competencies . . . IQ and expertise are no longer considered the best predictors of performance or lead-ership effectiveness." In fact, Goleman found that 85 to 95 per-cent of the difference between a "good leader" and an "excellent leader" is attributed to emotional intelligence (*Working with Emotional Intelligence*, 1998). We see this often today in how effectively change initiatives are implemented. There is abun-dant research that shows that even if the strategy for the change is the correct one, unless the leader can truly inspire employees to willingly give their discretionary effort to make the change a success, then execution fails. Effective implementation of critical changes is all about capturing the minds *and* hearts of followers.

So, what do today's leaders need to do if they are to ensure collaborative innovation? In the following sections of *The Firefly Effect*, I will share with you tools and techniques for embodying the incredibly powerful, two-fold role you play as a leader:

1. To create and maintain a safe, respectful environment where individual creativity can emerge to its fullest potential (Part II, Chapters 4–7); and

2. To focus that creative energy in the right direction based upon the core purpose of the team and the targeted goals (Part III, Chapters 8–10).

The first calling of an innovative leader is to create a fertile environment that will allow creativity to be unleashed. Like the firefly, creativity cannot exist everywhere. Did you know that you won't find the flash of a firefly west of the Rockies? It's too dry. Only a few scrappy ones can exist there, and they don't shine. Survival is their main objective.

One could say their true calling as Lampyridae (their official family name, which translates as "shining fire") is not fulfilled. The leader's role is to create an environment where fireflies— or individuals—can not only survive, but also thrive and truly shine.

So how do you create this motivating, collaborative, and innovative environment? Each member of your group must first acknowledge that not only is *he* or *she* unique and creative, but that every *other* person on the team has different strengths and talents, and that those differences have the potential to provide incredible value if capitalized upon. And while recognizing their peers' value lays the foundation for mutual respect and trust, leaders must ensure that team members spend quality time with each other building strong bonds. Finally, all members of the team must view conflict in a new way; not as a destructive, inevitable evil, but rather as a constructive source of creative abrasion. As Ed Catmull, co-founder of Pixar and the president of Pixar and Disney Animation Studios, captured this critical role of leaders so eloquently in his September 2008 *Harvard Business Review* article, ". . . getting talented people to work effectively with one another . . . takes trust and respect, which we as managers can't mandate; they must be earned over time. What we can do is construct an environment that nurtures trusting and respectful relationships and unleashes everyone's creativity . . . everyone feels that they are part of something extraordinary. If we get that right, the result is a vibrant community where talented people are loyal to one another and their collective work, everyone feels that they are part of something extraordinary, and their passion and accomplishments make the community a magnet for talented people."

The second role of the leader, which I will explore further in Part III, is to find a way to target this creative energy in the right direction. The first priority is to be clear about the role or purpose of every team member, and to establish guiding principles for how the members will work together. The second priority will be to develop a common understanding of what success for the team means, and how it will be measured. Finally, you'll want to create a timeline for the major milestones that you need to hit in order to accomplish these goals, with well-understood accountabilities and inter-dependencies, as well as a process for monitoring progress and course correcting.

In the following chapters, each of these components will be discussed in greater detail so that you'll know exactly how to capture the creativity on your team and catapult it into results. If you decide to embrace the new expectations, you'll find that this is an exciting time to be a leader. And as the research above clearly states, you will find a ready and willing labor force emerging who want to work together in a new way.

Chapter Four

No Dissing the Red Quadrant

The world as we see it is only the world as we see it. Others may see it differently.

—Albert Einstein

I have found through my own experience that at the core of every great team are individuals who recognize the differences among them, and have learned to see these unique qualities as a source of value to the group. I love the analogy that Marcus Buckingham uses in his book *The One Thing You Need to Know*; and I share it with my clients on a regular basis, because it creates such a beautiful and memorable image. Buckingham claims that skillful managers are like great chess players; they know the unique strengths of each player on the team, and are able to use those strengths to their greatest advantage. Mediocre managers, on the other hand, play checkers. Think about it; the pieces all move the same way in checkers. In a game of chess, however, a player must learn how each individual piece moves, and then use this knowledge of each piece to accomplish the work of the team. I have found that it is so much more powerful if everyone on the team—not just the leader—sees each other as valuable chess pieces, and not as simple red or black checkers.

Thus, truly effective leaders have moved away from the notion that treating everyone equally works and have embraced the idea that everyone needs to be treated differently, and as an individual. Enlightened leaders value the process of discovering the unique qualities of each person (including themselves), and create a safe environment in which every member of the team can knowingly and proudly claim those differences, and then apply them in an optimal way to achieve the goals of the team. I'm talking about differences that are not visible to others, those that are deeper than race, sex, job title, and even daily responsibilities. The kind of variation that I mean includes how team members think, what drives them, what kind of work they do best, how they like to be rewarded and recognized, and so on. It is a leader's role to light the way by making this kind of inquiry a priority, and by finding the tools and processes that will allow people to see each other in a new light. However, this is not solely the leader's responsibility; *everyone* on the team needs to get on board with this concept of appreciating the inherent individuality and worth of every other member. Then, they can focus together on how best to apply each team member's unique combination of skills and experiences to make the team better.

Speaking of diversity within a group—how many species of fireflies do you think there are? Would you guess 2 . . . 10 . . . 20? Would you believe there are more than 2,000 known species worldwide today? There are 170 in the United States alone, and more are being discovered each year. Who knew something that appears to be so simple on the outside could be so complex? And yet, how much more complex and unique are each one of *us*? How much greater is our individual capacity to shine brilliantly?

You have probably heard the familiar adage that leaders should hire people who are unlike themselves. Unfortunately, even when we get that part right, we then make the mistake of inadvertently—or even overtly—attempting to get these new hires to conform to the norms of the group, or to hide their uniqueness in order to fit in. On a more personal level, we often see this occurrence in many marriages; opposites attract, right? But then you run the risk of spending the rest of your lives trying to change the very differences that first attracted you.

I remember when I joined the human resources team of a large, very successful consumer products organization. There were several of us brought in from the outside at the same time. The company's intention was to hire us as change agents—employees who would really shake things up and help move the company in a new direction. Before I left two and a half years later, I remarked to a close colleague, "You know, it felt like being in the old sci-fi movie *The Blob*. They said they wanted change; but in fact, I felt like they just kept sucking me back in to conform and become part of 'the norm.' I had to make a choice." I so wanted to be valued for the different perspective I could bring, and the positive impact I could have. Perhaps I didn't know how to shape the message in a way that could be heard. As a consultant used to having the change happen on my timeline, perhaps I was too impatient. I was reminded how hard it is to stand out. If you don't have the leadership's support to truly be the different person that the company hired you to be, then you will either be sucked under or compelled to leave.

It is in our individual and corporate nature to try to deal with differences by eliminating them, and making everyone the same. However, the new role of leadership demands that you not fall into this trap, or you will lose the very elements you need for collaborative innovation. So what's a leader to do? Serve as a role model for appreciating the diversity you have on the team. The different members of a team can be a significant source of strength, if there is a safe environment for them to display and utilize their unique qualities to further the objectives of the team. As mentioned previously, I think we marry our opposites because we know that our greatest strengths, taken to an extreme, can indeed become our greatest weaknesses. Therefore, the teammates—and mates—who represent our opposites can help to counterbalance the team or union.

Author Jim Collins (*Good to Great*) has a well-known philosophy: get the right people on the bus, and *then* decide on the right strategy. When I share this idea with leaders and teams, I sometimes get this push back: "Hey, I didn't have a choice about who to put on my bus. The seats were all filled before I got here. Now what do you expect me to do?" I understand and agree that you may not have the freedom to unload the bus and start at a fresh bus stop. You do, however, have this choice to make—to look for, appreciate, and capitalize on what is right about the people you *do* have. The more you know about each of them, the more opportunities you'll recognize for getting some people to change seats on the bus for greater impact and personal satisfaction.

Now that you understand the critical task you have in making it a priority for you and your team to value the unique contributions every member can make, we can turn our attention to the tools and processes to help you accomplish this. There are a wide variety of tools and assessments out there—Myers-Briggs, DiSC, and the like. Perhaps you are already very comfortable and satisfied with your current assessments. I am not trying to convert anyone to another tool; I simply want to demonstrate how the one that I've chosen to use in my work with teams has come to be very effective.

I first was introduced to the Herrmann Brain Dominance Instrument (HBDI®) when I was an Organization Effectiveness Manager at Coca-Cola (which I will describe in greater detail in a moment). I had some team leaders who preferred the Myers-Briggs Type Indicator (MBTI), and some who preferred the HBDI, based on their familiarity and comfort level with the instruments. The MBTI, as you may know, is an assessment designed to measure psychological preferences in how people perceive the world and make decisions. It uses four different pairs of attributes to describe 16 different personality types: Introversion versus Extraversion; Sensing versus Intuiting; Thinking versus Feeling; and Judging versus Perceiving. While all teams felt that it was beneficial to learn about their personality assessments on the day of the team effectiveness session, those that used the HBDI continued to apply what they learned long after the initial event. I believe this was due to the HBDI's ease of use; in fact, I came to call the HBDI the user-friendly Myers-Briggs because of the common language it uses to describe our thinking styles, and the many business applications it provides.

Creative thinking pioneer Ned Herrmann created the HBDI during his time as head of management development at General Electric. Herrmann was struck by the differences in the "learning styles" of the participants (even before that terminology was in vogue). He examined relevant scientific research about how the brain processes information, and developed a four-quadrant model to explain the differences between left-brained versus right-brained and visceral versus cognitive thinking (see Figure 4.1). He then created an assessment instrument to measure people's specific thinking preferences in each of the quadrants. The overarching philosophy that Herrmann put forth as a result of his research is the notion that we all have preferences, none of which are inherently good or bad. We talk in terms of strengths and blind spots, not weaknesses.

Because of my background in industrial/organizational psychology, an instrument's validity was very important to me; and this assessment met that criteria. I also was impressed by the fact that using the instrument required certification—a signal to me of how seriously the assessment

Blue — "Analyze" (A)	*Yellow — "Strategize" (D)*
• Is critical • Analyzes • Is logical • Likes numbers • Is realistic • Likes to quantify • Knows how things work • Likes to measure things	• Is holistic • Imagines • Is flexible • Speculates • Is curious • Takes risks • Is spontaneous • Conceptualizes
Strengths of Each Quadrant of the Whole Brain® Model	
Green — "Organize" (B)	*Red — "Personalize" (C)*
• Takes preventive action • Establishes procedures • Pays attention to details • Gets things done • Organizes • Is reliable • Timely • Plans	• Is expressive • Considers impact on others • Is passionate • Likes to develop others • Is enthusiastic • Supports others • Is collaborative • Is empathetic

Figure 4.1. Strengths of Each Quadrant of the Whole Brain Model

and its results are perceived to be. As a facilitator who debriefs hundreds of different assessments each year, I also very much appreciated the fact that almost every individual would read the description of their profile, and be amazed at how well it captured them.

I think that being aware of our strengths is an inherent human need; this is made quite clear in the growth in popularity of online assessments and tools that are available to help us discover our unique gifts. When I walk a team through their individual HBDI profiles, I see fear and excitement about what they will find out personally—and what others will discover about them. I try to lessen that fear by explaining the thinking that each of the four quadrants represents. I pause at every step and ask the group to write down what they value about each quadrant—something that forces people to appreciate thinking in ways that might not be the norm for them.

It is a very positive experience for each person to realize their value—and then to hear that affirmed by the other groups. It is always a very eye-opening experience for the entire team. For the Blue (A) quadrant, I hear such things as "I value their logical, fact-based approach to problem-solving" or "I like that they know how things work." The most common attributes for the Green (B) quadrant are "They really know how to get things done" and "I like it that they are very organized and have a well laid out plan." Comments for the Red (C) quadrant often include such things as "I really like their passion and enthusiasm" or "They are very good at expressing themselves and relationship-building." And finally, the Yellow (D) quadrant often hears these words, "They keep us focused on the big picture and why we're doing something," as well as "They push us to take risks to make things better."

There is also an introductory exercise that I have the members of the team complete in order to help them to understand this idea of preferences. I instruct them to write their name in cursive with the hand they usually use. After a brief pause, I then ask them to write their name in cursive with the opposite hand. I immediately begin to hear groans and giggles as people try to adjust to simply holding the pencil with their nondominant hand. I ask them to call out how this feels.

"Awkward!" "Hard!" "I really have to think about it." "It looks terrible!" "I'm still working on it!" I then share with them, "This is how it will feel when you try to think in a less preferred quadrant; but you will all be able to do it. It just may take a little longer, and you will have to concentrate a little more, and it may not be as pretty; but everyone can do it." This is such an empowering feeling, knowing that you can tap into your full potential for thinking in a variety of ways, just by seeing—or holding—something differently. Our creative strength first comes from awareness, and then from experience.

Before the teams see their individual HBDI results, I use a tool called The Diversity Game as a means of helping them to gain insight into their own and each other's thinking styles. (Note: You can learn more about the HBDI and this game at www.HBDI.com.) I find the game is a great way to create comfort and prepare for the discovery of their actual HBDI results. The Diversity Game is not focused on representational diversity; that is, diversity in terms of what they can see with their own eyes—such as sex, ethnicity, age, and the like. The focus is on thinking styles diversity—recognizing it on the team, respecting it, and even applauding those who might have been "the weird ones." It is eye opening and gratifying for all to hear that there is inherent worth in everyone's method of thinking.

Here's a very brief overview of how I use the game in my work with teams. Everyone randomly receives cards with words and definitions on them that are color coordinated to match the HBDI four quadrants. For example, a blue card with the word "Analytical" or a yellow card with "Simultaneous," along with brief definitions. Their objective is to trade cards with the other people in the room to make their "best" hand; that is, the one that best represents their own style of thinking. I often encourage them that if they have a card that is "oh, so someone," to go to that person and try to negotiate the exchange of that card; but warn them that they better be prepared for the interesting dialogue that ensues. This process is a great way for team members to learn about each other; they see which cards they hold on to as being most like them and which ones they really, *really* want to get rid of.

Thus, the game is an interesting, engaging, and non-threatening way for individuals on a team to see each other through new eyes (because remember: they have already identified—and I have reinforced—the inherent value of each of the four quadrants). But be prepared—sometimes the results can be very surprising. I still remember one case in particular, during which I was working with the senior IT team of a telecommunications company. Two of the team members did not get along well at all. They spoke negatively about each other behind their back to peers and subordinates alike.

So picture this: we're gathered in a room playing the game, and I have designated a spot in the room for each of the four quadrants. I ask each person to get up and move to the quadrant most like them. Imagine their complete and utter shock and dismay as they each see the other moving toward the same corner. It was almost as if they were looking at each other and saying, "How dare you be in *my* quadrant?" Of course, this discovery of common ground—and the ability for each to see the other with a new perspective—gets to the very heart of this exercise. As a result of this two-day team effectiveness session, the interaction between the two continually improved and the leader of the group chose both of them to collaborate and lead a very innovative project together. This had a huge impact, not just on the two of them, but also on how well their departments collaborated to accomplish this critical work.

Of course, the participants are not the only ones who benefit when we conduct these exercises. I learned a very embarrassing but powerful lesson myself as well. I have found that many of the senior leadership teams with whom I work have a large gap in the red ("interpersonal") quadrant. This tends to be the case either because they do not have a strong preference in that area or because they are afraid to publicly own up to it at work since it appears to be so poorly valued by the rest of the team. As we walk through the HBDI model, I used these standardized words to describe the red quadrant—"emotional," "talks a lot," "touches a lot," and so on.

Almost immediately, the kidding would begin. "We're going to need some more Kleenex" . . . "Emotional—that has your name all over it!" . . . "Boy, talks a lot sure describes you." I would retort: "Get it out of your system now, because there'll be no more dissing of the red quadrant after lunch!" Sometimes the team leaders would be the very worst offenders, and have the greatest negative impact. A particular IT team had one individual with a strong red "tint" who kept trying to explain that he was just passionate about solving the customer's problems; but he still took a lot of ribbing.

Then something very surprising happened during a session—when a client told me that *I* was a big part of the problem! Although I was a bit shocked, I at least had the presence of mind to ask her to explain. "The words you use to describe the red quadrant are not business-minded words; so you are perpetuating the problem of not seeing this quadrant as one of value." I asked her to elaborate, and give me an example. "Well, what about using words like 'collaborative,' 'likes to develop others,' and 'enthusiastic' instead? Now, that sounds like something we would actually value on the team." Soon several more people were jumping in with recommended changes. "While we're on the subject, I don't think you've done such a great job with the yellow description either," said a high yellow quadrant participant. "It looks too playful, and there is too much emphasis on risk taking. Where are the other positive words that describe this quadrant—like conceptual or strategic?" I decided that it made sense to stop action right then and revise the offending words in an effort to show each quadrant's true value to the team's thinking processes in business, and I have been using this new language ever since. It just goes to show that we can *all* change the way we think about and see certain things; and that without even realizing it, we may be a part of the problem.

I mentioned earlier in this chapter that one of the reasons I really like the HBDI is the ease of understanding the model. This makes it an especially powerful method to help people learn about thinking styles—both their own and those of their teammates. After I have walked the participants through their individual profiles, I display the overall results for the team. It is amazing to see how quickly individual members can pick up on what these strengths are—and where they may have some gaps. We then talk about the impact of these findings on the role of the team, and how we might overcome these apparent deficiencies. For example, what would you expect the consolidated profile of an HR team to look like? A lot of red preference, right? Not always so. I believe they have become so focused on hard-core deliverables to the business, they sometimes bury their role as employee advocate and champion of engagement, which really will be a contribution, when you think about it.

There is one section in the HBDI team profile that is especially helpful in completing this particular step. It displays a variety of work elements—such as "Analytical," "Teaching," and "Implementation"—and shows how people rated themselves on the work they do best. This is a great opportunity for people to claim their strengths in front of their peers in a safe, nonbraggadocios way, since everyone will have at least *one* area in which they excel. I always try to convey the value of this information in terms of using it to assess how the team's work is accomplished. We then review the key accountabilities of the team and the way new projects are handled to see how we might be able to exploit (in a good way) each person's strengths to benefit the group.

This exercise provides an excellent opportunity for people to gain experience in areas that extend beyond their normal job function. On one team I worked with, for example, there was an individual who felt she was good at analysis, but not very skilled in teaching. In reviewing the strengths of the other members of the team, she determined that she could collaborate with another teammate who had complementary skills by taking her data and creating a powerful presentation to request additional funding for a project. How effective it is to match employee skills and interests to mission-critical projects. Great for the team; great for the individual.

What could you and *your* team do today to show that you recognize and appreciate the commendable differences that are inherent in each one of you? What distinctions in personality, ability, work ethic, and interests exist that can truly make your team a collaborative whole? When resources are stretched to their limit, is your time and attention best spent focusing on what makes us dissimilar? You bet it is—and the data bear this out. Do you know what happens when employees are recognized as unique with significant contributions to make? They become more engaged, work with passion and commitment, and feel a profound connection to their company. This is what we are hoping to accomplish, and we must never lose sight of it.

There have been numerous engagement studies conducted by a variety of organizations that consistently demonstrate that the more closely people are engaged in a task, the greater their productivity, discretionary effort, satisfaction, and retention are. Recent research by the Gallup organization shows that less than one in three employees are fully engaged; and this doesn't just impact the company at the individual level. In fact, there is a growing body of research that shows a positive relationship between high levels of employee engagement and superior business performance.

As if you needed it, Gallup has now given you more reason to care about engagement—information that is especially relevant given the focus of this book on team creativity. Their latest research found that:

- Higher levels of employee engagement increase the likelihood that individual employees will *generate new ideas.*

- In addition, engaged employees are more likely to agree that they *feed off the creativity* of their colleagues.

- Engaged employees perceived their companies as *being more encouraging and accepting* of innovative ideas.

- Engaged employees were much more likely to *involve customers in the innovation* and improvement process, stating that "we give our customers new ideas." What a competitive advantage for the company—and its customers!

Gallup summarized the information in this way: "Engaged employees are far more likely to suggest or develop creative ways to improve management or business processes . . . [and] to solve customer problems. . . . Company leaders who want to drive growth through innovation should first create an environment that welcomes new ideas—and should make engaging employees a key component of that strategy."

So—what can you, as a leader, do to create this environment of engagement? You must make it a priority to sit down regularly and frequently with *each* member of the team in one-on-one meetings. Many of the employees with whom I've talked find these types of encounters—if done correctly and consistently (i.e., not constantly dropped from the manager's calendar because something more important came up)—to be their most productive time with their leader. You might discuss how an employee views his or her performance; what their favorite tasks are to work on; what ideas they might have for new projects; what they think will help the team's work overall—all in a nonthreatening way. These topics will provide you with opportunities to steer employees toward those tasks they are best at, allowing them to show off their strengths to their best advantage—to themselves, the manager, and to the team. This, in turn, can form the foundation for *every* member to gain a deeper appreciation for what each other has to offer.

In this chapter, we have focused on recognizing and appreciating the differences that are inherent in each of us. I believe you will find what you look for. If your emphasis is on an employee's needed areas for improvement and weaknesses; then that is what you will discover. If instead you look for strengths and contributions to be capitalized upon, then this is what will be first and foremost apparent to you.

We each have so much that we can contribute individually, if we and others know what makes our light shine— or what our unique strengths are. Great teams are comprised of individuals who play to their own and others' strengths. The next step in our journey is to take this new acknowledgment to an even deeper level—one of establishing trust on the team, and seeing the total value in each person. I will show you how to do just that.

Chapter Five

Beware the Ferocious Firefly!

Trust men and they will be true to you; treat them greatly
and they will show themselves great.
                              —Ralph Waldo Emerson

What do we mean by *trust*? There is undoubtedly power
in thinking of trust as two sides to the same coin. The giver
of trust has made the choice (and it *is* always a conscious
choice) to have confidence in the integrity and capability of
another person. The receiver of this trust then has a responsibility that arises from the confidence that has been placed in
them. But what causes someone to choose to trust another
person? I've found that this is sometimes based on facts, and
sometimes on faith. When I'm addressing a group about this
issue, I will often ask for a show of hands after posing these
questions: Who believes that their trust must be earned? Who
believes that trust in others is theirs to lose? I almost always
find a split decision, and this can be a source of great dissonance on the team.

   Those who believe that others must earn trust can begin
to lay such a foundation by first focusing on the strengths
and unique contributions that each member of the team
can make. After all, believing that someone is competent at
a given task will increase the likelihood of your trusting

them—at least in the areas that use those particular skills. By leading with strengths, you are more likely to establish an environment of safety in which you can acknowledge and accept the weaknesses and human fallibility inherent in each of us. The more you see people as unique individuals—versus seeing them as just a person other than you—the easier it will be for you to trust.

This is why the last two chapters' focus on honoring each other through mutual recognition and respect of one another's unique strengths, talents, and innate creative ability is so important. In this chapter, we will build on that foundation, and take it to the next level: establishing a true sense of trust on the team. I will show you why trust is such a necessary ingredient of team strength, and will share the steps that you can take to build it. In the next chapter, I will explain how broken trust can be a source of destructive conflict—and how you can work to reestablish it once it has been damaged.

Teams develop *broad-based* trust (as opposed to one-on-one trust that may exist between individual members) over time through group interactions. While this may naturally occur in the ordinary workings of the team, it's much more powerful if you can jump-start the process and proactively take action to set the stage for establishment of trust. In addition, instigating groupwide trust-building endeavors will ensure that trust is not confined within pockets—a tendency that can create alienating cliques. I have seen this occur so often on teams. Simple proximity—either by location of desks, or as a result of working together for extended periods of time—can cause some individuals to build bonds which exclude others from this inner sanctum. While you may not want to stop this from occurring naturally, there needs to be a broader umbrella of trust that covers *all* members of the same team. My experience has shown me that this strong foundation forms the basis of truly productive conflict.

I will now share some trust-development techniques that I have used quite successfully with many teams. I will begin with some of those that are easier to facilitate—and safer for people to participate in. These initial interactions will lay the foundation for greater depths of trust to develop. One small, engaging activity with a surprisingly big impact is the personal introductions (I refuse to use the term *icebreaker*) that I have used with teams to initiate a session.

I was recently asked to make a presentation to a group of CEOs who had gathered specifically for the purpose of networking and learning and sharing best practices. Over the months since their inception, they had seen a series of presentations on a variety of topics, followed by Q&A—followed by less than satisfied CEOs at the end of the session. The sponsor of this group asked me to try to increase the meeting's level of interaction, since they were trying to create a place where these executives would feel comfortable sharing and seeking advice from each other. This request was music to my ears; I am a firm believer that there is *already* a great deal of knowledge when I enter most rooms where I will make a presentation. As far as I'm concerned, my role is simply to facilitate their recollection of this knowledge and their ability to share it with others in a way that can be heard.

For this particular group, my assumption was true—in spades. The CEOs very much longed to interact with and learn from one another. The title of my discussion was "High Performing Teams Start at the Top"; so I asked them to think for a moment about a leader who had a profound impact on them. (This is always a valuable tactic if you want to get great input from people; give them a moment to think, and then jot down some notes to themselves. Since they have their notes in front of them, they can turn their attention to what others are saying instead of remaining so intently focused upon what *they* are going to say when *their* turn arrives. Thus, the introverts have had the opportunity to prepare; and the extroverts have been forced to prepare.)

Their answers to this question became each CEO's introduction to the group that morning. With each story that was told, you could see people becoming more engaged—with each other, with the learning opportunity, with the connections to the issues that they faced at their own organizations—all because each person had allowed others a glimpse into what their unique view of what a leader is. There was *so* much communication during the introductions, in fact, that I ended up having to make some time adjustments for the rest of the presentation. At one point, I offered the group a choice— to either break into smaller groups to discuss a series of questions, or to stay together. The response was a resounding demand to stay together; they had bonded so well and learned so much through the memorable stories they had shared that they didn't want to lose that sense of cohesiveness. Moreover, the sponsors couldn't have been happier; this is exactly what they had envisioned when they had formed the group months ago.

You can generate the kind of connections that I created with this group of CEOs within your team as well. Because the stories that we share tell so much about each one of us, you and the rest of your team might make some discoveries if you too were to launch a staff meeting by posing this same question: What leader had a profound impact on you (present company excluded, of course)? To make sure this is an effective experience for everyone, follow my lead from the story above. Make sure people have a chance to think about their answer in silence and jot down their thoughts before you ask them to share. Ensure there is enough time on the agenda for everyone to share; you don't want the last ones to feel they are being rushed. If there is a limitation on the amount of time you can spend, then ask everyone to speak in headlines so that everyone has a chance to share. You could even have someone facilitate the process to keep it moving smoothly.

I conduct several team-building exercises that involve food, and not just because I love to eat, which I do. I truly believe food—any kind of food—can be a wonderful team-building tool. There is something about breaking bread together that makes people feel they have a different, more social relationship with each other. You will learn about a powerful exercise involving a shared meal later in this chapter.

For this next get-to-know-you exercise, I use M&Ms as a fun and easy way to prompt meaningful stories. I pass around a bowl of these candies, and ask each person to take one (or more, if you have the time for a longer session). After everyone has selected, I then unveil my list of questions associated with each color. For lighter weight introductions, red might be— what is your favorite vacation? Green—what is your favorite movie? Blue—your favorite restaurant. To set a more serious tone, you might ask participants to describe an event at work that made them proud; a time when they recognized someone for a job well done; or an instance wherein they were faced with a big challenge. It is amazing what teammates can learn about each other from simply sharing this kind of personal information.

Another way that food can be a team-building tool is with sharing a meal together. I have heard great stories of teams who held office potlucks and others who formed caravans to favorite restaurants. I have seen the impact on a very personal level as well. During my time at Coke, my colleagues and I made a trip to a farm that belonged to the grandmother of one of our teammates. The purpose was for business planning; but the results provided so much more. The trip made us feel as though we were going back in time. We felt free to be more open with one another in the unfamiliar and unassuming surroundings. The hay wagon, fresh biscuits, and our feeble attempts at milking a cow had such a powerful bonding effect on us all, which we very much needed to have, given the critical task ahead of us. In order to feel comfortable sharing what's not working and best practices with each other, you must have a common bond. This trip provided that for us—and led to our collaborating much more effectively on our specific client engagements in the future.

I've seen this kind of connection take place in my family as well, during our annual visit to Pawley's Island, South Carolina. As a result of much effort, we have been able to time it so that the entire extended family is there at the same time, and in close proximity to one another. Each year, all 30-plus relatives get together for dinner at our cousins' rented beach house. This year was going to be different, however, because this time, *we* were the ones who had rented a house with enough room to host the annual dinner. I will never forget the picture of all 12 members of the latest generation of cousins, sitting around this great big table eating spaghetti, laughing and talking. A different—and more significant—element of closeness within our children came as the result of this dinner. The kids trusted each other to be who they really were. My daughter, for example, told me, "I really like my cousin Brad. He's sorta quiet, so I haven't gotten to know him very much on our other trips; but I realize now he's really nice and smart." The steps in building trust that were taken simply by sharing a meal together led to collective experiences of crabbing on the beach, burying each other in the sand, and looking forward to new adventures the next time they get together.

When was the last time your team got together for a purpose other than holding a staff meeting, fixing a problem, or reviewing the budget to find ways to cut expenses? Time and again, during my efforts to facilitate a team effectiveness session, I hear one or more members remark that this is the first time in the last year they have gotten together solely to focus on their connection as a team. It *is* hard to take time away from the real work of solving day-to-day problems. Yet how much more efficiently and effectively could your colleagues solve those problems if they spent some nonproductive time just sharing a meal and building a deeper sense of cohesiveness?

Another very powerful team-building experience that centers on sharing food is something that I call the milestones dinner. For this exercise, I ask each person to come to dinner that night prepared to share two events or people who have had a significant impact on who—and where—they are today. I wait until the end of the first day to explain the exercise (I've learned my lesson that if I tell them too early, the dinner becomes their focus of attention for the entire day). Waiting until day's end also lets me assess whether there is enough security and trust on this team to protect the kind of vulnerability that I am asking of the participants. Another important point is that I only conduct a milestones dinner when I know that the team will be together again the next day. I want people to be able to look each other in the eye and remain comfortable with one another, in spite of what they might have shared the night before.

Many of the teams with whom I work have commented that this is one of the most powerful aspects of our time together, because it truly allows people to gain insight into what is important to others on the team, what they value, and why they might behave the way they do. I always prepare the team leader to go first, since I have found that his or her willingness to be vulnerable will set the tone for the rest of the team. Since the very nature of these dinners is one that emphasizes the importance of trust and confidentiality, I cannot share any specific stories of these dinners. I can say that the trust that one particular leader demonstrated by opening himself up to me and the others on the team served as the epitome of what these sessions can achieve. This is how powerful this dinner can be if it is done right; if the team leader is able to demonstrate trust first.

One of the things that I often find so amazing about this exercise is how *little* each of the members knows about what others are accountable for—even if the team has been together for years. I know this shouldn't be surprising during a time when everyone has been expected to do more with less; yet this issue of silos is a frequent complaint from leaders with whom I work. They wish that everyone cared about the results of the whole team as much as they do. But how can team members be expected to care about one another's work when they don't even know what tasks others complete, and how these tasks contribute to the overall success of the team? I will show in upcoming chapters how to use team meetings to break down these silos. For now, I just want to reveal one very cool and simple technique that a particular telecommunications IT team developed, called (not surprisingly, perhaps, given the industry) "Getting on the Grid."

This team knew that silos were an issue for them; these partitions were slowing collaboration and delivery on critical project milestones. To address the problem, they simply created a matrix with each team member's name and department across the top and along the side. Then, every time someone held a brown bag lunch or similar type of meeting for the sole purpose of getting to know the members and responsibilities of another team, you could place an "X" in the associated square for those two groups. This contest was called "getting on the grid"; and it really turned into a great tool.

When I shared this idea with an HR team at the same company, they took the concept in a different direction. They wanted to start on a more personal level by encouraging each member of the team to get together for one-on-one meetings in order to learn more about the other. The challenge then became sharing something that you had learned about your counterpart—that had not already been said by someone else—at the next staff meeting. People realized they had better get moving and set up these meetings in a hurry in order to have something unique to share. It turned out to be a great way to compete for a good cause. What might *your* team members discover about each other if you were to challenge each of them to "get on the grid?"

Now that we have discussed a variety of trust-building tools and techniques—from fairly simple and light to more involved, and from introductions to milestones dinners and breaking down silos—I want to share with you two more tools that are closely related: recognizing contributions and the feed forward exercise. There is also one final tool that a leader can use to role model the expected behavior and convey how very important it is.

How many of you have a note you've saved somewhere that was sent to you as thanks or recognition for something you did? When I pose this question to a roomful of people, almost everyone raises their hand. Hearing a kind or thankful word from someone is always nice; receiving a card or note of appreciation that we can keep for years to come is even more special. Now, imagine that we could receive this kind of note from the other members of our team. I use something that I've named the "Team Contributions exercise" as a way to remind each member of the team how valuable they are in making the team successful—and I have found it to be incredibly powerful.

I begin the exercise by asking each person to write their name at the top of a flip chart page and hang it on the wall. Everyone then writes one sticky note for every person in the room with the following information included: the recipient's name, the giver's initials, and something you truly appreciate about this person; something they do that makes the team stronger. After everyone has completed their notes, I ask them to go post them on the appropriate flip chart pages. I then instruct everyone to silently read their own chart. I love to watch the team members' faces as they read their notes. It is like they are seeing each other for the first time! Sometimes the value of this exercise simply comes from convincing everyone to take a moment to think about how each person uniquely contributes to the success of the team. I know for a fact that there are people on teams who have saved these sticky notes for years.

For those of you who might be wondering why I don't also ask the participants to share with one another how they can improve—I actually used to. Then I came across two separate client situations that changed my mind. The first involved a small high-tech start-up company whose leadership team was already having some difficulties collaborating. Maybe it was due to the pressure of the industry, the venture capitalists driving for results, or the very strong personalities on the team. But whatever the case was, when I conducted this exercise—and asked for both contributions on positive qualities and suggestions on how team members could improve for even greater positive impact—what should have been a positive and powerful experience went *very* wrong. The new head of sales—a woman named Suzanne—misread or perhaps misinterpreted what the head of technology had written about her in terms of an improvement area. This really damaged the connection they had been building, and since this was the last exercise of the day, it caused us to leave on a very difficult note.

I had a very different result with another client, a finance team for a telecommunications company that had been together for over a year. I told them about the activity during the agenda review the first day, and let them know that we would each be sharing on the topic of how we contribute to the team's success—and how we could improve. I kept hearing comments about it—concerned ones, at that—during the first day and into the next. Finally, during one of the breaks, the main person with whom I had been working told me that everyone was very uncomfortable with the notion of the exercise, and that it was distracting them from the rest of the things we needed to get accomplished that day. I thanked her for bringing it up, and assured her that I would discuss it with the group as soon as we returned from break. I told them again, and in more detail, what the Team Contributions exercise would be like, and enumerated the many benefits. However, they made it clear that they only wanted to do the positive part; and they figuratively crossed their arms and refused to do the improvement part.

I realized based on these two engagements that I needed to change my tactics. I knew I wanted people on the team to reap the benefits of looking for and finding the strengths and contributions in each other. I also knew that no one is blind to the fact that we all have areas in which we need to improve. Yet corporate America can be a dangerous place to show any weakness at all. How do I create a safe environment in which members of these companies could begin to forge the powerful bond of trust that develops when each person acknowledges to the other members of the team that they indeed *have* weaknesses? How could I compel these team members to share their input in a way that would allow others to hear and take action on it?

I discovered the solution in two words: feed forward. This technique, developed by management expert and author Marshall Goldsmith, places the emphasis on receiving suggestions for improvement *going forward*; not looking back to what has occurred in the past. I had the opportunity to participate in a feed forward exercise that Marshall conducted with 200-plus members and visitors at the Atlanta chapter of SHRM (Society for Human Resource Management); and I was amazed at the positive response that I and the other members of the audience experienced. I decided right then and there that this could be the answer I was seeking; this might be the way that I could get team members to own up to a weakness and seek input from other members of the team—all for the purpose of their own improvement, and for solidifying a stronger foundation of trust.

I have since had the opportunity to use Goldsmith's method on numerous occasions with various teams, and I've found that it's a great way to get people used to giving and receiving constructive feedback. It allows team members to see one another in a new light, and it helps people to safely acknowledge they have at least one weakness. In essence, this is a wonderful way to take trust to a new level; to go from simply *telling* someone about how they contribute, to actually *trusting* this other person enough to share with them an area you feel you need to improve upon (you see, even here I don't like using the word *weakness*). I do think people both want and fear this kind of insight from others. Feed forward is a process for making it safe to get it.

Feed forward works by having each person involved identify one specific area or behavior that they would like to improve upon. For one it might be "becoming a better listener"; for another it could be "learning to deal with conflict more directly." I tell each person that I am putting five minutes on the clock, and that when I say "go," they are to pair up with another person. I always encourage participants to choose at least two unusual suspects—people to whom they would not normally open up or request ideas from. One partner shares their area for improvement first. There is no explanation expected, or even allowed, for the reason this area was selected. The other person gives the first two suggestions for improvement, to which the initiator can only respond "thank you." Then, the roles are reversed. There is such power in not having to justify the need for improvement; and even more in not being *allowed* to tell the suggestion-giver all of the reasons their idea won't work or that they've tried these tactics and failed before.

The impact that this exercise has on the energy level and cohesiveness of the team is just amazing. When I ask participants to share highlights of how this felt and what they learned, the responses are always very positive: "Who would have thought getting feedback could be fun?" "I was surprised how good the suggestions could be when they didn't know my whole situation." "I like the fact that I am accountable for deciding which suggestions I will work on." The result is a new openness among the team members to receiving feedback from each other—and new insights into ways they can improve in their chosen areas.

One last critical component of building trust on the team is the leader's role in demonstrating his or her belief in the importance of facilitating these one-on-one connections between members of the team. One retail company executive had a very difficult time making small talk with the people in his organization. He came across as aloof and uncaring. "When I do try to go out and talk with the people, I hear later that they think I'm just checking to see who is still working late—you know, just checking for 'butts in seats.'" Being a leader is hard. All eyes are on you and people add their own meaning to everything you do.

Although "management by walking around" isn't talked about much anymore, I think there is tremendous value in this practice—*if* a leader can learn to do it without seeming like they're checking on employees, and *if* they can find a way to make it fit within their own style. For the executive mentioned above, I recommended that he try to alter the time of day during which he went out to talk with the people on the floor. If he did it throughout the day—instead of just in the evening—then perhaps his employees would stop assuming that he valued face time more than their performance. I also suggested that he come into the building and walk to his office in the morning via a different route every day. He was bound to run into different people that way, since most of us are definitely creatures of habit.

Now, what to do about the conversation that ensued when he actually stopped at someone's desk or cubicle. Informal conversation did not come easily to him, as I would suspect it doesn't come easily for over 50 percent of the population. (By the way, contrary to popular belief, this is not a male/female thing. I have coached just as many women as I have men in becoming more comfortable with interpersonal interactions. I could just as easily have shared a story about a female plant manager at a consumer products company who had her own issues with this level of one-on-one interaction.) I therefore shared with him some sample questions, recommended that he edit these to seem more natural to him, and suggested that he perhaps even develop some of his own. Examples of these questions were: What was harder today than it needed to be? What client (internal or external) issues did you encounter today? What could we do better?

Let me warn you there *are* good and bad questions, and good and bad ways of asking them. I do not recommend, for example, coming up to some unsuspecting employee in the finance department—as I recently heard a CEO had done—and asking him "What did you do today to increase our sales?" While this may be a perfectly legitimate question (after all, I believe everyone should have a clear line of sight as to how their job impacts—even if tangentially—the bottom line), if your intention is to build rapport versus fear, this approach would *definitely not* hit the target. Imagine how you would feel if your boss (or boss's boss) asked you the very same questions you are intending to ask those on your team; and then amend those questions accordingly. As you become more comfortable with these work-related questions, you can start to expand your scope to include even more personal interactions; perhaps commenting about a picture or some object on their desk. The more you open up to your employees, the more likely they are to open up to you. As the leader, you have to light the way by initiating this trend.

In summary, the more you know about someone—what makes them tick, what their values are, what their life outside of the company is like, what their daily pressures at work and home are—the more likely you are to trust them and give them the benefit of the doubt. When in doubt, you are more likely to check it out with them first versus talking behind their back with everyone else on the team to confirm that you are right and they are wrong. I firmly believe—and experience bears me out on this—that we give ourselves credit for our intentions, but hold others accountable for their results. Understanding each other on a more personal level helps us to give others credit for their intentions as well.

This brings us back to the choice I discussed at the beginning of this chapter. Will you choose to have confidence in the integrity and capability of the other members of the team? What's stopping you? What can you and the rest of the team do today to start building that foundation of trust that must be there before we can get to what's in the next chapter—productive conflict? Whatever this may be, the sooner you begin, the sooner your team will reap the benefits.

In the world of fireflies, there is one species in which the female is called the femme fatale. Why? Because they mimic the welcoming signal of another species to gain their trust. When the victim is close enough, it is pounced upon and eaten by this ferocious firefly. Likewise, trickery and manipulation can kill trust on a team. In the next two chapters, I will share with you examples of *human* behaviors that I have seen on teams that have worked to both establish and to destroy trust—that essential component of team strength.

Chapter Six

Conflict as Creative Abrasion . . . a Pearl, a Diamond, or a Mountain?

Many—if not most—people are very clear on their view of conflict: it is negative, bad, and destructive. However, conflict can in fact be a very powerful innovative force—if your team can come to see it as *creative abrasion*. The president of Nissan Design International, Jerry Hirshberg—the man who originally coined the phrase—felt so strongly about the power of this concept that he purposely hired people to design cars in pairs that represented very divergent thinking. Picture the people on your team. How diverse is their thinking? Are you proactively tapping into that diversity, or do you and your other team members treat it more as an irritant, like the grain of sand in an oyster?

I debated with myself which metaphor to use to describe accurately the fruitfulness I have seen creative abrasion evoke. I began with the oyster. Ah, yes, everyone has heard about that bit of sand that becomes a pearl; but let's extend the metaphor a little further. Unbeknownst to many, the oyster's true function is not to make the pearl. Thus, that grain of sand is pushed to the side and constantly covered with a shiny substance that smoothes out those rough edges, making the irritant tolerable but serving no useful purpose

. . . to the oyster. Humans, on the other hand, are more than happy to embrace this by-product of the oyster's attempts to make his environment more comfortable. Do you view the conflict on your team in the way that the oyster sees the pearl—as something to be buried or glossed over?

Let's take another metaphor—this time, a piece of coal. Do you know how that ugly lump becomes a diamond? Through intense heat and pressure. Is that the kind of environment under which your team works best? Is there always a new fire to fight? Do you suffer through white-hot high-conflict situations, and often find it hard to appreciate the diamonds that were produced?

Bear with me for one more metaphor, if you would, and picture two tectonic plates on the earth's surface—your way and my way, perhaps—grating against each other. Many people know that when this kind of friction occurs between plates, earthquakes often ensue. But what happens when these two plates—or viewpoints—come *together*? If the environment is right, they create a mountain—a third viewpoint that is a product of these other approaches and that is grander, loftier, and more powerful than either one was on their own. This is true synergy.

It isn't always easy to create a fertile environment for productive conflict, and it certainly doesn't come naturally. The leader must *guide the way*; and then every member of the team must *follow that path.*

Step One: Begin with a philosophical—but *realistic*—mind-set that conflict is natural, expected, and yes, even desired. And, if channeled properly, extremely productive. This is *creative abrasion* thinking.

Step Two: Acknowledge and discuss conflict that is already occurring, and determine its sources and impact. Is it one-on-one, leader and subordinate, or teamwide? Is it an annoyance, or is it debilitating?

Step Three: Get serious about addressing conflict. Develop a plan and approach for resolving it, and hold people accountable for making this happen.

Let's begin with the toughest step: the very first one, which requires you to make what may potentially be a very considerable mental shift in your personal view of conflict. I was working with one team leader who went so far as to ask me not to use that word *conflict*. Would I mind calling it *productive dialogue* instead? Abrasion is not creative unless a leader makes a conscious effort to make it so—and one necessary component of this is trust. In the last chapter, I made what I hope was a strong case for why trust on a team is so important to viewing conflict productively, and explained why the leader's role in creating such an environment is so vital. Then, everyone on the team needs to become more comfortable when conflict occurs—because it will. In my experience, very heated, passionate exchanges ensue about alternative solutions, pros and cons, and choosing the right path. You can still leave the debate with respect for the other person—both their intentions and intellect—if you have a strong foundation of trust. When trust has been broken, damaged, or never established in the first place, then it is very difficult to engage in a debate about ideas.

Another critical component that a leader can control is hiring and valuing a team that exhibits a diversity of talent and thinking styles. It is hard to encourage different perspectives if they all resemble your own. This is a well-known issue with managers, and believe me, we have all done it. You hire those people you like and to whom you can really relate; and if you aren't very careful, you often end up with a uniformly minded team. *Harvard Business Review* reported on a study that clearly demonstrated that teams that were homogeneous in thinking styles were *initially* very productive. This makes sense, since they all thought the same way, talked the same way, and in fact, could likely finish each other's sentences. After a short period of time, however, their level of productivity peaked. Why? For the same reason that success had initially taken hold—they were all thinking, talking, and working the *same way*. The lack of diverse experiences, opinions, and approaches stunted their growth as a team. However, the opposite occurred with those groups that were determined to be heterogeneous (thinking styles-wise). They were initially dysfunctional and less productive; but once they learned to value and capitalize on the differences on their team, their productivity level soared past the same-minded teams. The lesson here is clear: although similar viewpoints may seem to encourage team productivity at first, only a wide variety of opinions and attitudes can keep your team thriving in the long run. As Thomas Stewart, former editor of the *Harvard Business Review*, so aptly put it: "It is often said that sparks from opposing ideas ignite innovation." I haven't heard it said often, but I sure do agree with it.

On to step two. Conflict is like a 12-step program; you first have to admit you have a problem. Putting our head in the sand about whether conflict is occurring on the team or not is pointless, because I *guarantee* you that it exists. I have worked with more than my share of groups with leaders who assure me there is no discord on the team. I remember reading a survey that asked employees what New Year's resolution they most wanted their leaders to adopt. Want to take a guess what it was? "Do something about the conflict in the workplace!" Just because you don't see people yelling at each other and overtly expressing their dislike of others doesn't mean you don't have some degree of tension. Explicit expressions of anger are not the only way that conflict plays out on a team; oftentimes, it has gone underground or been glossed over (like the pearl).

I've found through years of working with teams that conflict can surface in many silent, hidden ways; like the passive aggressive person, or the femme fatale to whom I alluded at the end of the last chapter. You know the kind of people I'm talking about; they pretend to be your friendly colleague, a real team player who appears to agree with the team's consensus, but they are truly just feigning their cooperation and support. Instead, they will do just enough to get by, rather than giving their full energy and effort. It can be very deflating to the whole team when one or more members *act* like they are on board and truly are not. These people use others' trusting nature against them, and take advantage of the collaborative team in order to avoid responsibility and commitment. Not only does it defeat the firefly (or person) who has been eaten (or stabbed in the back); it destroys—sometimes for good—that other person's belief in the goodness of others, and the team's belief that this trust idea will ever fly. So, who—or what—is eating your team alive? What behaviors are proving to be toxic to the very trust you are trying to establish? Do you have a ferocious firefly that is harming the team and getting away with it? I will introduce various techniques for turning destructive conflict into productive conflict later in the chapter; but suffice it to say for now that the team leader needs to step up and address this situation head on, as quickly as possible.

Some of the hardest team members to eliminate are those who are getting great results for the business, but are doing so in ways that hinder or limit the team's overall level of trust and capability. Just as scientists aren't exactly sure why one firefly would kill another of the same species, you may not know why these particular members of the team would do things that damage trust on the team. It is the leader's job—with the team's support—to ensure clarity about what behaviors will and will not be accepted. Building a culture of trust demands that everyone accept this as a team value, and not in words only. It must be accompanied by actions. (In Chapter 9, we will discuss how to create these guiding principles for the team so that all are clear on the expectations for team behavior.)

There are three other ways that I consistently encounter with teams in which trust is damaged or limited, and unproductive conflict emerges. These are: (1) The individual who won't share personal information; (2) sarcasm disguised as humor; and (3) one or more disengaged members of the team.

In one instance, I was working with a leadership team at a telecommunications company. The leader, Scott, was sharing with me some of the current team dynamics, so that I could be prepared to facilitate their two-day team effectiveness session. He specifically told me about one member named Jerry who was new to the team, and came across as pretty aloof. He was a long-tenured employee of the company with known areas of expertise; but he had also been labeled a problem employee who had trouble fitting in. Scott had offered to take him on because Jerry had the technical expertise that he needed to complete a critical project.

At the end of the first day, I was explaining how the milestones dinner worked (i.e., sharing of two events or people who had a significant impact on who you are and where you are today) and the tremendous impact I've seen it have on teams. Jerry was not buying into this at all. "I will come to the dinner, but I won't share anything personal," he said. I asked him to tell the group his concerns. "Well, I think my work life is my work life, and my personal life is my personal life. I don't believe in mixing the two, so I won't talk about my personal life with my co-workers." This was not the first time that I'd seen this kind of hesitancy by a team member when I introduce the milestones dinner. I attempted to reassure him that we were not expecting any deep, dark secrets to be revealed; just something that would help us to see each other as whole people instead of just a name and a job title.

The rest of the team was getting into the act. There was one teammate siding with Jerry, saying he didn't feel like Jerry should have to do anything he didn't want to do. Others on the team tried to convey to Jerry that, considering he was new to the team, this would be a great way for all of them to get to know each other better. Jerry could not be moved. After we broke up for the day, and before heading to the milestones dinner that evening, Scott informed me that he would talk with Jerry just to see if he could convince him how important this activity was. He thought that he could perhaps alleviate Jerry's concerns by simply asking him to share *anything* of a more personal nature—even where he grew up, or something about his family. Although I hoped that Scott would be able to convince him to do this, I wasn't optimistic. That night, Jerry passed when it came time for his turn at dinner.

I did not have high hopes for Jerry's long-term success on the team. But I was wrong. This team, with the leader as a great role model, worked very hard to build the trust level for the members of the entire team. They incorporated personal information sharing into their staff meetings. They sought out opportunities to collaborate on projects. It was not an easy process, but it worked . . . over time. You have heard it before: Trust is something that can take years to develop, and then be destroyed in an instant. I disagree. If trust is built on a strong foundation, it will be able to sustain the natural human errors that we all make. But, it must be a priority, for both the leader and the team.

Is there someone on your team who is holding back, someone with whom others cannot seem to connect? If there is, your team needs to deal with this because even one closed-off member can distract a team from its primary focus: to use trust to do great work together. You can't have one person who is simply a bystander to the cohesiveness that is beginning to build. They will lose ground and never catch up to the work and connections that have been established. The entire team needs to convey the importance of opening yourself up to each other as humans, and make it clear that everyone is expected to work together in this way. Perhaps even more importantly, create a safe environment in which this can begin to happen—not all at once, but some forward progress must take place.

I also see a problem when one or more members of a team erode trust through their sense of humor. As you can probably guess, the only person who sees this as comedy is the one delivering the stinging remarks. Words matter; in fact, I would like to share a story about how mere words can destroy the very bond that I am there to help the team create.

I was working with the senior leadership at a hospital, a group that was used to throwing barbs at each other under the guise of humor. By the middle of the first day, I felt compelled to share with them that I thought this constant negative exchange was keeping a wall between them. Unfortunately, in this case the leader was the worst and deadliest offender, since he had been around the longest and knew so much about every one of them. I find this occurring a lot, especially on teams that have been together a long time and haven't had many members join or leave. They know each other's weak areas and soft spots, and they're used to poking so-called fun at each other. They've come to habitually deal with issues covertly through public humiliation versus overtly through direct private conversation. When I initially see this pattern emerging, I try to assess how much of a problem it actually is. I watch the faces and body language after a verbal dagger has been thrown in another's direction. When I can actually see the energy being sapped from that person—and I have determined that this is not person-specific, but rather a widespread situation—then I intervene.

My expressions of concern are initially met with, "Oh, you just don't know our team very well. We always joke with each other. Everyone knows we're just kidding." I ask them to take a moment and think about it—does this joking make the team stronger? Or, might it keep people from truly opening up to each other? I usually continue to receive push back, and I continue to bring it up every time a joke is made at another's expense. It makes them realize how much they are doing it, and who gets the brunt of it. I even have used the ground rule for these groups, "No heat-seeking missiles" versus with other groups it is simply, "Be hard on the issue—not the person."

Do you recognize this happening anywhere on your team? Are you perhaps the recipient, or are you the perpetrator? Are you the leader, or the ringleader? Let me be clear; I love good wit, as long as it does not erode the very team collaboration that you are trying to promote. The next time this happens, take a chance and bring it to light. Share this story and see if it resonates with the team. Then reach agreement on what changes you all will commit to make. It only works if everyone agrees.

Disengagement by one or more members of the team can be another significant barrier to trust within the team, and a tremendous source of conflict. This next example is more personal in nature. I was young in my career, only at my second job out of college, and I had just been promoted after less than a year. I was the director of Human Resources for a large, entrepreneurial, fast-food franchisee. I started taking on other areas of the company to manage, namely, facilities and administrative services. Unfortunately, I learned something about myself: I liked the exciting project work of creating new programs a lot more than I liked maintaining them. But, *man*, this job paid well. I came to really dislike the work, and it showed. Not only for me, but also for those around me. I was becoming a toxic firefly and poisoning everyone around me about the work, my boss, and my co-workers.

I will always be grateful to my boss for what she did. She first counseled me, pointing out my negative behaviors and the impact they were having, and then encouraged me to turn things around. I tried to have a more positive outlook; I really did. But I was stuck in a sour mind-set and no amount of effort on my part or hers could change that. Mind you, I was not grateful then, but isn't that the beauty of time? If we keep our minds open to it, and allow time to do its cliché thing of healing all wounds, then we (I) can look back on it and say that it was a gift—to give me 60 days to begin to look for other work.

To this day, I keep this personal experience in the back of my mind when I coach leaders to do what was done to me. If you have an employee that you think has some potential for success, then you have a responsibility to do what you can to help them change, or regain, their effectiveness. Put forth your best effort to help the problem employee who is no longer engaged or performing up to standard to turn the situation around, and make it clear what behaviors and results need to change. Then, if the employee is not able to deliver, and you honestly say that you have done your best as a leader and coach to help them succeed, it is time for that person to move on. The most critical point here is to let them leave with dignity; for their own sake, and so that you don't alienate the other members of the team. This sends a clear message to the people who are left behind that you value and expect results; but you will treat with respect those who cannot meet these standards.

Sometimes disengagement is not limited to just one person. Occasionally, real or virtual distance keeps members from building the bond of trust; and I am often there to facilitate a session to bring this very lack of engagement to light. Usually, I've seen these disconnected team members actually become involved once they feel valued. They may, in fact, be the very people who are the team drivers, but have not been valued before. I have seen a lot of bad team-building simulation activities in my line of work. One of my personal nonfavorites is the construction of a tower using a variety of props, including marshmallows, toothpicks, rolled-up paper tubes, and uncooked spaghetti. I am not quite sure what the purpose of this particular craft was, but I am willing to bet that it didn't do much to boost team morale or effectiveness.

Then I was introduced to the Jungle Escape simulation at Coke. We used it with our entire Coca-Cola North America HR team, so that we could be guinea pigs to test it out ourselves before we used it on our internal client groups.

In essence, each team gets a bag of helicopter parts made up of various size Lego pieces. The teams then need to build the helicopter in order to escape from a monsoon, using only a black and white picture and an actual model hidden behind a screen. The activity is intense enough to truly engage people— or bring their disengagement to light. That is when you can *really* begin to learn about the team dynamics. Soon after I started FireFly Facilitation, I purchased a set of the Jungle Escape from HRDQ (www.HRDQ.com) and had the opportunity to use this simulation with an accounting team at a regional bank. The leader had informed me prior to the session that his team was having a real issue with a division—and believe it or not, it was based on *floors*. You see, one part of the team was on the first floor—the same floor as the leader—while another was separated by just one level. This second-floor group truly felt like second-class citizens, which shows how significant a gap one floor can be!

As this team was putting together the helicopter, I noticed that Suzanne, one of the second-class floor teammates, was busily working away, using the model to write in the colors of the parts on the black and white picture. When she returned to the group to show them what she had done, they barely looked up from their work. Barbara, another member of the less popular floor, sat there with a propeller in her hand, twirling it between her fingers, a look of complete disdain on her face. It was amazingly clear to me to see what was going on. Three people, including the leader, were huddled over the helicopter; the three from the other floor were on the outskirts. Finally, the group had completed the building of the helicopter. There was subdued cheering—by some. Now, it was time for the real learning to begin.

I asked a few softball questions; and then I asked the participants how well they felt that they used all of the team members' talents. "Did everyone feel engaged?" I asked. The three who had been actively working on the building avidly agreed that yes, everyone had been really involved. I decided to address the proverbial elephant in the room. I knew that I had to take this chance, because the issue would continue to fester if I did not. "Tell me, Suzanne and Barbara, did you both feel like your talents were used?" Initially, they looked away and hesitated to respond. I pressed the point further. "Suzanne, what happened when you brought back the picture of the helicopter with the colors written in?" Bob, the team leader, truly seemed surprised to hear this. "When did you do that?" Soon, it all began to pour out. The second-class group came to realize that the neglect was not intentional; the first-floor group came to realize no matter how unintentional, it was still painful, and caused them to lose an incredible asset to their team.

The action planning that followed these team epiphanies was just as critical to the team's future success. Although combining the two floors into one was not an option, there were several changes—while small and seemingly insignificant—that combined to make a large impact. The location of staff meetings alternated between the two floors. Members of the different floors sought out and found opportunities to collaborate on cross-functional projects. The leader personally made an extra effort to reach out to those on the other floor, since he was now well aware of the negative impact that came when they didn't truly feel as though they were a part of one team.

So, ask yourself—in addition to encouraging team members to open up about their personal lives, eliminating (or at least lessening) the sarcastic humor that keeps everyone's armor on, and dealing directly with the disengaged and disenfranchised—what are some other ways that leaders can have a profound and positive impact on conflict within the team? What can you do to ensure that conflict is productive not only at the team level, but also in one-on-one interactions and between a leader and a subordinate? The next chapter will focus on exactly this.

Chapter Seven

Was It Something I Said?

There is no wasted energy in the glow of a firefly. Incredibly, almost 96 percent of the energy that a firefly uses to create light is actually converted into visible light. Compare that to a typical light bulb, which converts only 10 percent into light and uselessly expends the remainder. Fireflies know how to shine without creating heat—without wasting energy on unnecessary conflict. How about you? What could you and your team do today to turn that wasted heat of unproductive conflict into true creative abrasion? Let's look at your options for each of these layers of potential conflict: one-on-one, leader to subordinate, and team-based.

While our differences may sometimes be irritating, they can compel us to look at situations, problems, and opportunities more creatively, if we begin with a curious mind-set. Remember, everyone believes that their viewpoint is legitimate and reasonable. When you hear something that you disagree with, ask yourself "What would make someone think this or feel this way?" Then spend the rest of the conversation trying to discover the answer to that question. I admit that it is not easy; this is one I particularly struggle with. However, I truly find it helps to keep working at it, and congratulate yourself when you are successful. You must respect others' opinions as just as valid and valuable as yours because to those people, they *are*, no matter how much they diverge from how you see things.

There is a concept in the book *Crucial Conversations* (Kerry Patterson et al.) that has really resonated with me, and with the teams with whom I share it. It is easy to remember—and it works. When you are having a difficult time keeping that open, curious mind-set, ask yourself, "Why would a reasonable, rational, and decent person do what this person is doing?" It had a profound impact on me when I read this. There have been many times when I was in the midst of a conflict, and I began to attribute all kinds of terrible motives and reasoning for the behavior I was seeing. However, this one simple question forced me to stop myself and the self-talk about how absolutely right I was and how wrong the other person (aka my husband; yes, I sometimes use this on my own family!) was. By stopping that thinking in its tracks, you make the other person human again, instead of a villain. You compel yourself to think about why they are thinking or acting in the way that they are. I forced myself to walk the proverbial mile—even if only for a moment—in the other person's shoes. This, of course, takes me back to emphasizing why it is so important for all team members to have a more *holistic* view of each other—and know more than simply one's job title and where he or she sits.

The next step then must be for you to look at your own motives in the conflict—what do you really want the end result to be? If you begin with the right motives—what the authors call "starting with heart"—then you are more likely to get out of a victim mentality and begin taking accountability for your own contribution to the situation. (We will discuss this more in Chapter 13.) This quote may be trite, but I have found it be very true: "People don't care how much you know, until they know how much you care." If you begin by helping your opponent clearly see your *honest* intentions, then they may be more open to hearing your perspective and ideas for how to address the conflict in which you both find yourselves.

Okay, so let's say you have done all that and you are still having difficulties with another individual. Could it be it's the Venus and Mars issue, but instead of being between men and women, it is between HBDI Blue and Red or Green and Yellow? It shouldn't come as a surprise, after all, that differences in how people think strongly impacts the way they communicate. This dissimilarity is of course valuable, if we can overcome our natural resistance to this form of creative abrasion. This will be the very diversity upon which we are going to capitalize to tackle our greatest challenges and opportunities, if we recognize, understand, and make transparent our differences in communication style.

Remember our discussion of the Herrmann Brain Dominance Instrument (HBDI) from Chapter 4? Look at Figure 7.1 to see how differently people in each of the quadrants like to communicate and be communicated with—aka, "Communicating the Whole Brain Way." Because that's really what we're talking about here: learning how to converse in such a way that will truly allow us to convey our message to, and possibly influence, other people. We need to speak with others in a way that considers their dialogue tendencies. I have seen amazing

Blue "Analyzers" (A) like...	*Yellow "Strategizers" (D) like...*
▪ Critical analysis ▪ Facts—no fluff ▪ Technical accuracy ▪ Well-articulated ideas ▪ Goals and objectives ▪ Data—fact based charts ▪ Brief, clear, precise info	▪ Minimal details ▪ Freedom to explore new ideas ▪ Metaphors and visuals ▪ Connecting to the big picture ▪ New, fun, imaginative approaches ▪ Conceptual framework ▪ Aligns with long term strategy

Communication Preferences of the Whole Brain® Model

Green "Organizers" (B) like...	*Red "Personalizers" (C) like...*
▪ Detail time-action plan ▪ Thorough and timely follow through ▪ Rules and procedures ▪ Step by step approaches ▪ In writing in advance ▪ Contingency plans ▪ No digressing	▪ Group discussion ▪ Expressive body & voice ▪ Personal touch and informality ▪ Eye-to-eye contact ▪ Sensing how others are reacting ▪ Considering the needs of the listener ▪ No hidden agendas

Figure 7.1. Communication Preferences of the Whole Brain Model

transformation occur once people understand their own communication preferences, and how this might cause conflict with others.

For example, let's say your team needs to make a difficult business decision. If you prefer the Analyzer (A) quadrant, then you want to hear the facts, the figures, and the bottom line—all in a brief, clear, precise format. If you have a preference for the opposite—Personalizer (C) quadrant—then you want to discuss the context of the issue, the impact it will have on employees and other key stakeholders, what your gut or your intuition is telling you, all in a collaborative, face-to-face format. Can you imagine the potential conflict that could arise, all because of the variations in these thinking and communication preferences? Can you imagine the ideas that might emerge if all members of the team created a safe environment in which to share these perspectives? You get the picture.

I have only highlighted one set of opposites above, and I could have done the same with the Strategizer (D) quadrant—wanting the big picture, the visual, the alignment with strategy—as compared to the Organizer (B) quadrant—wanting the detail, contingency plans, and clear accountabilities. Does it sound like two sides of a coin—and very valuable currency at that? The leader can play a critical role in helping the members of the team see and value these different perspectives.

When I work with teams on developing constructive creative abrasion, we use a wonderfully simple tool that we created called an HBDI User Guide. Each person uses this page to summarize what they learned from their HBDI profile—their strengths, blind spots, how they behave under pressure, how they like to communicate and be communicated with, one area they would like to improve in their communications effectiveness, and more. Then we have each member share this information with the other group members, and often create a booklet with each person's user guide. This really helps to build team trust and awareness levels. I can't show you within the confines of this book how you personally would behave and communicate differently under pressure than you would normally; but that is one of the other valuable benefits of taking the HBDI online assessment. I always say this is a good thing to know for yourself and for your co-workers, especially if you are prone to a Dr. Jekyll/Mr. Hyde kind of transformation!

If you know that you need to have a tough conversation with someone to resolve a conflict, it is a good idea to prepare. I recommend that you actually plan what you will say in those opening one to two minutes. Although this might seem like a short amount of time to you, it will seem quite long to the other person. I like to use something we call the optimal flow for communication to help you to think through each step of how the conversation might progress. Here is what that looks like:

- **Yellow (D)**—Begin with a common goal that you and the person in conflict both have, even if it is just that this situation can be resolved to everyone's satisfaction. If there are points on which you can both settle, such as a common picture of the desired end result, then that is a great place to start (even if you initially disagree on how to reach that goal). Ask them if they agree with the common goal(s) that you have just stated. If not, see if a simple rewording would suffice; but don't get bogged down early on.

- **Blue (A)**—This is when you share the facts or the current situation as you see it. You might also discuss the impact that the other person's actions or current situation is having on others. Keep this as objective as possible, without emotions or exaggeration. Be careful that you have not made assumptions that you are presenting as fact. Make it clear you are sharing the way *you* see it; but acknowledge that they may see it differently. Separate the facts of the matter from your own interpretation. Be aware of the slant you may be giving to certain facts merely due to the ones you've chosen to focus on.

- **Red (C)**—Ask your counterpart to respond to what they've just heard. You might ask, "Do you see the situation differently? If so, how?" And then be silent. Try to keep breathing, and don't interrupt. Let them vent if they need to; what you have just said may be surprising to them, thus eliciting a very emotionally charged reaction. Remember the curious mind-set we mentioned above; ask yourself why might they be reacting this way.

- **Green (B)**—Focus on the points of agreement, and determine what the next steps might be. If you are in a position to begin to discuss alternatives for addressing the points of disagreement, then you can move back into the Yellow quadrant for brainstorming. Remember to keep a both/and mind-set, not an either/or. You don't want winners and losers. If tensions are high, you might want to set up a follow-up meeting for 48 to 72 hours from that point, to enable both of you to separate yourselves from the situation for a while and gain some perspective. Clarify what each of you will do after this meeting to resolve the conflict. Review what you've agreed to and what you still need to decide; don't leave that part vague, even if the exact path to a winning solution may be.

This should help you get a handle on dealing effectively with one-on-one conflict. But what if the situation has a twist, and you are a leader dealing with a subordinate? What might you want to avoid and to do? The major mistake I hear over and over again comes from very well-meaning leaders—and it can go in one of two directions. Option one: managers truly want their people to take greater accountability for solving their own issues. "Well, when they tell me they are having a problem with someone on the team, I just tell them to go work it out with that other person; that I don't want to hear about it. Isn't that what I am supposed to do?" While that may be what the manager *thinks* she is doing, the employee may perceive it in a completely different way: that the manager doesn't care. While neither is right here, both are.

Another option I often hear goes like this: "Well, when they come to me with a problem with another co-worker, I just pick up the phone and call that person to come to my office too, so that we can get it all out on the table and resolve this once and for all." Feels a little like being called to the principal's office, I would imagine. You now have, in most cases I've seen, a very angry co-worker who resents being asked to come to the boss's office, not knowing what for, or what has already been communicated. Not the best environment for a positive resolution of a tough situation.

So what is a leader to do? First, if you truly have a performance problem with one employee, you need to address that situation. How do you know if that is the case? Well, are you hearing the same or similar complaints from several (trusted) sources? Has this person been coached on this issue before? Do you know in your gut that you have been avoiding dealing with a situation that is truly your responsibility? If that is the case, then it is unfair to ask someone on your team to deal with a situation because you are avoiding it yourself. This can go on for a long time, and the result is usually that the rest of the team sees this one person as being responsible for everyone's problems. As long as they can keep blaming someone else for the group's ineffectiveness, then they don't have to deal with how they are hindering the team's progress.

Assuming, however, that is not the case—there isn't a problem employee, but rather a real problem—then the team leader needs to fully step into the role of coach and mentor. When one of your employees approaches you about a conflict with another one, it can be a prime opportunity for you to guide your subordinate on how to deal with this situation most effectively. Ask what the person has tried, what worked and what didn't, and explore their ideas for other options. If this is not an area of expertise for you, then simply walk them through some of the steps from the previous one-on-one discussion that most resonate with you. Recognize when a conflict between two or three people truly has to do with differences in style—thinking, communicating, or working— and realize that your role as the leader is to help them to learn to deal with these situations *themselves*. Help them to see this for what it is—differences that either can be viewed as dysfunctional or as sources of creative abrasion. Consider conducting a role-play to help employees prepare for a high-conflict discussion *before* it actually occurs. Use the optimal flow outlined previously. Jot down your opening statement to the discussion, which should be focused on the Yellow and Blue quadrants. You must clarify that unresolved conflict is unacceptable and detrimental to the team. Yes, it takes more time to help them to resolve it, but it is definitely teaching them how to fish.

The leader's role in effectively dealing with subordinates on the team in conflict goes hand in glove with how the leader can effectively address and resolve conflict in a *team* setting. How can you enable great discussions, keep conflict productive, and design a solution that everyone can live with and support? First, and perhaps most important, turn the energy accompanying the conflict outward. Great teams clearly know their competition, and they keenly focus their sights on how to defeat them. I was recently interviewing an executive at an insurance company in preparation for an offsite session. This was an organization struggling greatly in a downturn market. There had been layoffs recently that had left employees fearful and overstretched. "We have so much fighting going on right now between individuals and departments. Somehow, I need to remind everyone that the real enemy is outside our walls, not inside." I see this all the time when people have lost sight of the competition. People look at others on the team as their competition—for resources, a leader's time, for attention.

What if you were able to redirect that energy toward the *outside*? One picture of success keeps everyone mindful that the true competition is *external to the team*. When the team creates and remains focused on the common goal, everyone is committed to the same destination point on the horizon. Understanding each person's role and how they contribute to success is an important component to this. I have found an excellent exercise for helping teammates to learn more about—and hopefully gain an appreciation for—what it is like to spend "A Day in the Life" (from *Quick Team-Building Activities for Busy Managers* by Brian Cole Miller) in someone else's shoes. They gain respect for how hard the work is for their fellow members, as well as knowledge about the responsibilities of each other's department or team. In fact, I used this in a recent client engagement. When I arrived, the entire team was present, but none of them were talking to each other, save for some limited small talk and snide, sarcastic comments. Most were on their computers or cell phones. I was there for the stated purpose of trying to build their effectiveness as a team. They definitely looked ripe for improvement in that area!

Needless to say, my clients were not too excited about participating in this exercise when the time came for it during our session. They seemed to believe that they knew only too well what the other members were responsible for, but I prevailed anyway. I paired people up for the first round with the team leader's assistance. I was looking specifically for those who needed to collaborate better across functions; know more about each other's areas because of interdependencies; or who were doing battle all the time, and needed to form a stronger bond of respect for each other.

Once in pairs, one partner recalls in detail what their typical workday is like. The listener can say only, "Then what?" or "That's interesting. Tell me more." "Tell me more about that!" After 5 minutes, they switch roles and repeat.

If they struggle with describing a typical day because no day is typical, I recommend they describe yesterday, or pick one workday from last week. The trick is to have them use an actual date so that they can fill in the necessary details. When giving the instructions, warn them that five minutes will seem like a long time; but assure them you will be clocking it. The objective is not to just provide a quick run-through of your list of activities and meetings that day, but to truly share enough that your partner will get a good sense of what your day is really like.

Reinforce the key concepts at the end by discussing such questions as "How did you feel sharing these experiences with each other?"; "What did you learn about each other that you did not know?"; What challenges are they facing that you could help them with?; "What implication does this have for us back on the job?"

The transformation that began during the exercise continued through the debriefing and afterward. People were more relaxed. There were none of the snide comments, which I was concerned there might be. The information that they found out about one another—"I didn't realize that part of Sue's job was to negotiate contracts," "Now I know who to go to if I need help with creating a complex spreadsheet!"—truly brought them closer, both for today and for the future. It was a great way to get the people on a team to see each other with new eyes.

Another step that helps teams effectively deal with conflict is developing guidelines for working together before attempting to act on the problem at hand. In Chapter 9,

I will discuss the process I use to help teams develop their own guiding principles; standards that help people to understand the expectations for themselves and each other. Operating without these guidelines would be analogous to trying to conduct an effective meeting without clear, agreed upon ground rules. Additionally, I often work with teams to create conflict norms that are specifically designed to help the conflict generate more productive decisions to which all teammates can commit. I will discuss the process for this in Chapter 11. For now, I want to make some recommendations about what you can do if you are in a team meeting where conflict begins to surface.

First, remind everyone of your creative abrasion philosophy: Conflict can be very beneficial if we keep it focused on the *issues* and not direct our passion negatively toward one another. You'll need this passion when it comes time to commit to and execute the planned-for solution. I tell my clients to "Be hard on the issue, not the person"; and "Speak so that you can be heard." Both of these are meant to remind people that the *manner* in which you say things goes a long way toward helping others hear and accept your message, without automatically eliciting a negative emotional response. If things are getting too intense, take a brief break to give everyone some breathing room before resuming the discussion. When you reconvene, ask everyone to look for points of agreement, and then solve the disagreements together.

If the source of the conflict is a specific issue or problem, remind the team we are searching for the best solution, not a winner and loser. Remember to look for the third way that we discussed in the last chapter—a method that perhaps incorporates aspects and suggestions from a number of people. Such a solution shouldn't be based on the tyranny of either/or, but rather takes into consideration both/and. How do you do that? Ask people to spend as much time understanding other people's viewpoints as they do advocating their own. Consider asking them to paraphrase what the previous person said before voicing their own idea or opinion; or request that each person say what they like about another's idea before giving any criticism. Help them to clarify what is a *want* versus a *need*. I do not recommend—and many teams challenge me on this—that you only allow facts; this causes people to misrepresent one for the other. You should instead ask your teammates to be clear on when they are stating a fact versus an opinion.

Make sure to keep the conflict a group issue, not a sparring match between two competitors. Encourage others to share their points of view, especially those who may have been silent up to that point. Be careful, however, not to put someone on the spot by calling on them. I ask them to do this as a means of balancing participation: "I am going to ask you to think about your participation level in this discussion thus far and self-police. If you have 'over-participated,' please make room for others to add their voice. If you have 'under-participated,' I am asking you to take this opportunity to make your perspective known." To make sure all sides are being adequately represented, you could have someone argue the position of the opposition; or better yet, divide the group based on point of view, and have them argue the other side. Ask what they learned, and how they can use this new perspective to develop a better solution.

As much as I might hate to admit it, I agree with Galileo, who said, "You cannot teach a man anything; you can only help him find it within himself." In these last two chapters, I have attempted to illustrate the value of creative abrasion, and describe the ways in which your team can achieve it. Some of these ideas may be new to you; some may be simply a different slant on suggestions you have heard before. Some you may agree with, and some you cannot imagine actually doing yourself. In the end, *you* have the choice to make—as you always do. What actions will I take based on what I have read? How will I handle the next situation that is ripe with the potential for conflict? How will I take those sparks that arise from opposing views . . . and use them to ignite my creativity in handling this situation better than I ever have before?

I hope that you've been inspired to find the answers for these questions—and so many more.

Part III

The Leader's Role—Targeting Team Energy

Chapter Eight

One Team—One Picture of Success

This chapter is about what happens when everyone unites for a common purpose, like going on a firefly hunt. Everyone knows why they are there—to catch as many as you can. There is one clear purpose, one clear goal. Don't you wish it could be the same for your team? Oh, the power we could harness if everyone focused on the same target with as much energy and excitement as you had chasing fireflies as a kid. How clear are you on why everyone is on your team? Does everyone have a common vision of what success looks like? It is very important that they do; and this chapter will share my approach to ensuring that this happens.

In December of 2002, my husband and I were on our way to Costa Rica to celebrate our 10th wedding anniversary. As often happens, he fell asleep shortly after take off and I pulled out my airplane reading. This time it was Patrick Lencioni's newly published *The Five Dysfunctions of a Team*. I was immediately captivated by this phenomenal book, because I totally believed in and agreed with the author's model for how an effective leadership team should function. I had already read so many books that stated if members of a team were not *truly* interdependent, then they were not a team; they were just a group of people. They also contended that this was even the case for high-level executive teams. Prior to reading

77

Lencioni's book, I had always thought companies were paying these leaders way too much money to *not* have them functioning at a higher level than that of a simple group of individuals. They should be expected to act like they care about the success of the whole organization, not just their own silo. I now had a model to support this theory, in a very well-written story—what I call a page-turner whenever I introduce it to teams. I immediately began sharing this model with the teams that I consulted with, and they too saw the power in it.

Over the following years, as I shared Lencioni's book and model with numerous teams, I was struck by one common theme from the participants in the session—the paradigm shift of who is your *number one* team. They had not realized how closely they had been focusing on their *own* team—that is, the one that reported to them—and the significant impact this had on their perspective of the needs of the business, the lack of attention they gave to the problems and opportunities of their teammates, and the power that could be unleashed if they truly began to look at the business synergistically as one team.

I specifically remember one marketing leadership team that had been organized in a highly matrixed grid-like formation, which allowed this company to address multiple business needs using multiple command structures. This particular team had some members who had dual responsibility to both their core marketing team as well as the geographic unit they supported. When I asked them to identify their number one team, I saw one person who, in the space of 30 minutes, went from saying that it was not possible to do so, to saying that it *must* be so in order to deliver the greatest value to their true number one team and the overall organization. Clearly, there was quite a bit of confusion surrounding reporting relationships and a sense of divided loyalties, and this was adversely impacting their ability to fully bond as a team and to achieve the level of effectiveness that a matrix organization is designed to accomplish.

I was able to feel the power of a clear, one-team mindset firsthand at Atlanta's Society for Human Resource chapter meeting, and participated in something called the Music Paradigm experience. I say experience because it isn't something that you just watch—everyone attending becomes involved. Program creator and conductor Roger Nierenberg travels around the country and works with members of an orchestra in a variety of cities. Then, during the performance, the players are actually physically seated among the 200-plus members of the audience. It was truly a mind-altering experience to be able to see these musicians, their instruments, and the looks on their faces in such close proximity, and then hear the beautiful sound that envelops you when they began to play. There was one point in the program during which Nierenberg went out into the audience to allow one person to experience the impact of conducting this magnificent orchestra, and that one person happened to be me. He took my hand and led me to the stage, stood carefully behind me and placed his hand over mine—the baton held aloft—and we began.

Both power and humility overwhelmed me at the same time, and my face apparently was conveying the very strong range of emotions I was feeling. Nierenberg asked me to give words to this. "I can't believe how different it felt and sounded to be at the front of the orchestra versus being immersed in it. You can see all of the individual musicians; but you are more aware of the whole. This must be what it is like for the leader of an organization."

How I wish every leader could be in two places at one time—giving the vision speech at the front of the room, and hearing it in the audience like everyone else. What might they feel or do differently? Could they develop a deeper appreciation of how difficult it is for everyone to be on the same page with the vision? By the same token, I wish that every person in the audience—or on the team—could take on the role of the leader of the orchestra, even for just a few moments, to feel the awesome power and humbling responsibility of leading a group of virtuosos. How do you know where to take them? Well, the good news is, you don't have to—and shouldn't—decide alone. Unlike the conductor who decides what music will be performed, or where the team will go, the best leaders engage their team members in creating a shared vision for the future.

I truly believe that when done correctly, strategic planning can be one of the most exciting and effective team development tools available to a leader. (I must tell you that when I use the words *exciting* and *strategic planning* in the same sentence, many of the teams I work with think I should have my head examined; but I promise that you'll see why I have found this to be true.) Two key components drive powerful teams: where they're going and how they're going to work together to get there. The answers to these questions are inextricably tied. This is not kum-bah-yah, touchy-feely team effectiveness. It is simply asking, you want to capital-ize on team members' unique differences to *what* end? You want to promote creativity and innovation targeted toward *which* business objectives, problems, or opportunities? Both strategic planning and building team effectiveness require always having to keep a sharp focus on the business priorities. A clear link between these items—for the leader *and* the team—ensures that everyone will stay committed when the work gets harder. Some teams I work with have the benefit of a crisis, a situation that has allowed them to see that they need to do something different at the very core of their business. It can be much harder for leaders—even very enlightened ones—to convince their team that chang-ing their behavior is needed when there *isn't* a glaring problem; that it's just for the sake of being even better.

We can learn an important lesson from the world of the fireflies. Did you know that one of the reasons the population of fireflies appears to be diminishing is because of ambient light, or as some call it, "light pollution"? That's right—there are too many distractions; all these unnecessary bright lights keep fireflies from performing at their best. They can't focus on their real target when they are blinded by these irrelevant ones. How similar and true for the people on our own teams, if we don't have a common vision of success to focus our time, attention, and resources.

Another important point to keep in mind: Don't presume that everyone is already on the same page. Too many leaders have said to me, "Well, we don't need to do this exercise. Everyone already knows what we do and what our targets are." When I probe further, I learn from the leader (and from the members of the team) that while there may be varying degrees of clarity on specific project goals (usually owned by one or two members of the team), there is not *one driving purpose* or clear vision for success (of which these various projects are a very tactical part). You know how the saying goes . . . "If you don't know where you're going, any road will take you there." I assure you that people want a destination; they don't want to be on just any road. They want something more unified that binds them together. Challenge me on this— ask your team at the next staff meeting to write down what they think is the role of the team and how it adds value to the business. The answers that you receive will make you want to read the rest of this chapter.

I am going to share with you the strategic planning process that I have used with hundreds of teams over the last 15-plus years; one that I have consistently refined to capitalize on what I learned along the way. (See Figure 8.1.) I'll first give you an overview of the process, using a metaphor that really seems to resonate with people—which, of course, also has the benefit of making it easy for them to remember.

- The *mission* or role of the team is the road we are on.
- The mountain in the distance is our *vision for success*.
- The mile markers are the *key milestones* that will measure our progress.
- The guardrails are our *guiding principles* that will clearly lay out how we will work together to reach that mountain.

With this overview in mind, let me take you through the steps of this process in more detail, and share my facilitation tips for helping you to create a clear, compelling plan for your team's success at each one—not just a SPOT (Strategic Plan on Top Shelf!). Just as importantly, I will provide you with the details necessary to ensure that you get the true benefit of the team's thinking; and that it is not just a simple regurgitation of what you would have come up with on your own.

I've seen my share of company leaders debating about who should attend a strategic planning session. I will give you a typical consultant answer to this question: it depends. If it's a small, departmental-level meeting, I think you should bring everyone—and I mean *everyone*, from individual contributors to managers to support staff. There's no better

Figure 8.1.   The Firefly Path to Success

opportunity to educate and involve the full range of your employees in setting the department's—and organization's—priorities than during this session. With larger sized firms, you will likely want to hold a higher-level strategic planning session first that will set the vision and plan for the overall organization. Then the next levels down can hold their sessions based on the outcomes that the higher levels have achieved. This creates a crystal-clear line of sight between each plan and the organization's overall strategy.

One particular instance demonstrated very powerfully for me the positive impact that inviting everyone on the team can have on a gathering like this. I was facilitating a strategic planning session for a nonprofit organization. As a part of the opening segment, I asked each person to cite a time during the past year when they had been particularly proud to be a member of the organization. A program manager named Sandra talked passionately about a recent lunch with her friends in which she explained how their company was help-ing people to get into affordable housing, and how that posi-tively impacted their own sense of self-worth and gave their kids a feeling of permanence. We later came to Jill, an admin-istrative support person for the team. She was very hesitant to say anything, and in fact passed at first, claiming that "I don't see how what I do impacts people." It was so gratifying to me to see her teammates respond to this, and how everyone rallied around her. One especially supportive colleague in-formed her, "Jill, you capture and consolidate the data about the impact of our programs so accurately; we can always speak to our donors and the media with confidence." It was amazing to see Jill transform; she literally became more engaged, leaned forward and more actively participated in the breakout discussions, and listened more attentively. As she became more engaged, she became more engaging to her teammates. I am positive that the change I saw before me transcended to her interactions with others outside the team when she returned to her regular job.

The moral of the story is that people want to *know* they have an impact on something of significance, something that matters. Do you think the people on your team know how they contribute? What about the ones who are not client facing with only internal clients? If you're not sure, this is a great time to find out, and a wonderful way for the team to rally together to encourage and give voice to the value of those who may not be so sure.

Now, back to the process. If the budget makes it possible, I also recommend you try to hold your meeting off-site. You would be amazed how a different view gives you, well . . . a different view. That is really what will separate this from regular budget planning or a crisis management situation—the longer-term nature of the perspective that you gain.

I apologize up front if the following point appears to be self-serving; but I really do find it to be true. If possible, get someone other than yourself as the team leader to facilitate the session. You cannot truly contribute at your best if you are as worried about process as you are about content. Even worse, it is very hard for you as a leader *not* to dominate and overly express your opinion on the issue at hand. I should know; I'm a facilitation expert, and I can even find it challenging to control the dominance of some leaders. Additionally, if you are facilitating the session, you need to be at the front of the room; the exact *opposite* place that I recommend the leader sit when I am facilitating. I suggest that leaders sit along one of the legs of a U-shape of tables. This way, the people in the room can't easily see what he or she is thinking, or how he or she might be reacting to comments they might make. Remember: The whole purpose of bringing your entire group together is to hear what they really think and get *their* best ideas, right? Invest in a professional external facilitator, or find a talented one internally. I promise you that the return on your investment will far outweigh the lost opportunity cost of a substandard strategic plan and decreased morale. Enough said.

So there you all are, in a separate location (or for heavens sake, at least in different seats in the same room)—now what? This is a great opportunity for the leader to share the overall strategy of the organization, the state of the competition, the overarching business priorities, and the goals for the coming 24 to 36 months. I am always amazed how much members of the team love to hear this type of information, and how *little* they actually get the chance to. Now is your time, leader, to truly remind people of the difference the company is trying to make in the world. You may be thinking that only the younger generation needs this, but I can tell you the older generation needs it too, even if they've simply given up hoping that someone will tell them. There is such power in people believing that they are part of something grander than just what they can see. This is a great opportunity for you to truly test, and perhaps even stretch, your ability to inspire your team. It is critically important to be able to help the team link what they do to the achievement of this greater good.

It's also important to keep in mind that this is an opportunity for you as a leader to set expectations for the process and results of the session. If you know or firmly believe that there are some things that are nonnegotiable, off limits, or in some other way outside the scope of consideration for this group in the strategic planning process, then you need to clarify what those are up front, and explain your rationale. I sometimes hear leaders say that they are concerned about doing this because they're afraid it may be disempowering to the team. I have actually found the opposite; that it frees them up to focus on those things they really *can* have an impact on. Now, it could very well be that the team may challenge your rationale and thinking on why something is off the table. But what a compelling discussion to have. It may, in fact, open your thinking and allow you to explore alternative approaches to achieving goals of which you had been unaware. But it's always better to explicitly state these issues from the beginning than to have to covertly attempt to shift the direction of the group if it strays into (albeit unbeknownst to the rest of the team) off-limits territory. Your kick-off as the leader of this team is vitally important to the success of the whole undertaking. (No pressure!)

Members of your team are now aware of what the overall organization is working to accomplish; so how do you all help to make that happen? What is the role of the team; how do we contribute to the overall success of the organization? I sometimes ask this question to prompt team members' thinking: *If this team ceased to exist, what critical work wouldn't get done?* Give everyone a few minutes to think individually and jot down their ideas (this ensures that the extroverts do not out-talk the introverts, causing you to lose their equally valuable input). Then conduct a round-robin of sorts, to hear what everyone thinks the team's role is. There will be several opportunities to conduct this round-robin exercise, and I recommend starting at a different location each time. I like to do it without giving the participants forewarning; it keeps them on their toes! For both the mission and the vision, I sometimes send out prework in advance with questions to prompt their thinking, so that they can come prepared to discuss their thoughts at the start of the session. More often, I just make sure that all team members receive a high-level agenda in advance of the session, so that they know the objectives for the session and have a general idea for how the day will run.

I encourage you to instruct everyone to listen actively while others are sharing what they jotted down about the role of the team. Not only will it ensure that they stay engaged in the process, but you will also be asking them to listen for common themes or anything that I call a gut-level response. This means anything that truly connects with them—well, in their gut, or viscerally. My experience has been that if you can first connect their hearts with the role of the team and later the vision, then the head follows more easily. In fact, these gut level responses often capture more eloquently what people are truly working for and toward.

After the last person has given their input, I then ask people to help me capture on a flip chart what common themes and gut level responses they heard. The leader should spend an appropriate amount of time at this stage making sure that everyone is on the same page and has a common understanding of the newly defined team role. Since I've been facilitating strategic planning sessions for a while, my approach at this point has changed somewhat over the years. I used to spend quite a bit of time with a team really refining this (and later the vision statement too), making it, as I would say, suitable for lamination. You know how that goes. Create one statement that everyone can finally agree to, and it ends up reading like it was created by a committee, which it usually was.

However, that is no longer my approach. I now believe that it is more important to be in agreement *directionally* and less so to be in agreement *literally*. In other words, I have found that this early stage of the process is not so important for the statement that is produced, but rather for the conversation that it sparks. Maybe it's a lack of patience with the process, or the need to move faster in these rapidly changing times; but mission and vision statements on little wallet cards don't really seem to contribute to the bottom line anymore (if they ever did). Full participation in the process and a complete understanding of the intent is what is needed for the plan's successful execution.

Now that we know what road we are on (*our mission*), we turn our attention to the mountain in the distance—our *vision for success*. Stated another way: if we have been true to our mission, how will we know we have been successful 12 to 18 months down the road? I actually have a strong opinion about how long this horizon should be, based on the level of the group. If you are planning for an entire organization, it needs to be longer than you might make it for just one team. The bigger the company, the longer the time frame; you know what they say about steering a battleship! The long-term vision for Coca-Cola or Wal-Mart, for example, may need to be 10 years. For medium-sized, fast-moving companies in rapidly changing industries, that can be abbreviated to three years. When it comes to the actual planning phase, I like to have a much shorter time frame. An ideal timeline would therefore be a three-year vision of what success looks like on the horizon, and then creating a concrete action plan to cover the next 12 to 18 months.

It's very effective to frequently change up the process I use for each step of creating the plan. Perhaps because we are focused on the future and team members need to use their imagination even more, I use what I call a visioning process to actually *create* their idea of what the future looks like. I say something like this to the group . . .

Close your eyes and imagine it's two years from now, and we are having a huge celebration.

- Where are we?
- What are we celebrating?
- Whom do you see as you look around?
- What are people saying in their speeches?
- What have we accomplished?
- What is the look on everyone's faces?
- What are people talking about?
- Where are you in this picture?

I then distribute a handout with these same questions on it, as well as space for them to jot down everything they saw, felt, and heard. I then use a process similar to the one that I used with the mission setting, and conduct a round-robin (starting at the opposite end of the U) to ask each person to share what they wrote down while others actively listen. Again, we flip chart common themes and then debrief to reach a consensus on what our future picture of success looks like.

As I mentioned before, I don't get hung up at this point on a specific vision statement unless the client says they *absolutely* want one. I am actually finding that more companies are opting to move away from the campaign slogan–type vision of the past; possibly because they know employees are jaundiced. So I encourage them to think of the mountain in the distance—*the vision*—as a mountain range, instead of just a single mountain (i.e., a specific vision statement). Successful leaders prefer to convey their intent by their actions rather than the words on a T-shirt. I have found that people don't have the patience for generating these kinds of statements; and the end product didn't justify the time it took for a large group of people to wordsmith such a declaration. Even asking a subgroup to craft some kind of maxim and report back later with these morphed alternatives makes it difficult to get other members of the group excited about creating it. You have to decide for yourself, and the team, if you need a specific statement at all to guide the strategic decisions that come next.

This is the process that ensues if I use the knowledge that is in the room—and most of the time, given the teams I work with, it is. In the vast majority of cases, there isn't a need to collect additional market data or conduct another employee survey before teammates can come together to create their common picture of success and decide on their priorities and action plans. However, I *have* had teams collect data after the fact to help them set tangible and realistic goals or measures for the vision for success, and hone it to become more focused.

One caveat to this rule might be if a team is entering a new market or considering taking a completely new strategic direction and doesn't have the necessary data to make sound, fact-based decisions. Then I would suggest that you do collect the data, consolidate it, and send it out in an easily digestible format at least three to five days in advance of the session for the participants to review. People need time to truly understand the information, to formulate questions, and to think about the implications for their own areas of responsibility and for the whole team.

There is one last question that you might want to ask yourself in regard to the vision for success that the team has created: How would your team's customers—internal *and* external—view this vision? Are they able to see how it benefits them and meets their needs by way of your success in actually achieving this vision? It can be a very valuable exercise to put a name to a client (and yes, I mean pick one of your toughest customers), and actually imagine reviewing this vision with them once you leave this meeting in order to gain their support. What do you think they would like about it and encourage? What might they question, or even strongly oppose? You and your team need to decide what changes to make to the vision based on looking at it from this viewpoint, but you need to have this very candid discussion among yourselves first. I am not advocating that you change your vision to make it safe and easy for your customers to accept. However, you need to carefully reconsider how you will gain the support of your key stakeholders in your success if you find areas of possible contention.

The next step in the process is to conduct something that I call a force field analysis. Think of a T chart on a page. On the left hand side of the T are all of the forces that work *for* our success in achieving our vision, and on the right side are all of the forces that work *against* it. I give each person a handout (or ask them to draw a T on their paper) and ask them to write down everything they can think of that might impact our success—either for good or for bad. I then ask them to put a star beside those critical three to five items on each side of the T. Think of it this way: what forces working for us must absolutely *keep* working for us to be successful? Which are the ones that, if we get to the end of our planning cycle and we have *not* been successful, are the reasons why?

The leader (or anyone on the team, for that matter) can then summarize these key forces on a chart at the front of the room for all to see. I advocate working on the forces *for us* first, and those *against us* second. I ask each person to give me one of their top reasons, and then share their rationale for why they chose it (why they believe it is supporting or hindering our success, and what aspect of it makes this so). I continue going around the room until everyone's most pressing reasons have been captured for both sides of the T chart.

You may instead choose to conduct this compilation and discussion of forces using small groups (as opposed to going straight to the leader flip charting them), for one or both of the following reasons. First, if you think that some people on the team may be hesitant to candidly share what they believe are obstacles to the entire group, then it's probably best to break participants into small groups of four or five people to create a group T chart. The smaller groups have a tendency to create a degree of safety and anonymity that allows people to more openly discuss these tough issues. The other reason to use small breakout groups (cross functional if possible) is that it gives the members a chance to work together and rub elbows in a format that differs from their typical interactions. Each person is thereby exposed to the thinking and perspectives of others, thus accentuating the team development aspects of the strategic planning process.

Let me digress from the explanation of my process for just a moment to share two perspectives. The first is my use of the force field analysis versus the SWOT analysis, a process with which many of you are probably familiar. As you likely already know, a SWOT is laid out in four quadrants, with Strengths and Weaknesses (that which impacts us internally) on the left side and Opportunities and Threats (that which impacts us externally) on the right side. After using SWOT for years, I found that people in the planning session were getting way too tied up in debates about which quadrant to put something in, versus deep discussions of the implications of these forces. Proper labeling became more important than the ensuing discussion. I have found that the simple format of the force field analysis keeps the focus where it needs to be—on the discussion itself. In fact, I will often find people discovering that something is both a force working for *and* against the team and it is fascinating, and very helpful, to discuss what aspects of this single facet can be seen in those two ways.

The second has to do with the order of the process that I've laid out. Must you first conduct the visioning exercise and then examine the current reality using the force field analysis, or can you reverse the two? In the vast majority of situations, I have found that it is better to envision the future picture of success first, before diving into the current reality. However, many strategic planning books propose just the opposite method. They claim that "you cannot possibly think about the future until you know where you stand today." But in fact, if this picture of the future is clear and compelling enough, then you'll create a powerful state of cognitive dissonance for the team by just as clearly laying out the specific forces working for and against this vision. This works in direct opposition to conducting an indiscriminate SWOT or force field analysis that takes a very broad or generalized look at these forces.

Having said all of this, however, there *have* been some instances when I do feel that it was in the client's best interest to comprehensively understand the current reality first before moving to the visioning stage. For example, during the presession interviews for a recent client, it became clear to me that members of the executive team who would be participating in the strategic planning session had very divergent views of the current state of the business and the marketplace. I decided it was critical to first bring these conflicting perspectives to light in the session—and resolve or reconcile them—before we could truly create one picture for the success of the company that all could sign on to. The bottom line: If people are clear enough on a common view of the current reality (again, another good reason to send out any necessary data in advance to lay the foundation for this common view), then I recommend you start with creating the compelling vision for the future, and *then* conduct a targeted force-field analysis specifically against that new vision.

So you have now collaboratively created a compelling team mission and vision, and tested it against the current reality using the force field analysis—no easy task, indeed! In the next chapter, you will build upon this foundation by learning how to make those tough strategic choices about where to focus the team's attention and resources. Because, as you know, if everything is important . . . then nothing is.

Chapter Nine

How Will You Know When You Get There?

Your team is now poised to take the mission and vision to the next level—an action plan to make it become reality. You know what is working against you; so now you need to decide where you're going to focus your attention and resources, and what specifically must be done. I will share my recommendations on how to broadly communicate your plan, follow-up on the progress being made, celebrate your successes, and course correct. This is what will ensure that you execute with excellence.

You'll recall that the last chapter ended with your identification of the key forces working for and against your vision for success. The next step I usually take during my sessions is to ask the participants in the room to look at all of these key forces, and identify the critical few strategic priority areas upon which we need to focus. I like to call these the big buckets of work that need to be done; and as unsophisticated and nontechnical as that may sound, people actually get it. It might include areas like infrastructure, operations, marketing, products and services, finances, facilities, and more. At this time, these are only meant to be labels for the buckets; they don't represent what we will actually *do*, or how we will measure our success. If it helps, the team can also think of these areas as the umbrella under which all of the various initiatives and projects should fit. But these strategic priority matters still need to be limited to the three to five highest priority ones. Focus is key here, because strategic planning is not truly *strategic* unless you are deciding what *not* to do along with what *to* do.

The process I use is very simple. First, make sure that everyone understands what is meant by a strategic priority area. Give each person three sticky notes, and ask them to look at the array of positive and negative forces that you've just assembled. Then legibly write one strategic priority area per sticky note. Even though you might eventually end up with five, I think that giving people only three choices forces people to pick their truly highest-priority items.

I am often asked if the group should focus solely on the forces working against us. Instead, I encourage you to have your colleagues really attempt to look at the totality of the picture when they are developing these priority areas. In this way the team does not myopically look only at the negative— the normal human instinct of fixing a problem—but also considers how to use those forces in our favor to keep driving toward success, and maybe even to overcome those negative forces. Another key point in this regard: I often find that teams put the same issue on both sides of that T chart. It can be seen as a force for good or evil, as I like to say—it all depends on which aspects of it you look at. You would likely lose sight of that if you only look at one side of the equation.

When everyone has identified their top three priorities, which should take about three to five minutes, there are several different approaches that you can use to categorize similar ones, depending upon the size of the group. You might ask a team of six to eight people, for example, to bring their sticky notes down front and place them on two flip chart stands. Then everyone can work collaboratively to group like ideas together, until you have some fairly clear buckets (and perhaps a few outliers). Reach a pretty quick consensus on what you want to label each bucket. This is an especially good approach if people have been sitting for a while, and they really need to get up and be energized again by physically moving around the room.

You might want to break a larger-size crowd into smaller groups of four to five people, and then have them conduct the classification of sticky notes in these subgroups. You would then need to debrief as a large group to discover the similar buckets across the groups. One other approach would be for the leader (or another participant) to ask for one sticky note from an individual, read it aloud, and ask for others that are similar to this one, thus building your priority buckets as you go. However, I must warn you that based on previous experience, this can be a somewhat arduous task, especially with larger groups.

Once you have reached a groupwide decision on the three to five top strategic priority areas on which you need to focus your attention and resources, I recommend that you break into clusters of two to three people and assign one group to each strategic priority area to work on fleshing out the details. Either you can let the clusters select the area upon which they want to focus, or you can assign them based on creating cross-functional teams. The pro of letting them pick is that they get to follow their passion—and perhaps expertise as well. These are the ideal people to potentially champion the work to be done for this area after the session. The pro of assigning them is that you can insert some ignorance into each group; in other words, sometimes the best questions and suggestions come from those who are ignorant of what everyone else knows is absolutely true. They prompt us to question our mental models and paradigms of what is and is not possible. Yet another alternative might be to execute this step in the large-group setting, facilitated by the leader or another member of the team. A word of caution about this approach—it can really begin to drag if the facilitator doesn't make a conscious effort to keep it moving.

You now need to decide what success looks like for each strategic priority area as it relates to supporting the vision and addressing the forces working for and against your success. You then must develop metrics for measuring that success. You must decide the end-point time frame for this planning effort (which should be the same for all priority areas). I often recommend that the time frame coincide with your fiscal year, especially if you are looking at a time frame of about 12 to 18 months out. I feel strongly that it is very powerful for people to have a fixed point in their mind toward which they can plan.

Let's be clear: we are not saying that the strategic priority will be completely *accomplished* by this point in time. We are only trying to determine what *could* potentially be accomplished by that time.

We've now come to a point where you have subgroups working on each priority area. Each knows the time frame against which they are planning, and they have reached a consensus on what success will generally look like at this point. Now you need to establish some metrics to use so that you will actually know it when you achieve success.

I believe that many members of corporate America have gotten too hung up on using quantitative measures exclusively without considering the benefits of qualitative measures. I recommend that you remain open to using both types. I have seen quite a few teams exclude a given priority area simply because they couldn't put a number to the measure. Hitting a target date also is another way to satisfy this need to measure success. Take a look at what can be measured *now*. Will this adequately meet your needs? If not, is there another way to measure what you are trying to assess? Is the investment of time and resources to create/revise a process or tool for gauging and gathering worth the added information that you will get?

I recommend including both leading (that which gives you insight in advance of something actually occurring) and lagging (that which you track after the fact) indicators in your set of measurements. Why? Did you know that right now across the earth there are scores of people—scientists and volunteers—who are systematically measuring changes in the firefly population, and they have some concerns. So concerned in fact, that more than 100 entomologists and biologists recently gathered in Thailand for an international symposium on the "Diversity and Conservation of Fireflies." Similar to a canary in the coal mine, they believe these significant declines in the firefly population could be indicative of destructive changes in the surrounding environment—changes that might not only be harmful to fireflies, but to humans as well. What should you be measuring now that will help you to foretell and hopefully forestall something that could deter your team from successfully achieving your plan . . . and ultimately your vision for success?

I often recommend at this point that a team determine what critical items they want to track on a regular basis. This can then very effectively be turned into a team dashboard to review frequently and consistently. Consider an actual car dashboard. What is your equivalent to the speedometer; could it perhaps equate to the achievement hit rate for major project milestones? What about the fuel gauge? Is this the voluntary turnover rate, or maybe the measured engagement level of the employees? Could the odometer or the mileage trip counter be a longer-term goal or objective for the team? You get the idea; but I really think putting it in terms that people on the team can visualize and relate to makes it much more impactful.

The next step is to create—while still in the strategic priority subteams—very concrete action plans that include key milestones, timelines, and accountabilities. Ask your team: knowing what success looks like (i.e., what needs to be accomplished by the end of the planning period) and given where we are now, what must we accomplish along the way? Then have them write down each of these key milestones on a sticky note, along with a due date and the person or department accountable. Use a different colored pad for each priority area.

These should not be the specific interim steps, tasks, and activities; but should instead capture the desired end result. For example, if you were going to conduct an employee survey, you would not write down "Send the survey out to employees" unless, for some reason, that was going to be a significant undertaking in its own right. You might simply write, "Conduct the employee survey," which presumably includes all of the substeps—like selecting a vendor or creating your own survey; deciding who will participate; determining whether it will be online or paper and pencil; and so forth. The next end result might be, "Agreement reached on recommendations from survey results"; which again presumes the substeps of gathering the data, analyzing it, developing recommendations, and holding meetings with key stakeholders to discuss results and finalize recommendations for implementation. All of these substeps and their timing will be fleshed out after this session by the people accountable for executing on the key milestones.

Here is the process I use for creating and then debriefing the timeline:

1. Tape up several blank flip chart sheets in a row across the front of the room.

2. Draw a horizontal timeline across the middle of the page (I usually show breaks on this timeline for each quarter).

3. Along the left side place a colored sticky note that corresponds to the color for each priority area, and write the name of that area on it.

4. Invite the subgroups to come up and place their sticky notes along the timeline (in a horizontal line adjacent to the colored sticky note with their area name on it). You will end up with different streams of sticky notes, one for each priority area. It is very visually impactful to see these multicolored notes on the timeline.

5. Finally, take each area one at a time and ask someone from the group to walk us through the corresponding sticky notes. Do keep track of the time and allow each area about 10 minutes max for their debriefing, or it will really begin to drag.

6. While that person is walking the group through their area's timeline, ask everyone else to actively listen for interdependencies, overlaps, resources needed, and support offered. Fill out new sticky notes as needed to capture new milestones and put them on the timeline.

In terms of next steps after this debriefing, the team will often decide on priority area champions or two-person sub-teams to lead the charge on tracking the progress of their selected priority area. This can be a wonderfully bonding experience for two people to work together on a subteam to achieve this goal. The other added advantage—which appeals particularly to the team leader—is that with this approach, it is no longer the leader's plan . . . it is the *team's* plan; and they have increased accountability to execute it with excellence.

While everyone is still in the session, you need to give significant thought to what and how you will communicate this strategic vision and plan to the various stakeholders involved—some of whom might include the next level up boss, direct reports of those in the room, and internal and external clients/customers. In addition to capturing the key output of the day—and especially the timeline—into a word document, I also suggest that as a group you capture a few vital messages that convey the essence of the session's output. What were some of the more critical decisions we made? What has changed about how we will focus our attention, efforts, and resources? How will people's roles transform based on what we decided?

It is said that however much your team or organization is communicating now, when you're in a state of transition (which you should be, if you have truly done a good job of making strategic choices about what you will and won't do) you can multiply this by 100; and you are *still* not communicating enough. Simply sending out the book *Who Moved My Cheese?* and informing people that change happens and they need to get over it is *not* the way to get everyone comfortable and on board with the changes needed to make the new vision for success a reality.

What *should* you be communicating; and to whom, how, and when? To answer these questions, I create a communication matrix that captures all of this information in one easy document:

- Column One: List all of the various *audiences* with whom your team must communicate.

- Column Two: List each of the key *messages* and the *purpose* of the communication for each audience (and there may be multiple purposes for a single audience)— to inform, to engage, to implement some aspect of the plan, to influence, to solicit funding or other resources, to gain their input, and so on.

- Column Three: Here, you want to list the top *vehicles* of communication for each audience—those that are most impactful for each audience and message—like face-to-face meetings, town hall meetings, e-mail, newsletters, phone calls, and so on. Be sure to include both one-way and two-way communication methods, and see if you can locate any internal surveys that might have been conducted that show how people in your organization value these different methods. This information can be very helpful in the planning phase.

- Column Four: Decide on the *timing* for each communication vehicle for each audience. Remember: you can't just say it once in one format and think that everyone will get the message the first time out. If you truly must get everyone on the same page, then you will likely need to communicate the same message at least three different times in three different formats over an extended period of time for people to take seriously any shift in direction or focus.

- Column Five: Be sure to capture here *the person or people accountable* for each of these messages, and who needs to approve, provide input, or respond to the drafts before sending them out.

If your strategic plan was created by a leadership team but needs to be executed by a much larger team of people who were not present during its original creation, then you must develop an approach to share and gain the executors' input on the strategic mission, vision, priorities, and dashboard. In fact, you might not even want to determine the milestones and create the timeline in the small leadership session. Instead, bring the team together to gain buy-in and/or create the above strategic plan elements, reality test them, identify key challenges, and engage *everyone* in solving them. This is true, two-way communication; and it is vital to helping everyone connect the dots between what they do on a daily basis and how that activity contributes to the overall success of the organization—in other words, that what they do really matters. In his book *The Three Signs of a Miserable Job*, Patrick Lencioni makes a very strong case (in his always-compelling fable style) that employees who don't know how their work impacts the lives of others will experience irrelevance, and will not be fulfilled in their jobs. Remember Jill from Chapter 7, and the importance of hearing from her co-workers how she positively impacted their jobs? Similarly, everyone coming out of this session should have a clear line of sight into at least one (and hopefully more than one) metric to which they can directly contribute. This information will then allow them to take it all the way down to determining their individual objectives and setting budgets.

The final step in the process is to figure out how the team will follow up, celebrate successes, and course correct. There will need to be regular and consistent progress tracking on the team dashboard and on the milestones in meetings, of course. This needs to be an area of focus—not in a report out fashion; but in genuine, problem-solving mode (and I will show you how to do so in upcoming chapters). In addition, I strongly recommend that you have at least one half- to full-day session (preferably off-site, or at least in a different meeting room) after three months, and again after six months. As I am sure you well know, what gets measured gets done. The purpose of these sessions is for the leader to keep everyone, including themselves, focused on the right things. Making it clear that these sessions are on the calendar and will not be canceled ensures that everyone understands the high priority of executing the plan.

The team should accomplish the following critical undertakings during these sessions:

- *Celebrate success.* One of the chief complaints I hear from team members is that they don't stop to truly rejoice in what they have accomplished together; and often, the team leader is the biggest culprit. Engage the team in figuring out how to really reward and recognize what they have done (and it doesn't always have to involve money!). I have seen teams celebrate with company-bought pizza in the conference room for a Friday lunch; or perhaps everyone takes off for a team outing at a bowling alley or for putt-putt golf. Remember to keep the focus on a team celebration—not everyone simply getting off early for the day and going their separate ways. That may be individually satisfying, but it does nothing for reinforcing the excitement and reward of a true team accomplishment.

- *Identify where the reality is falling short of plan, and why.* If you don't know what got you here, you won't be

able to course correct. Were the assumptions too con-
servative or too extreme? Was the data faulty; or was the
wrong data used? Have there been unforeseen circumstances that negatively impacted the plan? Has it been a
case of bad execution? If so, what was the cause? This is
not a time to assign blame, but rather to truly learn from
what has occurred and agree on a course of action to
make sure that the same mistakes aren't repeated
again.

- *Replan as required.* You must keep the plan real, or
  people lose the motivation to carry it out. Neglecting to
  openly acknowledge the changes that need to be made—
  and not encouraging the team to help to face this challenge together head on—is a slippery slope down to a
  very disengaged team that will not be so quick to participate the next time you want to hold another off-site!

Imagine you are on the shoreline of the beach, watching
the waves come in. You see a big one approaching. It crashes to
shore. And then . . . nothing. Calm waters behind it.

I recently shared this analogy with an operations team at a
consumer products company during a strategic planning
session, and used it to explain to them that as soon as you
are getting close to the end of your vision horizon, you must
begin to plan for the next one.

There will always be a new wave to replace the one that
just hit the beach. You need to be able to see in the distant
future—not necessarily to each and every wave, because you
do need to have time to catch your breath or it will overwhelm
you like a rip tide. But if there is too much time between one
big wave and the next, you can grow complacent, get bored,
and then be taken by surprise and knocked over when the
next one comes. The time to come together, celebrate your
success, and begin the process all over again is just before that
next big wave hits; or you will find yourself surrounded by the
dead calm that settles over the ocean after that last big wave
washes everything away.

Chapter Ten

Guiding Principles as Guiding Light

Do you know how fireflies communicate with each other? Each species (and remember there are more than 2,000 of them!) has its own unique signature, so to speak. They have a characteristic sequence of flashes and pauses, almost like a species-specific Morse code. Their flight patterns differ as well—some low to the ground, some high among the trees. Have you seen fireflies only at dusk? Well, if you are a patient and inquisitive night owl, you can also see a different type closer to 10 P.M. The color of their glowing light is also somewhat different, with some flashing yellow, green, orange, and yes, even the eerie glow (you guessed it, *blue*) of the "blue ghost" firefly. These various patterns are so precise and species specific that researchers often use them as a means of mapping the population, and the fireflies use it as a means of finding their own kind. Their very survival depends upon it.

So, while fireflies may be naturally wired to know how to communicate and collaborate with each other for a common purpose, humans have not (thankfully) been preprogrammed to behave in such a way. We bring our own life's experiences and expectations with us when we join a team. For us to work together at our best, we must develop a clear consensus of what makes for an outstandingly effective team; and then we must have guiding principles to light our path to getting there and staying there. There are two approaches that I have used in my work with teams that ensures that there is a common picture of what makes a great team—and how *this* team will work together to become great.

But first, a quick recap. In the last two chapters we discussed how to create a common view of the team's mission (the road we are on), the vision of success (the mountain in the distance that we want to climb), and how we will measure our progress toward success (the mile markers). This is what every leader wants—all oars rowing to the same beat, toward the same point on the horizon. In this chapter we will focus on the *guardrails* on our road—the guiding principles for how we will work as a team, and the means to the end.

Close your eyes and take three deep breaths. Now remember the greatest team you were ever a part of. Who was on the team? What results did you achieve together? What role did you play in that success? How did you deal with conflict? How were decisions made? How did it feel to be on this team?

This is the way I begin a team visioning exercise. I believe that when people bring themselves back to this point in time, they actually can put themselves in the room and recall exactly what it felt like to be a part of that team. I remember exactly what it felt like to be a part of a great team when I was a member of the Organization Effectiveness group at Coca-Cola—the best team of my life. Why? We felt we were on a mission to make a great organization even better. This was a very diverse, smart, talented group of individuals who understood and respected the unique contributions that each person could make. Some of us had been internal members of the organization for a number of years, and knew the culture very well. Some of us came from the outside—specifically, from the consulting industry—and could introduce best practices from a wide variety of organizations. No one person was more valued than another; this combination of experience and perspectives granted us the opportunity to participate in creating the team culture that would allow us to thrive personally and to do great work for the organization. We all learned creative new approaches, and it was fun to learn them together. We would bring our problems to the team and get these great minds working on them. It was a truly rewarding time in my career.

I would suspect that every member on your team can remember a similarly gratifying team experience. You can tap into the tremendous power of each of these by deciding, together, what you want to incorporate from those diverse experiences in order to create a unique, once-in-a-lifetime, best team experience right now. You just need to find a way to draw on these; and using the visioning approach I shared above is a very effective technique.

The next step is to ask each person to record what they saw, felt, and heard when I took them through this visioning exercise. I then ask them to share what they wrote down with the rest of the team, and no one is allowed to say "Ditto" or "Everyone has already said everything I wrote down." This is a moment of vulnerability for everyone on the team, and it's absolutely vital that you hear each person's unique voice and perspective. Things such as: "Everyone knew why they were there." "We were like family." "We didn't always achieve every goal, but we gave it everything we had." "We had good arguments, you know; they were about important things." I really want them to remember—and form a gut-level connection to—what it felt like to be part of an extraordinary team, and that it is possible to have this again. There is something very powerful about jointly creating this shared vision for how you will work together.

After each person has shared their story while others are listening for the common threads, you can then identify the most frequently cited qualities that are required for the makings of a great team. Next, you have to do the tough work of melding these diverse perspectives and recurring themes into clear rules of engagement that all can live by. I recommend keeping the number small and directly related to this team at this point in time. You don't want a long list of mom and apple pie kinds of things; you want to select those critical four to six guiding principles that will steer your individual behavior, and your behavior toward each other. Some examples might be:

- Team meetings are important times to come together. We will keep this time sacred, and come prepared to do our best work.

- We value and need each person's input to create the best solutions and to make effective decisions. Our team will be known for its strong environment of trust and candor.
- It is important to keep our commitments to each other. Personal accountability is expected on this team.

After you have created these guiding principles, I recommend your group brainstorm any barriers that might arise in your attempts to follow these guiding principles, and decide how the team should address those. One common challenge that I often hear about in many of today's complex organizational structures that necessitate mixed or dual reporting relationships is, how do you deal with the tug of war that can arise? How do you stay true to the guiding principles of your number one team? The problem most often becomes significant and a true conflict when someone on the team individually decides that a particular matter takes precedence over another, and then doesn't make their thinking explicit to the rest of the group. For example, let's say that one member is asked to be in two meetings at one time—both of which are gatherings that are critical to those respective teams. If the team has previously had candid discussions about pressure points like these—and have together created the criteria for how to make the right decision about which team's requirements will take precedence—then the group will understand the choices that are made.

If, for some reason, the previously explained visioning approach does not resonate with you, then you might want to consider using the online assessment tool that Patrick Lencioni's consulting firm, The Table Group, has to offer (www.TableGroup.com). This instrument is based on the very compelling and popular team effectiveness model in Lencioni's *The Five Dysfunctions of a Team*. I have used this approach successfully with dozens of teams, and have found that it is especially relevant if:

- The team leader and/or members of the team have read the book and really gravitate to the model;
- The team needs or wants hard data on how bad things are;

- The team is too contentious to create a common model for what team effectiveness looks like, in which case Lencioni's model can serve as an example.

Some of you may be wondering if it's even necessary go to all this trouble. Why is it so important to spell out these guiding principles for a team? Aren't we all adults here; don't we all know the right way to behave on a team? But, that's just the problem—if you have two people on a team, you will have two different perceptions on *how* a team should work together most effectively. Neither one is necessarily wrong or right, but they are *definitely* different. This can be a source of extreme, unnecessary conflict, and I'm not talking about conflict in a good, creative abrasion way. I am talking about the kind that denigrates into personality-based disagreements, all because the team did not take the time to determine and clearly lay out the expectations for working together to achieve results. Taking the time to do this demonstrates more plainly than words ever could that yes, results matter; but how you *get* the results also counts on this team.

I happen to know firsthand of one organization that learned this lesson in a very painful way. The company had surpassed incredible growth and profitability targets in the past, and the new ones they had just received promised to be even higher. They had just received the bad results from their employee engagement survey. Let's just say they weren't . . . engaged, that is. Both the leaders and the results were dismal. This is where I came in.

I was hired to work with the head of the IT function to improve his team's effectiveness and employee engagement. He told me himself: "Yes, we get results; but we leave dead bodies in our wake. We can't continue in this way anymore." This CIO got it—how an employee's job satisfaction fit into the equation for business success. Their current path to achieving incredible results was not sustainable. Sure, this may work for a while when the job market is tough. You may be able to keep those who can't find a job elsewhere or aren't sure enough of their skills to attempt to leave; but are those the ones you most *want* to keep?

Of course not. You want the ones who have choices, and *choose* to stay with this company, this leader, this team. You want to attract those who say, "I have options, and I pick this company because I will be able to do my best work here." Most employees who I speak with know how hard it is to find an excellent team and a truly great environment in which they're given the chance to use their unique gifts and talents to contribute to something important. If you as a leader can cultivate this kind of setting, then you are set for an incredibly creative, productive team for the long term.

Okay—at this point, you have worked together as a team to create these guidelines. Now what? How are you going to make sure that the team upholds these principles over the coming months? Well, first of all, by keeping them front and center at all times. I worked with one team that came up with the idea to put them at the bottom of each team meeting agenda so that they could be *visibly* reminded of what they had agreed to every time they met. And I do believe that the times when the team gathers is exactly when you will see who is walking the talk of these principles. Are they just words on a page, or does everyone truly see them as an essential component to the team's ability to do its best work?

Another key to cementing the team's belief in the procedures is for everyone—not just the team leader—to hold every other member of the team accountable for living up to them, and confronting those who don't uphold them. This begins by first reminding the offender of the principle, and giving them the benefit of the doubt—after all, to err is human. Repeat offenders, however, are no longer team problems, but a performance management problem that it is up to the leader to solve.

What are some of the other team issues, in regard to following the principles, which the leader needs to address? I'll share this next one by using a fact from the scientific world of the fireflies. Some people have commented to me that they don't seem to see as many fireflies as they used to growing up. Scientists have studied this, and one of their conclusions is: there is too much light in the surrounding area. For fireflies to be drawn together to do their best work, there cannot be a glaring spotlight nearby, for example. I would propose that the same is true for us humans; that is, if one member of the team is emitting a glaring light, then the other members of the team will be overshadowed. Thus, they will not want to come together in the spirit of camaraderie and a shared cause. This person might be the team leader's favorite, the one who's chosen for the best assignments, who enjoys a special rapport with the leaders, and who doesn't seem to have to play by the same rules as everyone else. We have often seen this kind of unproductive situation on sports teams—such as basketball, baseball, and football—that depends on the players' keen interplay. The result can be a lot of glory for this one member's results, but the team as a whole does not win the game.

The star expects to be treated differently—and often is. Results tend to matter more than the way in which they are achieved. Others ask how the leader can allow this to go on; is he not aware? But instead of evoking feelings of under-appreciation, these star performers can serve as mentors to others—if they are willing to share the limelight and glory with others on the team. They bring out the best in others and, in fact, enhance the productivity of the entire team. One firefly on a summer night is not magical; but a whole *team* of fireflies is what inspires us.

Is there someone on your team who needs to be the center of attention, or is seen as the favorite? How do you think that individual impacts the team's performance? More often than not, these *stars* keep the team from focusing on improving, because their view of how things could get better is being obscured by the glare of this disruptive force. As long as the focus remains on this person as the source of the team's problems, then we don't have to turn the focus on ourselves. When are we at our best? When do we illuminate? What brings out the worst in us, and causes us to glare or obscure the work of others? The leader may be forced to make tough choices. If there are people on the team who have gotten great individual results, but are failing to live up to the principles and contribute to the group's success, then something must be done. It begins with coaching; and it may need to end with letting that person leave with dignity.

It is clearly the team leader's responsibility to address any member of the team who causes a disruptive and unproductive glare. But what happens when the leader keeps *too* tight of a hold on the behavior of the team? Perhaps they are using the guiding principles as a club to demand or elicit behavior from the members of the team. How might that play out?

I saw this firsthand when I was in the audience at the Music Paradigm experience, which I first mentioned in Chapter 8. There was one point in the program when the orchestra leader Roger Nierenberg asked the violinist to stand so that he could conduct her solo. The audience members were not aware of any change in manner on Nierenberg's part, but the violinist certainly was! And it came through very clearly in the resulting piece.

Nierenberg posed the question: "So, tell me, what do you think of the way I conducted you?"

The violinist replied, "Well, I sure didn't like it! You were so exact in the way you expected me to play; you did not allow any of my individuality and my own interpretation to come through. So I said to myself, if you're just going to tell me how to perform, then you'll get that and nothing more."

Oh, my gosh—how many times had I seen this occur with my own and other leaders' management style? To use the firefly metaphor: the conductor had the lid on the jar too tight, and there was no room to breathe since no air could get in or escape. The firefly's glow would soon die out in this environment.

If, like this conductor, you have a group of virtuosos, then your job as the leader is to bring out their best. You are not solely responsible for team members living up to the guiding principles—everyone is. Enlist their support!

I believe leaders sometimes keep this tight lid on the team because of the way that they view their role and others' expectations of them. I saw this very clearly during a recent workshop that I conducted in a small town in southern Georgia. I was addressing a group of supervisors at an automobile parts manufacturing plant. The purpose of the workshop was to get them all working together as a team to hit the customer-driven—and almost inconceivable—goal of zero defects. It was going to require a lot of changed behaviors.

I began with the visioning exercise. "Picture the most effective team you were ever a part of. It can be a group from work, sports team, or perhaps in your church or community. Does everyone have one in mind now? Okay, remember how decisions were made on the team . . . how conflict was handled . . . how the roles were assigned . . . what you accomplished as a team." We then formed small groups and they shared what they had written with the others at the table. During the large group debrief, I was struck by a huge contrast.

Those who used a sports team as their example talked about decisions being made and roles assigned by the coach. Conflict was not tolerated; you were told to deal with it. On the other hand, those who used a corporate example described teams who openly discussed topics before making decisions. Conflict was handled fairly and individually first, and only brought to the team leader as a last resort.

Since I didn't have much experience playing on a sports team growing up, I decided to ask my husband to help me understand these stark differences. He explained to me, "Well, in Little League and high school teams, coaches are more directive and authoritarian; perhaps because they are dealing with young kids."

"But," I protested, "What about the inspirational coaches that I read about? You know, the Vince Lombardis and Bear Bryants?"

"Well," my husband patiently explained, "later on in college, and in professional football, the coaches can treat them more like adults, get their input, and take a more collaborative approach to the team."

Then it hit me—how many leaders in corporate America today have a great team from their youth as their role model for how a team should function effectively? Do they now see themselves as the coach giving orders to the players on the team? Are they members of the team, waiting for someone to tell them what to do? Is conflict being viewed negatively, because it was never tolerated on the team before? If there are such different perceptions of how an effective team functions and the right role of a leader—and they remain unspoken—how potentially damaging to collaboration and a shared mind-set for how all the members should work together. That's the whole point of this chapter—to bring to light those diverse perspectives and combine them to create the best team now.

I would like to close this chapter, and this section of the book, by bringing the key points together using the metaphor of a catapult. Some people actually wondered why I chose to use such an archaic weapon in the title of this book. I did so because it beautifully symbolizes something that I believe about great teams. When you think about how the catapult actually works, you can see how it applies. After all, you need a team to roll the catapult into place, to gather the stones, and to assess how effectively you can hit the target. It isn't like throwing the proverbial spaghetti against the wall and seeing what sticks; it's much more purposeful than that. And the catapult itself is much more effective than individual weaponry, like a slingshot or bow and arrow. Yes, these items have a place in the team's arsenal, but there is more power when these individual efforts are supplemented with a team approach—the catapult. I therefore encourage you to now gather your best resources, reach agreement on your target, take aim, and send those results flying!

Part IV

Everyone Firing On All Cylinders

Chapter Eleven

Team Gatherings—Time to Shine

I believe wholeheartedly that a team gathering can be the most productive and exciting time in the life of the team. And though I believe this, I sure don't see it happening in many of the organizations I work with. If you remember back to the firefly metaphor I shared in the very first chapter, this is the feeling of joy and pleasure that being a contributing member of a great team evokes. It is all about the process of coming together. But how do you make this magic happen? In this chapter, I will turn your attention to the greatest challenges and problems I see occurring on a regular basis when teams get together; and then give you specific, targeted, and—most importantly—*doable* actions that you can take immediately.

Why are you coming together as a team? Why do you meet? Do you have different purposes for each type of meeting? I can't emphasize strongly enough the energy that comes from openly discussing these items and hearing everyone's candid expectations for these meetings, especially the dreaded (and often dull) staff meetings.

Let's see if this story resonates with you. I was working with the leadership team of a mortgage company on improving their effectiveness. During the interviews I was conducting to understand their particular group dynamics and issues, I was struck by what I kept hearing about their staff meetings. Each thought these meetings were serving the *others'* purposes. The leader told me he held these meetings so that *his staff* could know what he already knew through other means. He wanted his staff to learn about the current status of each other's areas, and gain insight into the critical connections and interdependencies between the various projects and initiatives. Makes sense, right? Now, what do you think I heard from the team members who attended these meetings? They thought he held them so that *he* could learn what everyone was doing, and thus didn't have to hold time-consuming one-on-one meetings with each of his direct reports. They weren't really paying much attention to their teammates report outs; that's not the reason they were there. Hard to believe, right? Obviously, this is one meeting that wasn't adequately serving anyone's needs—and nobody knew it. If someone interviewed your team to find out why they think you are meeting on a regular basis, how might they respond? Are you confident that they're clear on these reasons?

So step one to improving your team meetings is to get everyone to agree on *why* you are even there in the first place. Let me state this categorically: don't let that purpose be report outs! My belief is that in these types of meetings, nobody is listening . . . unless they are talking. And even then, I think they are on automatic pilot, hastily sharing whatever's off the top of their mind when it is their turn to give the team an update. What do I hear teams say they *wish* was the purpose of these meetings? To learn more about the strategic direction of the company; to develop their effectiveness, as a group, in identifying key problems and collaboratively solving them; to wrestle with longer-term issues and reach critical decisions that will impact the priorities and plans of the team.

Step two is then to design the agenda so that it is in alignment with your stated desired purpose. Over the years, I have discovered that although people with different thinking styles want different things from a meeting, most gatherings are designed based on the leader's preferences, or on the way that *their* past bosses ran staff meetings. So, a vicious cycle of ineffectiveness is perpetuated. What is *your* agenda design based on? I conduct a fun effective exercise that uses what group members learned from each other's HBDI preferences (see Chapter 4 and Chapter 7), to actually *redesign* the staff meeting. I instruct people to focus on their favorite quadrant and then design the team meeting as though only people just like you (i.e., the other members of your quadrant) were coming to the meeting. And I tell them to have some fun with it. One team comprised of analytical, Blue-quadrant people, for example, said that everyone would have to bring a computer to the meeting; and the only thing participants would be allowed to do was show each other graphs and spreadsheets. If someone had a question, you could only IM the other people in the meeting; no informal interpersonal communication allowed whatsoever!

After everyone has a good laugh, we then discuss the Blue team's concepts to see what we would actually like to adopt from their ideal staff meeting. Someone might note that the team really doesn't spend much time, if any, getting a strong enough grasp on what the numbers (the core business and team metrics; maybe even the team dashboard results) are really telling them—and what they should be doing about this. While you might think that only analytically oriented people might see this as a weakness in the current meeting structure, in fact, I see suggestions such as these can come from any quadrant, once they recognize the value of Whole Brain® thinking.

On the opposite end of the spectrum, the Red/interpersonal quadrant's ideal staff meeting might spend the first 20 minutes hearing about everyone's weekend, with the expectation that each member would bring something for a potluck meal. Although that's another extreme, what would we want to adopt from that? Perhaps the inclusion of a brief icebreaker to kick off the meeting and to keep learning more about each other by creating a safe, trusting environment where people can gain comfort and confidence in sharing what they *really* think. The Green/organized quadrant may bring to our attention the importance of having an agenda and premeeting information sent out in advance, so that everyone is fully prepared to discuss and reach a decision on an important topic. From the Yellow/future-looking quadrant, we might gain an appreciation for thinking big picture and asking *what if*. It is amazing to see how the desires of each quadrant differ based on what each believed should be accomplished in a meeting, and how much more effective the meeting is and engaged the people are when you take those diverse perspectives into account and try to structure the meeting to achieve them.

I must warn you that one of the unintended consequences of engaging in this type of exercise is the potential realization that you need to schedule additional meetings, each of which are designed to serve different purposes. For example, one team recognized that they always put the more strategic issues toward the end of the agenda; issues that, as a result, weren't adequately covered. The leader confessed to me that one particular topic had been on the agenda for three months now. When I discussed this with the team, they finally came to realize that they needed to start having quarterly strategic meetings to deal with the more complex topics on the agenda. And this was not the only team I have worked with that has made that decision. I would suggest that you give some serious thought to this idea because I've found that it's very difficult for most teams—and for members themselves—to go back and forth effectively between a tactical, operational issue and a longer-term strategic issue. I promise you, the tyranny of the urgent will overwhelm the important every time.

I highly recommend designing the ideal agenda first, based strictly on what you learned from the discussions about the purpose and meeting desires of the participants, regardless of how long or how often you meet now. I learned this through my own error in working with a telecommunications company IT executive and his team on redesigning their staff meeting. I made an error in judgment by asking how long their meetings were now. "They are currently scheduled for ninety minutes, but they never go that long," the leader told me, "so don't you design this to be any longer!" In fact, once we identified all of the items that the participants stated they wanted to accomplish in this meeting, we saw that it was going to last 2 hours and 10 minutes. No one wanted to cut it any shorter—not even the team leader!

You see, I believe team meetings suffer from poor attendance and slack participation and get canceled or cut short, because they are not designed to serve the objectives of those in attendance. Every agenda item should have a clear deliverable or outcome that is important to those present. Some of these may be standing agenda items that are addressed each time; which is fine as long as they are still providing the results they are designed to deliver.

I have even had some teams color-coordinate the agenda items to correspond to the four quadrants of the HBDI Whole Brain model. This serves two purposes. First, it encourages everyone to consider the topic from the same perspective. If, for instance, the focus was, "Brainstorm new marketing approaches to deal with the rising competition in the Chicago territory," it would show up in yellow, prompting everyone to be in an idea-generation mind-set. No reality testing of the ideas (blue) or action planning (green) is allowed at this stage. This approach also ensures that thinking from all quadrants is represented, which will give all team members a sense of comfort that the discussion will turn to one of their most preferred quadrants at *some* point during the meeting.

You might want to place any particular team weakness at the very beginning of the agenda; otherwise, you might never address it. I have encountered several leadership teams that were, shall we say, somewhat weak in the interpersonal/Red quadrant. One senior team in particular knew that they were not good at recognizing their employees on a regular basis (because their employee engagement surveys told them so). This team recognized the direct connection between the employees feeling underappreciated and poor customer service ratings. So what did they decide (on their own, I might add) to do about it? Each leader started writing thank-you notes to the people on their team who deserved to be recognized. And at the start of every meeting, they would pass these notes around the table for the other leaders to also read and sign. Not only did these surprised employees receive these personal thank-you notes signed by all of these execs; they were also stopped in the halls and received e-mails to congratulate and thank them for what they had done. The impact—both on the individuals who received the recognition and on others who heard about it as these stories spread—was amazing.

And, as you might expect, the leaders were impacted as well. I often find that senior leaders are not comfortable making chitchat with employees that they don't know well, if at all, especially in other departments. This gave them a reason to seek out these other people. Even if they were initially doing this with a *Blue* intent (to reinforce the results they wanted to see more of), there was a *Red* impact on both the giver and the receiver of the recognition. And maybe, just maybe, this leader would be a little more comfortable expressing their appreciation of the efforts of others (maybe even on their own team!) without needing the crutch of a thank-you note.

I'd like to offer you some other, easy-to-implement agenda design tips. I suggest that you time box (i.e., assign specific times with limits) the discussion, keep a tight rein on the number of items on the agenda, and put the most critical topics first. Engage others on the team in taking responsibility for some of the agenda items. This demonstrates clearly that everyone has a role to play in the meeting's success, and it is a great way to get some of the less demonstrable members to practice (in a safe environment) being in front of the room, making presentations, and leading a discussion. Isn't that part of the leader's role—to mentor and coach people so that they can expand their skill sets? I promise that when you take the time to seek everyone's input and then together design the meeting for success, you will find this investment of time—in both creating and conducting these team gatherings—to be *well* worth the result.

Okay—so you have now set yourself up for success by being clear on the purpose of the meeting, and perhaps even created an additional meeting or two to address other critical purposes that aren't served by the original one. Each team member has learned what is particularly important for them to get out of the meeting, and the agenda has been designed to meet those needs. Now what?

The next thing to do is to focus on what is happening when you actually have everyone together. The following are the top three dysfunctional behaviors that I see most often—and hear the most complaints about—in team meetings. These have the greatest negative impact on the effectiveness of the meeting; therefore, I have provided my suggestions for how the team can deal with them.

The first of these is *lack of participation*. This can take the form of one or more people who consistently arrive late or not at all; who show up unprepared; or who generally fail to contribute to group discussions. If a single individual behaves in this way, then the leader should have a direct conversation with this person to point out the impact that their disruptive behavior is having on the team. Truly seek to understand the causes, both those that are most readily apparent, and the underlying ones as well. Take a collaborative approach to solving any barriers that are preventing a team member's full participation. Reach agreement on the actions that need to be taken to overcome this problem; make it clear that changed behavior is expected; and readily demonstrate your support and confidence that this situation can be resolved. Don't let the problem fester. I assure you, the other members of the team are watching how you handle this to see how serious you are about truly building an effective team and holding everyone accountable for their participation in achieving this objective.

If the lack of participation is a widespread and consistent problem, then you need to deal with it as a team. If you have not yet discussed the meeting's purpose—and designed the agenda to meet that purpose—this would be the place to start. Do you have team-guiding principles that you can use to help reinforce the expected behaviors of members of the team? If not, get the team engaged in helping to create them, paying special attention to developing one related to meeting expectations. (See Chapter 10 for the approach I use with teams to create these principles).

I would also encourage you to insert as much variety into your team meetings as possible. Change where you meet, or at least, for heaven's sake, change your seats. It is amazing how sitting in a different seat next to different people for each meeting can change one's perspective and transform one's mind-set. The team leader can role model this behavior; after all, if you change your seat each time, then everyone else will have to also. Get others—both on and external to the team—involved in relevant agenda items. Bring in speakers from outside the company who can share insights on best practices, trends in the industry, new business books on the market, and so on. Change up the processes you use to deal with agenda items. If every topic means a PowerPoint presentation followed by open discussion that maybe eventually ends in a decision, you will have a very boring staff meeting on your hands. Invest in sending yourself or someone on the team to a facilitation class or reading a book on effective group processes to widen your options for dealing with the topics. A last suggestion (though certainly not a last resort): ask the team to help you solve the problem of low participation levels. You just might be surprised what you discover!

Since our clients tell us that more than 75 percent of their meetings have at least one virtual participant—and that they only see that number increasing in the future for a variety of reasons—it's important that I provide you with some quick tips on how to get greater participation from your virtual teammates. Here are some very doable suggestions for engaging these remote contributors:

- If at all possible, arrange for people to meet in groups at the remote locations; and even a twosome is better than nothing. This helps to lessen the sense of isolation, and encourages people to begin talking before the meeting actually starts.

- If off-site members can't meet in groups, then overcome the wallflower phenomenon by engaging virtual teammates in some small talk at the start of the meeting. Hearing your voice in the room early on gets people poised to contribute during the meeting.

- Add a visual component to the meetings. Many teams I worked with had this capability and never used it, and these were often the same IT teams who had set it up in the first place! Technology is often such a barrier to high-touch; turn that trend around and truly use these tools to your advantage to promote greater team cohesiveness.

- Level the playing field, and occasionally have everyone participate remotely. They will truly understand how tough it is to be engaged when they have walked half a mile in their remote teammates' shoes.

- Make it clear that when the meeting is over, the meeting is over. One of the greatest frustrations I hear from the remotes is about the conversations that ensue after the disconnect button has been pushed. Those who have called in to the meeting are unaware of the key discussions and decisions that have taken place in those

10 minutes or so after the meeting is officially over when people in the room linger and continue talking about the meeting topics. And when these discussions and decisions are referenced later, the virtual people have no idea what their colleagues are talking about.

- Send information out in advance; this is more important with remote participants. You can't hand them something in the meeting, and they may not be in front of a computer to be able to receive it in real time. Use technology such as team rooms where they can view and add to team documents—something that will foster premeeting collaborative behaviors on the part of all team members.

- This next idea may sound silly, but it works. If you can't have your off-site team members present using video technology, then go low tech. Create a simple name tent for them, and place it in front of an empty seat at the table. This may even work better than using a conference calling system; after all, how many times have you completely forgotten there is someone on the speakerphone? Well, no more!

- Use a variety of techniques to encourage everyone to give their two cents. For example, I like to conduct a round-robin where I go around the room to hear each person's perspective on a particular topic. Change the person you start with each time, and don't tell them in advance where you will begin. This really keeps people alert!

- Establish a rule that forbids multitasking. (Of course, this also should go for those in the room—no peeking at your e-mails on your device under the table!) This is one of the biggest distracters for virtual participants. You know how it goes ... push that mute button and you can keep plugging away at your real work. And when they call your name to respond to a question or contribute in some way, all you have to say is "Could you repeat that? I couldn't understand you. I must have bad reception."

- This leads to my next point—don't allow remote team members to even *use* the mute button. Not only does this encourage multitasking, but also it severely limits participation. Yes, there may have to be limited exceptions to this rule (e.g., if absolutely no quiet spot can be found in a noisy airport); but most of the excuses we all hear are just, well, lame (such as, "My dog barks every time he hears a noise"—*well, one of you should move outside*). It's just easier to hit the mute button; and then no one *really* expects that remote person to contribute. Let's face it: it takes energy to lean forward and unmute that call in order to say something. And then the remote person starts an internal debate with themselves—"is this really worth saying?" In those few seconds of delay, their moment may have passed, making it much more difficult to consider it worth it the next time.

- Invest in bringing everyone together in the same room at least a few times a year. Nothing can replace actual human contact for building team effectiveness. This doesn't necessarily mean going to the same main office location every time. A lot of goodwill is generated when the team mixes it up and holds their gatherings in the various remote locations.

- Finally, if you have people meeting virtually, ask them how effective the meetings currently are for them. Just acknowledging that you understand that their experience as remote participants is different from those in the room will go a long way toward making them feel a valued part of the team. Acknowledge the fact that increasing their ability to participate fully is a *team* problem, not just one impacting the remote people. This will allow them to see that you all truly believe that you make better decisions with everyone's full participation; and that you are committed to making this happen.

Okay—so we have spent quite a bit of time talking about how to increase the participation level of the meeting attendees, and the various efforts we can make to truly engage them. Now let's focus on the opposite problem; what happens when some people—or a single person—*dominate the meeting*. How do you deal with this? Well, let's assume for a moment that the person controlling the meeting is not, in fact, the team leader. (That issue is so critical that I devote a whole chapter to it. Interested? Turn now to Chapter 13!) I like to give people who attempt to overtake meetings the benefit of the doubt, and assume that they may need to be protected from themselves. Some of us—me included—have very outgoing personalities that, left to our own devices in a meeting, can take an ugly turn toward dominance, something that is truly *not* our intent.

So if you believe this person is not *purposely* attempting to outshine others, what can you do to help them? First, limit the time they spend seated near the front of the room. This is another side benefit of regularly changing up the seating arrangements to increase participation (see my earlier suggestion). The front of the room gives them far too big of a stage upon which to perform. I actually like to seat them right next to the more reserved people. Their extreme extroversion may become apparent, even to them. Also, be sure to have a rule in place that asks people to self-police their participation levels. I like to remind people of this at the meeting's start, and then ask them to do a gut check on their participation level when they come back from a break. Too much? Decrease it. Too little? Pump up your participation.

Because, you see, this really is a two-sided coin. For some people, silence is horrible; so they fill that void easily and quickly. Getting the more introverted and quiet members to increase their participation level really helps to balance things out. But how do you accomplish that? By modifying the process for dealing with agenda topics. Don't allow every item to be addressed through open discussion; this is fertile ground for the dominant player to take over, and, well ... dominate. Conduct more round-robins to make sure you hear from everyone. Ask that people speak in headlines and limit their comments to two minutes. On meatier topics, insert some time for individual thinking before opening it up for general discussion. You will find that this allows both the introverts and the extroverts to think through their perspective on the question at hand.

You can also follow individual thinking time with small group breakout discussions. You will find that most people will become a lot more talkative—especially if the topic is of interest to them—if they are in groups of three or four versus a large group discussion comprised of 10 or more people. I have also seen this technique handled very effectively by some leaders; simply ask the quieter participant to share their thoughts on a topic. If they have not spoken for a while, it is quite likely that they have been taking everything in and have some keen insights to share. Be careful not to push it, though, if they don't have much to say. What you saw as quiet introspection could have been their daydreaming about what they will order for lunch!

The last, but certainly not least, dysfunctional behavior in a team meeting is *not starting and ending on time*. How on earth do you fix this one? Well, your team meetings must first become known for starting on time. When the meeting invite goes out, make it clear that it starts promptly at X time—and then stick to it. I assure you if the leader shows up on time and expresses an appropriate level of displeasure at latecomers, everyone will get the message.

But, you say, that is only half the problem. How can you possibly keep a meeting from running long? Well, I have one trick that I use religiously, and it will only cost you the investment in a simple kitchen timer. People know when they invite me to facilitate a meeting that we will get a lot accomplished and we will have fun doing it. For those who don't know me, it is always a shock when I tell them we will have a 15-minute break—and then I pull my timer out of my black facilitator bag and set it for 15 minutes, followed by my words "I have a timer and I know how to use it!" At one meeting with a mixed group of those I had worked with and those I hadn't, one participant laughed as soon as I set the timer and said, "You better believe she means it! I heard she even came and banged on the men's room door at the last meeting!" (That was only a slight exaggeration!)

I truly believe that use of the timer sends the message that I am very goal-oriented and that I will do everything I can to ensure that the meeting will accomplish what we all came for. It also reinforces the message that the participants' time is valuable—and I will treat it that way. This is actually one of the foremost complaints about ineffective meetings—that they don't start or end on time. No one likes it when the entire meeting is held up because one person is still on a cell phone call. If we still have a lot to accomplish before the end of the day, I will tell the group "We are running short of time. Can you live with a seven-minute break?" You would be surprised how fast people can move when they know that their break time is limited, and that we will be starting back on time. This choice of seven minutes is very strategic. I call a five-minute break a *bio break*—short for biological break. In other words, go if you need to, but be back fast. This is not an e-mail or cell phone break. If you say a 10-minute break, it sounds loose, like 10 could stretch into 15. But seven minutes tells everyone you really mean it. This has only backfired on me once—when I was the one late returning to the meeting after the timer went off—and a couple of smart alecks decided to teach me a lesson and locked me out!

I promise you that getting and using a timer will be one of the least expensive, most effective time management tools you've ever encountered. The timer can also serve a dual purpose, by not only clocking breaks but also seeing how long people can talk. It is a gift to others to keep long-winded people in check! (Even my daughter has a timer. At the age of 13, she is now on her second one. I might have even put it in her stocking for Christmas. We use it for tracking time spent studying, breaks from said studying, and for reading in bed at night. She loves it—she really does!)

So—how do you end a team meeting in a manner that ensures maximum impact and effectiveness? I recommend doing two things: reconfirm next steps with clear account-abilities, and conduct a brief meeting evaluation. While action planning can be very elaborate—and believe me, I have seen my share with LCD screen projectors and detailed Microsoft Project templates—most of the teams I work with don't have the time or the stomach for this. I prefer a very simple flip chart at the front of the room with the words: *Who? What? By When?* written on it. This provides a very clear listing of the agreed-upon next steps coming out of today's meeting. Nothing makes personal accountability more real than seeing your name (and I always put the name first!) and a deadline date associated with it. All of a sudden, there is a heightened sense of interest in the words that go up on that page. The best approach is to capture these to dos as you go, while the topics are fresh in everyone's mind. This prevents you from running out of time to complete this step; then, at the end of the meeting, the leader is simply reminding—and reinforcing—the assignments to which everyone has already agreed.

Finally, reserve five minutes at the end of a meeting to conduct an evaluation, and capture valuable information about how to improve the next one. Again, my approach here is the simpler the better, and the more likely to get done. I ask each person to take a sheet of paper and draw a T chart—with a + sign on one side and a Δ or delta sign on the other (a triangle symbol that stands for change). Give everyone three minutes to jot down the things that worked really well in this meeting on the left side, and the things that could be changed or improved on the right. The leader should then have all participants star the top three things in each column that they think had the greatest impact on the success (or lack of it) in the meeting. If time is short, simply collect these sheets for review later. These can be anonymous assessments—or not—depending upon how safe the environment is. When in doubt, I recommend erring on the side of anonymity and candor. If time permits, capture these notes on a flip chart in the front of the room and make a decision as a team about those things they want to keep and those they want to change. If you really want to get uptown, you can conduct a more formal assessment and track progress over a period of time. Remember, it is not just the leader's responsibility to fix any problems; it is everyone's, so engage them in the process.

Think of the last team meeting you attended where you glowed with anticipation about what could come out of this meeting. Has it been too long since you've had a feeling like this? Then I encourage you and the team to take the steps I have previously outlined. Maybe your team meeting time will truly become one of trust building, problem solving, and collaboration—and will be a spark in the dark for others to follow. Because, you see, what your meetings look like as a team leader will greatly influence what the meetings of your direct reports will look like. How exciting could *that* be?

Chapter Twelve

Team Decisions: Fact or Fiction?

Several years ago, I began to see a trend in my consulting work. People tended to be very uncomfortable dealing with conflict in a team setting, something that was negatively impacting their ability to engage in effective discussion and to execute decisions with commitment. It was a particularly intractable problem with a certain IT leadership team at a telecommunications company; and they had quite a few projects that were in jeopardy because of it. I decided to design a new exercise for their upcoming team effectiveness session I was facilitating. During the off-site meeting, I asked the participants to remember and jot down their thoughts about the last time this team had a really *great* discussion that resulted in a very effective decision. I also asked them to list all of the factors that contributed to the effectiveness of this discussion and decision. I noticed people doodling on their page, squirming nervously in their chairs, and glancing around furtively; but no one was writing down a thing. I asked them if the question wasn't clear. Did I need to explain it further? "No, it's clear," one member said. "It's just that we really don't make decisions as a team. We'll start to talk about something here, and then a few members of the team are assigned to take it off-line and deal with it. Most of the time we don't even know how it got resolved."

I was amazed. This group was missing out on one of the most exciting and rewarding parts of being a team: working together to solve problems creatively. At first, I thought that perhaps the problem just affected this one team. But, after engaging a few more teams in this exercise, I realized that this was in fact true for the majority; and I think that the teams were even surprised by the results of this exercise. I'm continually stunned by how few decisions teams actually make—but need to. I think the vast majority need to make more decisions as a group, but oftentimes don't view decision making as the work of the team. Their gatherings or staff meetings are more likely to serve the purpose of reporting on what they have been doing, and providing highlights of what's coming up—not to tap into the collective knowledge and creativity of the team to solve really tough issues.

Some teams and their leaders have justified this situation by explaining that their organization is just too siloed; they simply don't have enough information to make decisions as a team. Besides, things are happening too fast; you can't slow down to get everyone's opinion on every little thing and make a group decision. Of course, the execution of the decision suffers on many occasions, because team leaders didn't have time to seek the input of others; but that is just the price you have to pay in a new environment that is organized for speed and efficiency versus effectiveness.

Most humans likely consider their problem-solving skills trump those of our feathered, four-legged, and finned counterparts. Yet when we look at the animal kingdom, we can find ample instances of incredibly effective *group* decision-making taking place. It's called *swarm intelligence*, something that profoundly influences the behavior of ant colonies, schools of fish, flocks of birds, and herds of horses; and something that is being applied today to improve the efficiency of traffic patterns, responses to 911 calls, and searches of earthquake-damaged buildings for survivors. Cornell University biologist Thomas Seeley's discoveries, which explored the mysterious decision-making ability of honeybees, were described in an article in *National Geographic* magazine: "The bees' rules for decision-making—seek a diversity of opinions, encourage a free competition among ideas, and use an effective mechanism to narrow choices—so impressed Seeley that he now uses them at Cornell as chairman of his department." (If you want to see the fireflies' version of swarm intelligence—where individual actions come together to have a much greater impact than any one could alone—then you will love Chapter 19!)

So—how much does *your* group resemble this swarm of honeybees? How many decisions do *you* make as a team? Too few; too many? I would guess it is the former, rather than the latter; and if you aren't sure, ask the team to participate in the same exercise that I conducted with the IT team. If you get great feedback, you can skip this chapter and go on to the next one. If you don't, then I have a few suggestions for a process (which I explore in greater detail in this chapter and those following) that will help to improve the decision-making ability of your team:

- First, the team needs to believe that they will *find more creative solutions and make better decisions* if they have purposefully created an environment that promotes each person's ability to bring their unique strengths—and offer their diverse perspectives—to the team.

- Second, there needs to be an *agreed-upon process* for making the decisions—and the team leader needs to clearly explain this process—along with the rationale for choosing this approach, immediately and up front.

- Third, team *leaders* need to be *mindful of their role* in the decision-making process; and must acknowledge that they can be a force for either good or evil.

- Fourth—as mentioned above with the example of the honeybees—there needs to be a wide *variety of ideas freely offered* before making a final decision.

- Fifth, there needs to be *clarity* when the team has reached the point where they *should make*—or *have made*—a *decision*; and accept that it is time to move on, getting people to commit to a plan for executing the decision.

- Finally, there needs to be a *mechanism for tracking* the effectiveness of the decisions that the team has made—one that makes members comfortable with revisiting and revising decisions based on new information.

Much of the work described in my chapters leading up to this point will guide you in creating this kind of safe environment; one that allows *a diversity of opinions* to be heard. Team members need to acknowledge that both their own and others' opinions have value, even if they are vastly different. The team needs to find ways to discover and continually emphasize these diverse perspectives. Not only will this stimulate better decision making, it will also, in fact, be better for each person's individual job satisfaction. Research shows that when people get to do the work they do best more often, superior productivity, discretionary effort, engagement, joy, retention, and loyalty result. Great teams play to their strengths; they clearly know who the competition is, and keep their sights focused on what they do and how to defeat them. They expend as much effort as they possibly can to being their best as individuals, a team, and an organization.

After you acknowledge the inherent value of each person's diverse perspective, the next step is to assure everyone that it is okay if this creative abrasion leads to conflict—as long as these differences of opinion remain focused on the issue or problem at hand do *not* get personal. I would expect and want people to passionately debate and share their ideas, as long as they don't denigrate another person's ideas (and thus, that person) in the process. You will be able to make better and faster decisions if the team has collectively created an environment where each person feels equally safe to share their honest perspectives, without a sense of the artificial harmony to which Patrick Lencioni refers in *The Five Dysfunctions of a Team*.

This is the way I describe that behavior to teams. Do you remember the bobble-head dogs that people would place in their car rear windows? You get the picture—they nod relentlessly. Well, if you as the leader ask the question, "Is everyone on board with this decision and our plan of action?" and you see anything even slightly resembling a bobble-head from the people on your team and not a question or a word of concern ... then you might be experiencing artificial harmony! So what do you do if you see this? Don't take them at their word (or nonwords, so to speak). Ask questions of *them*! Ask them to tell *you* all the things that could go wrong, all the iffy assumptions that have been built in, who we *must* convince this is a good idea . . . and then you bring the renewed energy, candor, and creativity of the team to bear and address those challenges together!

For this process to be truly effective, however, several necessary pieces must be in place for the team to create a fertile environment for productive conflict. One obviously critical element is for the team leader to role model what this looks like; and I will discuss this in more detail in the next chapter. But what about the rest of the team; what can *they* do to promote this inviting environment? Well, just like you have ground rules to make your meeting more effective (e.g., start and end on time, limit side bar conversations, forbid multitasking), a team also needs to create *conflict norms* that beget productive discussions that will lead to decisions to which everyone can—and *will*—commit. So let me return to the exercise that I talked about at the beginning of this chapter.

After I got over my initial surprise about the IT team's lack of group decision-making—and the corresponding dearth of *norms* to which they could refer back—I helped them to take the only logical next step: create them. I truly believe that generating these principles themselves enhances any team's commitment to uphold them. Several people said they had some ideas of what the guidelines might be, even though this particular team had never used them before. I suggest that you and your team do the same; don't get hung up on whether you currently have any rules. Simply move on to create them; and use them going forward.

But how do you do this effectively? You might begin by asking each member to write down three to five norms that would lead the group as a whole to more productive conflict and make better decisions; that is, conditions that would need to be in place for this to happen. Don't worry about the exact wording at this point; just get the gist of an idea. If the team has many members—or if the environment doesn't make this kind of open, candid discussion realistic quite yet—then have members create small groups of three to four people to share what they wrote down. They then can discuss and agree upon the suggestions that they think are best for this team at this stage in their growth. Again, don't worry about wording at this point; we are simply looking for trends across the various groups. Are we seeing any kind of pattern? Are you hearing the same repeatedly? If so, then you know you have hit on something. Another way to approach this step is simply to hand each person five sticky notes and a black marker, and then ask them to jot down one idea per note. There is great anonymity in the same color notes and markers. You can then group together the notes that seem to be addressing the same issue.

You have now identified some general themes or concepts for what these norms might be. What next? While you could keep the whole group together to wordsmith each one, I prefer a simpler and more engaging approach. Let people form (new) small groups to work on the single theme about which they feel most strongly. This incites the favorable consequence of having internal champions who will ensure that others adhere to these norms, since they were so deeply involved in their very creation. After about 15 minutes of work, ask the groups to share their draft norms. You want people to react to these by asking them questions such as: "What do you like about it? What would you change? Will we be able to know if someone is living up to the norm—that is, can we see it in action?"

This last point is very important. Beware of vague mom and apple pie norms like "Show respect." After all, how will you *really* know if someone is showing respect? The very definition of the word respect can vary greatly from one person to the next. As much as possible, leave little room open for interpretation, and make each rule measurable and actionable.

I have had the opportunity over the last several years to work with dozens of teams in creating these conflict norms. Next are some of the general categories into which they tend to fall, and examples of each. Sometimes, when I need to jump-start the process or if I have limited time with a team, I will simply hand them this list with these corresponding instructions:

Choose four to six conflict norms that you think would help this team have productive conflict and make more effective decisions. Feel free to alter the wording, or write your own.

- *Common Goal*
  - Establish a common goal that the group fully understands
  - Ground the group by stating the objective of the discussion
  - Define the topic, problem, or opportunity
- *Environment*
  - Provide an opportunity for every voice to be heard
  - Ensure open and respectful dialogue—do not belittle people or their ideas
  - Create an environment in which team members feel safe to question and/or challenge
- *Participant Behavior*
  - Speak so others can *hear* your message
  - Remain engaged and attentive, and consider everyone's input
  - Seek first to understand, *then* to be understood
- *Decision Parameters*
  - Acknowledge the necessary speed or timeline in which a decision needs to be made
  - Confirm if it is a decision to be made by the team or simply a request for team *input*
  - Provide guidelines and boundaries for each decision to be made
- *Decision Process*
  - Provide appropriate advance information to people in time for effective discussion and decision making
  - Act on facts and data without analysis paralysis—don't get stuck admiring the problem
  - Clarify pros, cons, and risks of options or potential solutions
- *Commitment to Outcome*
  - Be decisive and make certain that all members commit to a decision
  - When we leave this room, we all speak with one voice

- Although consensus is not necessary, full *support* of the decision is required

An important factor to consider is that cultural differences may exist within a group, particularly in relation to individual levels of comfort with conflict arising during a team meeting. A variety of reasons can influence people's perceptions of the value of and the appropriate way to handle conflict, such as the country or region in which they were born, their nationality or ethnic makeup, how they were raised, and various other life experiences that have shaped them. This makes the need to reach agreement on the norms that dictate how *the team* will deal with conflict that much more critical. Just because conflict may not overtly explode during decision making does not mean that it doesn't exist. It could mean that dissent has just gone underground and is biding time until it can come out later in the form of undermining decisions and delay tactics. By keeping the conflict below the surface and neglecting to address it in a straightforward manner, you run the risk of gaining compliance, but failing to achieve any true commitment to these team decisions. Thus, even though some members may not have joined the team with a high level of comfort with conflict, the team as a whole must become adept at facing and managing it.

I have seen the impressive impact on teams who make the courageous choice to embrace conflict. I was working with a particular group of leaders for a wonderful school, who had exerted a great deal of effort to overcome their natural tendency to gloss over conflict. The norms they created were very effective, because they reflected what *they* most needed to keep in mind and improve upon when making decisions. I came back about a month later and passed one of the team members in the hall. Louise was very excited to see me. "We just had a great fight in our staff meeting this morning. You would have been so proud of us!" When I ran into the team leader a short while later, without my even asking him about it, he said—with a rueful smile on his face—"Well, the team is certainly more *animated* than they've been in the past!" (Remember the old adage—be careful what you ask for, you just might get it!) These team members were now able to express a sense of passion—and yes, even passionate disagreement—about their work with which they had never before been comfortable; one that would help them face and resolve their most pressing issues.

Now on to my second point: that there needs to be an *agreed upon process* for making the decisions. Perhaps I should be right up front here: I am not expecting that *every* decision truly be a team decision. However, *almost* every decision could benefit from receiving robust team *input*. Although there will certainly be some instances in which the leader should decide alone, I promise you that this should very much be the exception rather than the rule.

So, with all of these caveats in mind, how do you know the best approach to take? I have two words for you: Vroom-Yetton. Most teams to whom I utter these words have never heard them before; but I promise that you will find this decision-making framework (named for its creators Victor Vroom and Phillip Yetton) to be simple and invaluable.

Vroom-Yetton is a powerful tool for determining and making explicit how groups will make decisions. It provides the leader with a thought process for determining the optimum level of involvement of others in the decision, which will then allow the leader to make that rationale explicit to the team. I've usually found that team members know they won't be making every decision, and they don't mind *not* having the absolute final decision-making authority, as long as they understand the decision process up front and view it as fair. What the team does *not* appreciate is being under the impression that the leader wants them to make the decision, and then having that authority taken away. When a manager takes the decision back, it can leave members feeling as though they did something wrong, which seems like failure to the team. That is *never* a good place to start if you want commitment to the final decision.

On the other hand, you as the leader can use this framework to help you think through which level of input you want from the team, before you even engage them in the discussion of the issue. Thus, you are much less likely to need to yank that authority back from them and you can more clearly share your expectations with them, right up front, at the outset. The levels of the *Vroom-Yetton Decision Making Model* are as follows:

- **Autocratic**
  - A1: Leader solves the problem alone using information that is readily available to him/her.
  - A2: Leader obtains additional information from group members, and then makes decision alone. Group members may or may not be informed of the final decision.
- **Consultative**
  - C1: Leader shares problem with group members individually and asks for information and evaluation. Group members do not meet collectively, and leader makes decision alone.
  - C2: Leader shares problem with group members collectively, but makes decision alone.
- **Group Based**
  - G2: Leader meets with group to discuss situation. Leader focuses and directs discussion, but does not impose will. Group makes final decision.

So with all of these levels to choose from, how can a manager decide which is the most appropriate for each decision? Here are some of the factors to consider when making this choice:

- **Need for complete buy-in:** The more commitment needed from the team to ensure effective execution, the more involved they should be.
- **Learning opportunity for the team:** If the team can use this problem to improve its capacity for making effective decisions in the future or to gain greater knowledge of the issue at hand, then ask them for more input.
- **Criticality of the decision:** If the decision is extremely critical, the leader may not have the freedom to allow as much involvement as might otherwise be the case. On the other hand, the leader may decide that, given the importance of the decision, there needs to be *greater* involvement by the team to ensure that they've fully

vetted all options. Be sure to explain the rationale for whichever choice you make, and if you decide upon limiting team involvement, then identify other ways of gaining their commitment to executing this critical decision.

- **Breadth of impact of the decision:** The broader the impact, the broader the involvement should be. This will give you a greater opportunity to take all of the critical constituents' viewpoints into account when you develop the solution, and when you plan implementation of the decision.

- **Difficulty of execution:** The more difficult the execution, the greater the need is to get the entire team involved. You do not want to be pushing that boulder up the hill all by yourself, and you cannot possibly foresee all of the things that will need to be done if you make the decision alone. You don't want to count on others' engagement if they didn't have skin in the game when the decision was made.

- **Complexity of the problem:** This factor can prompt you to go either way. One might argue that the issue is *so* complex that you need to get the full involvement of the team because no one person—the team leader included—can have the necessary knowledge and breadth of understanding to make this difficult decision on their own. On the other hand, this very complexity may make it too difficult for the leader to explain the situation to the rest of the team, and thereby give them a credible role to play. This would require the leader to make the decision individually.

- **Individuals' knowledge or credibility on the topic:** If the leader has limited knowledge on the topic, then bringing the rest of the team into the equation obviously makes great sense. If a member of the team were the one who lacks knowledge, then I would still recommend including that person in the discussions for two reasons. First, it will broaden their understanding of the topic; and second, a certain amount of ignorance about an issue can sometimes be a great vehicle for challenging the assumptions that everyone else accepts as true.

- **Timing:** If speed is of the essence, then the leader may not be able to involve the whole team. When the building is burning, you don't want to be debating alternative escape routes if one person absolutely knows the one best way. I find, however, that people tend to use this need for speed as an excuse for expediency versus effectiveness.

The third part of the equation for effective team decisions is the role of the team leader. This element is so critical to the creative exploration of solutions, effective decision-making, and successful execution, that I have devoted the entire following chapter—"What to Do if the Leader Is Keeping Too Tight a Lid on the Jar"—to it.

I will therefore move on to the next critical phase—ensuring that you are remaining open to a wide variety of ideas before making a final decision. As I have stated repeatedly throughout this book—while our differences may sometimes be irritating, they can spur us to look at situations, problems, and opportunities more creatively if we begin with a curious mind. Unfortunately, I have seen the opposite occur in many group-setting situations. When people know that they are attending a meeting where an important decision will be made, there is often a lot of jockeying for position that occurs before anyone steps foot in the door. People sell their ideas beforehand to save time instead of truly coming to learn about potential, viable alternatives.

How do you deal with this kind of preconceived decision making? By reinforcing that curious mind through a balancing act of inquiry and advocacy. I initially learned about this wonderful technique when I was an Organization Effectiveness Manager at Coca-Cola. We were learning how to use a variety of tools from Peter Senge's *The Fifth Discipline Fieldbook*. This book introduces a very straightforward concept for teams to understand and use—one that, despite its simplicity, seems almost revolutionary to many a leader.

The unfortunate truth is that most team members have already formed a conclusion about what they think is the right approach; and it can take a great deal of effort to put that mind-set aside and openly request the other's point of view. We are too often working our hardest to convince each other of the correctness of our conclusion, position, or actions. But true creativity and conflict resolution screams out for inquiry, not for the other person to simply stop talking so that you can interject your opinion. After all, it's hard to hear others above the voice speaking in your own head—isn't it? Inquiry prompts you to focus your energy on truly listening and comprehending another's point of view instead of on defending *your* position.

It has been my experience that the vast majority of people have no problem advocating their opinions; heck, that's what you expect a real leader and strong team member to do, right? Well, I would like to suggest that *true* leadership is something different. When someone offers an idea for a solution that you disagree with, you stop yourself from saying "That wouldn't work." Instead, begin with inquiry by asking, "Can you help me to understand your thinking on that?" or "What leads you to suggest that would be a good alternative?" and then really listen to their response. You just might be surprised.

I have found two other procedural techniques that go a long way toward ensuring a lively discourse on alternative solutions. The first is very simple: send information out to the participants in advance, and expect them to read it and come prepared to learn and share perspectives. One particular team was struggling with the fact that most of its members were hearing about something for the first time during the meeting, and were expected to offer feedback on the spot. They have since implemented a mandate, which stated that anything requiring a decision at the meeting had to have preliminary reading sent out a minimum of 48 hours in advance. This was a terrific way of ensuring a more level playing field for informed discussions and decisions.

This team then went one step further, which brings me to my other procedural recommendation. For significant strategic decisions with far-ranging and longer-term impact, you cannot expect a decision to be made when the topic is initially raised. This team leader has now implemented what he calls a rule of 3, meaning that these higher-level issues will be discussed in three separate meetings, with a decision expected in that third meeting. This gives the team an opportunity to learn about the relevant issues in the first meeting; bring additional information that spurs investigation of a broader search for alternative solutions to the second; and finally, to making an informed decision to which all can truly commit at the third. This leader knew the value for this team of allowing an appropriate amount of time between the productive conflict and the decision making. (Note: In this chapter, I have focused on ways of inviting a broader range of solutions that are procedural in nature. For true creativity boosters that will really jar team members thinking about a problem in totally new ways, see Chapter 16: "How Could You Forget the Toys?".)

This brings me to my fifth point on this topic: knowing when you have reached a point where the team is prepared to make a decision and begin planning for its implementation. I didn't realize how hard this could be until recently when I worked with an IT leadership team at a financial institution. We were discussing why some problems kept resurfacing and never seemed to get fully resolved during a recent strategic planning session. To use HBDI-speak, this was a very Blue-Green group ... a combo of analyzers and organizers. One team member named Joseph hit the nail on the head when he said, "We like to admire the problem." Everyone laughed; but it was that kind of uncomfortable laugh when you know something is true even though you don't like admitting it. This line became code for when we were spending too much time analyzing the problem and needed to go green to solve it. I have used this same line with other very blue-green groups, and it really resonates with them.

At the beginning of this chapter, I mentioned that problems can arise when some members of the team are asked to take the problem off-line and solve it. However, I am not so naïve or unrealistic as to believe that after reading this chapter, you will address every problem you face as a team—or not at all. I don't necessarily think that is the right solution. I *do*, however, believe in finding the optimum balance and the right criteria for determining when decision making should be taken off-line. And it's just as important to have an agreed-upon process for reintroducing these decisions to the team later on to inform the entire group of how an issue was resolved. I often recommend that there be a placeholder at every staff meeting for updating the team on how these off-line decisions were resolved, and then thinking through the impact these decisions will have on the other members of the team.

There is one more (slightly surprising) issue that I have encountered on a couple of teams: they don't know when they have made a decision. I truly believe that everyone reaches a point when they are just talked out, and most team members simply hope that someone else has taken action based on the dialog in which the team has engaged. Well . . . don't count on it. If you aren't quite sure about whether a decision was made or not, simply ask the group: "Can anyone tell me where we landed on the XYZ issue?" When in doubt, seek it out. (I will talk more about the leader's role in effectively bringing a discussion to closure in the next chapter.) And always make sure to assess the rationale for the choices that *are* made. I heard once that all decisions are emotional ones, and that people simply try to justify them with facts *after* they determine their point of view. Being clear on the reasoning behind your team's choices will substantially help if you need to revisit your thinking later. It will also provide valuable content for the communications going out to others about the decision.

One clear sign that your team has made a decision is that you start the concrete planning stage. Nothing says action better than writing *Who? What? By When?* on a flip chart. Something happens to people when they actually *see* the expectation and the due date recorded right there in front of everybody. They suddenly become very concerned about what they are being expected to do, and they want to scrutinize every word that is written down, which is good. It seems a lot less like smoke and mirrors.

I have seen my share of lofty approaches to conducting action planning; yet I keep coming back to asking, "What are the teams I am working with most likely to *do*?" Keep it simple, I say. Ideally, you post the flip chart page at the front of the room with three columns and those words (Who . . . What. . .By When) at the top. Then, as the group makes choices and members volunteer—or receive assignments—for various tasks, add them to the action list. If your team meetings tend to run long, then it is preferable to keep this running list than to wait until the end when you may not have, or make, the necessary time for action planning. If you do opt to complete this part of the process at the close of the meeting, reserve at least 5 to 10 minutes for a recap of action items and assignments. I have seen more technologically adept teams summarize these to dos in a spreadsheet on a laptop that is projected on to the wall. Whatever works for your team and gets the job done is the approach that your group should take.

After you have identified the plan of action for implementing the team's decisions, your final step is to ask one very simple question that I learned from one of the team leaders with whom I worked: "Who is *not* in the room that needs to know what we just decided?" This is a great way of getting the team to identify the key stakeholders in their decisions. The more essential their sincere commitment and ensuing actions are, the more time and effort you need to spend in rigorously considering how to attain truly engaged input. How are you going to get their support to achieve the decided-upon goals (commitment) versus simply instructing them to do it (compliance)? From an HBDI perspective, this is a time when those with Red quadrant preferences (remember, these are the ones who are very good at all things interpersonal) are particularly invaluable for helping you to both identify these concerned constituents and understand what it will take to gain their support. They can lead a discussion on how this decision will affect these key stakeholders. Of course, you should always keep in mind everyone's favorite radio station—WIIFM or *What's in It for Me?* Your stakeholders, who are likely be different for each of your decisions, might include people who:

- Will be directly affected by this decision
- Have final sign-off authority
- Have to implement the decision
- Could sabotage the process

The next logical step is to figure out how the team will communicate the decision to these people. What are the key messages, what are the right vehicles, and what should the timing be? The more power each stakeholder has to support or derail the decision's approval and implementation, the more thoroughly you will need to plan the communications, and the more closely you will need to monitor their effectiveness. When you have come this far, you can't leave this last part to chance. Use the team's creativity to determine the most effective means of reaching your most critical stakeholders.

So there you have it—a tried and true process for ensuring your team makes better and faster decisions that include everyone's most creative input. In the next chapter, we will focus on the leader's role in making certain that these are indeed the best decisions. In Chapter 14—the final chapter in this section—we will explore accountability, and figure out how to assess whether team members are fulfilling the commitments they've made. *Because a decision without action is really just a hallucination!*

Chapter Thirteen

What to Do if the Leader Is Keeping Too Tight a Lid on the Jar

Do you remember capturing fireflies and placing them in a jar? Why did we do this? To have control over them? To keep their magical light close to us? As so often happens in cases like these, we were our own worst enemies. Held captive in the jar, with no means of escape, their light begins to fade until eventually there is no light at all. Oh, yes, if you really shake things up, you might get a brief flicker, but it sure seems to have lost its magic when it is forced like this, doesn't it? The firefly doesn't die, not right away, but it doesn't thrive either. This glow was not meant to be bottled up and kept for the delight of just one person. It is in the DNA of this tiny firefly to be free and shine its light for all to see and enjoy. The analogy for us as humans is all too clear.

I'm curious to know: Are you a leader who is reading this to learn how to better manage your own behavior in order to elicit creative ideas on your team, and enable better decision making? Or, are you one of the members of the unfortunate team who really gravitated to the title of this chapter, especially the part about *too tight a lid*? Whatever your situation, you will benefit from reading what comes next. After all, how do you strike a balance between guiding your team effectively while simultaneously not keeping too tight a lid on the jar—and leaving team innovation gasping for air?

In Chapter 11 on team gatherings, I highlighted several varieties of dysfunctional behavior that occur in meetings, one of which is the tendency for a single person to dominate the meeting. The *real* danger zone, however, exists when the person dominating the meeting is the leader. You may well have discovered this for yourself (if you are a team leader) if you took my suggestion in that chapter to ask team members why meeting participation levels are so low. I often find one of the main reasons this occurs is because the leader is keeping too tight a lid on the team meeting by exerting too much control. Now, when I suggest this to team leaders, they sometimes react defensively and say, "Well, then I just won't say anything. Let them create the agenda and run the meeting. I'll just sit there and listen." I then make a giant sucking sound and tell them this is what will happen if they completely abandon their role as the team and meeting leader. Most teams become very dysfunctional when a power vacuum has been created. You need to figure out how to *manage* your impact, not completely abandon your role. When the team is used to your playing a strong directive role, you can't simply disappear one day.

But how can you tell if you are being overly dominant in your team meetings? One clear sign is lack of interaction and member participation when the team discusses urgent topics, and especially when you are sure that people in the room are knowledgeable on the subject and have strong opinions that they aren't expressing. If there is a group member to whom you are particularly close and who you know will talk straight with you, then ask them. Tell them that you're afraid that you're shutting down two-way communication on important issues; and that is *not* what you want to do. Ask them to clue you in on whether this is true, and if so, when they see it happening the most.

If there is no one on the team who can serve in this role, you have two other options. Invite a close colleague from outside the team to attend your next team meeting and silently observe the interactions. (You could always explain this person's presence by saying that you want to get an outsider's perspective on the meeting's effectiveness.) The other option is to ask the team members directly if they feel you are dominating. This is a delicate matter, and may be difficult ground upon which to tread. So you first need to clearly indicate to them that you really do want the *truth*, and that you will act on what they say. You may prefer to solicit opinions anonymously, perhaps by asking them to write their comments on three-by-five cards. Nothing says anonymity like a white note card and a No. 2 pencil!

So what are some things leaders *can* do that will ensure they don't dominate a meeting? I have listed a few simple solutions below. I will also share some best practices later in this chapter that are directly related to the decision-making process.

- *Beware the dominating power of a seat at the front of the room.* If you are in a room with a board table down the middle, you should choose a seat in the middle of one side of the table. This is as close as you can get in these seating configurations to King Arthur's round table. Better yet, change your seat each meeting. You will drive the person who is constantly jockeying for a prime position next to you crazy!

- *Use positive reinforcement to encourage participation.* This can be expressed both verbally and nonverbally with smiles, positive head nods, and leaning forward and listening intently. But be sure to spread it around equally; you don't want to look like you are playing favorites.

- *Be careful not to get into a prolonged conversation with only one or two other members of the team.* Nothing kills the energy, enthusiasm, and participation level of the whole team faster than feeling left out and then tuning out while these few go on and on . . . and on. And after an interchange like this, it is incredibly hard to get everyone reengaged and back on task.

Okay, so now you understand—and can hopefully eliminate—common behaviors that team members might perceive as overbearing. How do you deal with people's natural tendency to defer to the leader, even when he/she isn't dominating—or, in fact, is consciously trying very hard *not* to? As the leader, you must go out of your way not to unduly bias the people in the room, especially when discussing controversial topics and making decisions. An easy solution: always share your opinion on a topic last. The only caveat I would give in this regard is if you know there are some options or ideas that are not open for discussion; then make that clear before any dialogue on the topic begins. But that should be the exception, not the rule; and it goes a long way toward being acceptable to the team if you can give clear, fact-based rationale for why these particular things are off limits for the topic at hand at this time.

Beware as well that you are not telegraphing your opinion on a subject or your unfavorable response to something someone said through telltale facial expressions and body language. You may be more of an open book than you realize. In fact, one team leader told me about a time when he was videotaped during a meeting. He couldn't believe it when he later watched the tape and realized how clearly his face and body told the story of how much he disliked what another person was saying; in fact, how much he disliked that very *person.* He told me he became much more aware of his behavior after that. Maybe all of us could benefit from being videotaped during a meeting. One approach is to at least pretend that someone has a camera on you, and taking this into consideration before you allow your face to betray your thoughts!

You can also alleviate team members' tendency to defer to you by altering the process by which you deal with agenda topics. Most teams I've encountered seem to feel that every item should be addressed through an open, free-flowing, large-group discussion. In fact, this can be one of the *least* effective means of ensuring that diverse opinions are brought forward (aside from the natural tendency of people to defer to the leader). This becomes even truer when the topic at hand is especially controversial, sensitive, or of particular importance to the leader. So what are you to do? How about trying one or more of the following approaches in your next meeting?

- *Have the team write down their thoughts first before sharing them aloud.* This gives each member a moment to consider how best to phrase their points in order to ensure that others receive the message as intended. It will also help to keep comments tight and on point versus sharing rambling thoughts off the top of their heads, or being ill prepared to disclose any topics that they feel are worthwhile.

- *Have a small-group discussion first, followed by a large-group debrief.* There is safety in numbers. If something difficult needs to be said, the spokesperson can defer to the group's thinking without taking personal responsibility. Together, they can also figure out the best way to raise a delicate issue before bringing it to the entire team's attention.

- *Have the team leader leave the room for part of the discussion.* Now, I don't normally advocate this technique; but I have used it on a couple of occasions involving extremely sensitive issues. I've also opted for this course of action when team members thought that the leader's retribution against some or all members of the team was likely. In one situation, a manager whose team saw her as overbearing and unreasonable wanted to know what they expected of her as a leader. She thought they would be more open in sharing this if she were not in the room; and she was right about that. Their respectful but candid feedback, which she accepted graciously and without defensiveness, went a long way toward building a strong bond between them.

- *Submit comments anonymously.* If this is a highly sensitive subject, anonymous comments are a great way to solicit input. See the above suggestion about protecting anonymity by distributing paper and pencils for everyone to use so that there is no guessing about who wrote what. Of course, be sure to mix up the papers after you collect them prior to sharing them with the group.

- *Use round-robins.* This is a great way to make sure that you give everyone equal airtime. Depending on where you are in the discussion cycle and how much time is remaining, you might need to ask people to limit their input by asking them to speak in headlines; that is, as you might read it on the front page of the newspaper. Do not use this approach, however, if you have not fully vetted a topic. People may feel pressured to summarize their position in a headline without providing some rationale as to why they feel this way.

- *Always offer your opinion last.* As I said before, this is one sure way not to influence the direction of the discussion. Don't let the team know what direction you are leaning on a topic until you have heard from everyone. Who knows—you might even change your mind! And when you do share your opinion, be sure that you clearly show that you value what others have said before you. Be candid and honest with your opinion—as they all were—but keep in mind that your perceptions carry extra weight with the group, so measure your words accordingly.

Not only do you not want to dominate; you in fact want to be a role model for effective listening that everyone on the team should try to emulate. What exactly does that look like? It means that you make eye contact with people when they are speaking, and you don't interrupt them when they are talking. Instead, you ask them questions about, or paraphrase what they just said to ensure your understanding. You don't multitask, become easily distracted, or engage in side conversations when others have the floor. Now—be honest—which of these behaviors do you demonstrate on a regular basis in your team meetings? If you could use some improvement in the effective listening department, I would suggest that you make a concerted attempt to try out one or two of the positive behaviors listed above; or eliminate one or two negative ones during your next meeting. You might be surprised by the response. I assure you, if you display more productive listening behavior, and make it clear that this is what you expect of others on the team as well, then you will definitely see a change in the group dynamics at future meetings.

After you've addressed any meeting-dominating behaviors and have begun to demonstrate effective listening, people tend to become much more comfortable offering up their ideas and opinions. In fact, they may have now gotten so comfortable, you are moving into what is perhaps uncharted team territory—really open and passionate debate about the topics on the agenda. Whoa—you weren't really prepared for this! But it's happening real-time, so how do you handle it now and ensure that the conflict stays productive without denigrating into personal debate? How do you handle these strong emotions that may be rising up within you and your teammates? Here are some suggestions for ways to remain calm and lead a productive discussion, even when passion about the topic begins to rise:

- *Relax and stay focused on the goal.* Force yourself to slow down physically, and your emotions and mind will follow. Take a couple of deep breaths, sit back in your chair, and keep your facial expression as neutral as possible. Remind yourself that you wanted this open dialogue, and that it really will help you to achieve your goal of a more engaged discussion and a better decision to which all team members can commit.

- *Put those effective listening skills to work.* Maintain regular eye contact, remain engaged in the dialogue, and don't interrupt the flow of the conversation unless it's clear that opinions have been misconstrued or the tone is becoming very personal or negative. Paraphrase and ask questions to get things back on track or to clarify misstatements, erroneous assumptions, or opinions stated as fact.

- *Offer encouragement and guidance to the team.* Tell them that this kind of passionate, engaged discourse is what will help us to make the best and most informed decisions. Remind them that each team member believes strongly that their point of view has value and that, to them, it is the *correct* option. Reinforce the use of the conflict norms (if you have these in place). Ask team members to balance the advocacy of their own position with inquiries to gain deeper understanding of other positions, and even to tip the balance in favor of the latter. Allow people to share both facts and feelings on the subject. (I am actually not one who believes in allowing people to talk only about facts during these discussions. I think that this method only encourages them to try to represent how they feel about something as a fact, when really it is just an opinion.)

- *Make sure all members stay engaged.* Consider changing up the regular process. For example, ask everyone to take a moment to jot down their current perception of where we are on a given topic; then conduct a round-robin to hear everyone's perspective. Or, solicit feedback from one or two members who have been less vocal (but be careful not to make them feel they have been put on the spot; or that they are being asked to be a tiebreaker).

- *Call for a break if needed.* If tempers are really flaring— or the conversation has become a debate between a few, vocal minorities—ask for a 10-minute break. Make it clear that they are to use this time to think about where they currently stand, and return with suggestions for how to proceed. Talk to the parties individually during the break; remind them of the importance of the discussion, and the need to reopen their minds to discovering other alternatives. I don't suggest tabling the entire discussion for a later meeting (the only exception might be as a last resort, or if the benefits of a cooler head and more information outweigh the possibility of negative feelings and opposing opinions hardening even further).

- *Ask the team if they are ready to make a decision.* The timing of this can be very delicate, so get the group to help you figure out if you are ready to decide. Gain clarity on areas of agreement, as well as any topics that are still under dispute (and how serious these are). Offer up a rough proposal for what you understand the team's decision to be, and let them react to it. Ask others to share their own, alternative proposals. Test for consensus; is this a decision that they can all live with and support? I personally like this phrasing: "I believe this is the best decision for the organization at this time, and I will support it."

- *If you can't decide now, reach agreement as a team on next steps.* Delay for the right reasons; for example, to gather and disseminate critical, relevant information prior to reconvening. There might be other knowledgeable and influential people who should be included in the discussion. Make sure, however, that participants aren't simply looking for time to gather forces and return to the next meeting even more firmly entrenched in their original viewpoint, and now armed with a legion of converts who've adopted their thinking, thanks to the informal discussions that were held in the interim. Only allow the team to defer to the leader for the decision as an absolute last resort. Doing this on a regular basis sets a terrible precedent for future tough decisions with which the team needs to grapple together.

- *Once the team has made an effective decision, congratulate them.* Make sure everyone is in clear agreement about what was decided. Recognize that it takes hard work to reach a positive conclusion when there are such diverse opinions that need to be considered. Thank them for sticking with it, even when it became intense. Remind them that we all now must support our teammates in the implementation of the decision no matter what our personal opinions, choices, or ideas might have been going into the discussion. When we walk out of these doors, we leave here speaking with one voice.

The team leader plays a critical role in ensuring that all voices are heard; that their own voice does not dominate the discussion; and that the conflict stays productive. They must be highly attuned to the delicate balance between needlessly delaying a decision and pushing to forced consensus too soon. I like to say, "Go slow to decide … go fast to execute." Good dialogue will not only inform a better decision, but will also ensure greater commitment to implementing the decision— and will result in a stronger, more cohesive team.

Chapter Fourteen

Shining the Light of Accountability

Over the years, I have discovered that accountability is a subject best viewed through three separate lenses—personal responsibility, the role of the leader, and the team's collective accountability. In this chapter, I will provide some best practices for positively impacting all three.

Are you as good as your word? Can others trust you to live up to the commitments that you make? What does exceptional personal accountability look like to you? Do you think that everyone sees it the same way? I hear a lot of team leaders complain that "We need more accountability on the team," or "We have a problem with people on this team not taking responsibility." I ask them to describe what this looks like when it's done well, something that's usually very hard for them to do. I have therefore found that it is much easier to ask each person to remember a time when they saw an outstanding example of someone taking accountability or being answerable for their actions. I ask each person to describe the situation, what the person did, and why they thought this was a good example of accountability. This can be a very powerful experience for a team, especially when each member is able to see the similarities and the differences in expectations about the individual meanings of accountability.

There is a wonderful book I use with clients entitled *QBQ: The Question Behind the Question* by organizational development specialist John Miller. It is a short, pithy, easy read; but it tackles the tough topic of personal accountability with exceptional clarity and an orientation toward action. It's almost like giving each member of the group permission—and a guide—to turn their attitudes around, and make positive change happen in their lives.

Miller's book shows people how to regain a sense of control over their actions and reactions to the world and people around them. It instructs readers *not* to see themselves as a victim who blames others for their circumstances, but instead to take ownership and action by asking the simple yet serious question, "What can I do to improve this situation?" This is what Miller calls "the *correct* question" versus "the *incorrect* questions," such as "Why does this keep happening to me?" or "Why don't people just do their job?"

Miller provides several easy tips for turning any incorrect question into a correct one. *Incorrect* questions begin with "Why," "When," or "Who"; *correct* questions begin with "What" or "How." *Incorrect* questions contain the words "them," "they," "we," or "you," while *correct* questions simply contain the word "I." *Incorrect* questions dwell on the current situation; correct questions focus on action. Thus, any one of us, when faced with difficult circumstances or demanding people, can *choose* to change our response from *incorrect* ("Who dropped the ball on this?") to *correct* ("What solutions can I provide?"). The beauty of changing our questions—and thus, our mind-set—is that we're able to turn laserlike focus on our actions and ourselves. We can then use this information to impact the way in which we view and react to the events and circumstances of our lives. We all know, but always forget, that we can't change other people; we can truly only change ourselves. We can choose to tap into our inherent creativity and turn our energies toward finding solutions that address these issues and problems; and *that* is the first step toward reclaiming control over our current situation. As Miller says in *QBQ*: "Personal accountability does NOT begin with you. It begins with me.... Personal accountability is about each of us holding *ourselves* accountable for our thinking and behaviors and the results they produce."

I firmly believe that accountability must start at the individual level, but that those who become leaders must demonstrate and reinforce it. So what can managers do to be true role models for excellence in accountability? First, we will focus on how a leader should behave during one-on-one situations, and then move to discussing his or her role in driving accountability across the whole team or department.

One of the most effective ways to hold someone accountable is to improve your delegation effectiveness. This simply means clarifying what success looks like at the end of the task or project, outlining any assumptions and nonnegotiables, and defining any known key milestone dates and targets that must be hit. You should also define quite clearly your team members' scope of decision-making authority.

Leaders are likely to have greater luck getting their employees to commit to completing a job with excellence if they provide reasons for the particular delegation. By taking the time to explain *why* they are assigning this responsibility or project to this specific person, they are far more likely to enhance the impact that its success will have on the team and other ongoing projects, and thus achieve some broader departmental or organizational goals. People like to feel that they are "in the know." They don't like receiving a task without understanding how it fits into the larger scheme of things. Ask yourself, if your boss told you today to go gather certain information without telling you what this information was for or how it was to be used, would you want to—and could you even—give it your best effort? I think not. So don't expect those who report to you to feel any differently. Such an explanation will likely only take a few minutes more, but can cause a completely different attitude and result for those to whom you are delegating.

Other important points for the leader to consider when allocating responsibility are the resources and support that can be provided to help ensure this task's successful accomplishment. Do you need to send a heads-up to someone that this work is under way? Is there an influential player who could really help to smooth the way for this individual to obtain the information or cooperation needed? How can you, as the leader, get them on board with this? Think about others that need to know what is going on, and inform them as soon as possible.

Agree on deadlines, and how progress will be tracked. Identify the key points along the way when those to whom you have delegated tasks should check in with you. The less certain you are of their ability to perform the task and/or the higher the criticality-level of the task, the more frequent the follow-up needs to be. If you clarify at the outset when these touch points need to occur, and which of you will initiate them, the less apt this is to be a point of contention later on. Finally, leaders should ask the individual to summarize their understanding of the task or project. Focus especially on what success looks like at the end, key delivery dates and metrics that must be achieved, and the progress-tracking procedures.

Let's turn our attention to what might happen during these tracking sessions. One of the most frequent—and negative—ways for someone to lose their leader's and fellow team members' trust is through the element of surprise; as in, "Surprise, I'm not going to hit that target date" (and that date is tomorrow). Or, "Surprise, this project is going *way* over budget" (which you discover only moments before a meeting with your boss to review the financials). Your first priority is to deal with the situation at hand; the second priority must be to have a candid discussion with the individual. Try your best not to jump to conclusions about this person's intent or motives, because as I like to say: "We give ourselves credit for our intentions; but hold others accountable for their results." In other words, we are always aware of our own reasons for doing, whereas we only see the effects of others' actions. Your main goal should be to understand what caused the delay, and why they didn't give you more advance notice about the problem. Help them to understand the ramifications of their actions—for you personally, for the task or project, and for others on or outside the team. The better you comprehend what occurred, the more you can help them to learn from the situation; so try to keep your conversation positive and future focused. On the other hand, if this is a recurring problem, then you might need to take further action; because leaving these issues unaddressed and unresolved will likely mean this will happen again in the future.

However, what about the opposite situation, when you need to commend your employees for a job well done? Let's say you've reached the end of the project, and it is a success. How are you going to reward and recognize this accomplishment? So many books on the market describe a multitude of ways to show your appreciation to employees, so I won't go into detail in that regard here. But there are two critical points to keep in mind. First, appreciating differences in others means discovering how individuals like to be rewarded and recognized for their contributions, which is really just an extension of treating each person like a unique individual. Do you know how your employees *like* to be recognized? It may be different than you think. Know how to find out? Ask them. You might fear that each of them will say they want money; money you don't have to give. However, it might surprise you to find out that there are other ways to express your appreciation—a day off to spend with their family, a gift card to a movie or local restaurant. It might even be something as simple as a personal, handwritten thank-you note. If you saved at least *one* note of thanks that you received over the years, then you are like most of the people I have asked in my team effectiveness sessions.

There was one particular senior IT team that took this question to heart. They had been notorious for not expressing appreciation for a job well done, something that was obvious in their low employee engagement scores. They realized, in fact, that they were rewarding and holding people accountable for the *wrong* things. They called their culture a hero-worshipping one; for example, you were a hero if you worked all night or all weekend to fix a problem. Even if you were the very one who caused the error in the first place, you were the one held up as exceptional. They knew they were operating in a fire-drill mentality—I suspect like many of our teams—and that this pace was not sustainable. They needed to force themselves to engage in the longer-term advance thinking that would allow them to find more holistic solutions, and prevent any further emergencies. Yes, they needed to deal with the fire; but they had to work hard as a team afterward in order to keep the flames from igniting in the future. They had to *go Yellow* to look at the bigger picture to discover the problem patterns and then brainstorm solutions, instead of staying stuck in a Green, action-oriented mode. They needed to send a new message.

Now, this leadership team did not have strong preferences in the HBDI Red interpersonal quadrant. As I mentioned in Chapter 11, this team started writing thank-you
notes for those individuals who had truly demonstrated the
right behaviors; the kind they actually wanted to reinforce,
such as working collaboratively across departments to resolve issues before they became full-blown forest fires, and
taking more time to do the necessary (though not as exciting!)
up-front planning. Each senior leader brought their handwritten note to the staff meeting, and spent the first five
minutes sharing these success stories, and passing the cards
around for all of the leaders to sign. When the leaders saw
these individuals after the meeting, they would reinforce the
positive message—and the positive impact—by specifically
thanking them for what they had done. Well, the word spread,
and not just about the thank-you notes and long-awaited
recognition that they symbolized, but also about *what* was
being recognized. You could literally *see* change happen
among the leaders as they really thought about what they
should be rewarding and among the employees as they received the recognition they had been missing.

Hopefully, you've realized by now the importance of
personal accountability, and how leaders can reinforce it in
one-on-one situations that will lead them to reward and
recognize success. Now, let's turn our attention to the leader's
role in reinforcing responsibility at the *team* level. One of the
most important things that a leader can do is keep the team
focused on the *real* competition; those who exist outside the
walls of the organization, trying to win their customers over
every day. Team members can unleash their creative juices on
solving the real problems of the team and the broader business. Making this the focus keeps people from clashing within
the group. When this focus is lost, infighting and bickering
among the team members thrives. It's no longer us against
them; it is us against us. We have met the enemy, and they are
sitting in the same room as we are.

I was working with one leader at the mortgage division
of a large regional bank who very much wanted to break down
the functional silos that had cropped up on the team. As the
external marketplace was becoming tougher, the internal
finger-pointing and blame was steadily increasing. The leader

wanted to put a stop to it. I conducted individual confidential interviews to learn about the current team dynamics so that I could effectively design and facilitate the upcoming team development session, and this is what I found out.

Each member of the team knew that the leader wanted to create a "one team" mind-set. The new business realities required them to work together and support each other in a way they never had before. The leader was under tremendous pressure from corporate officials to hit the numbers. The employees got it. Rather than causing them to band together to achieve these goals, the manager was actually driving a wedge between them. He was so used to driving their individual accountability that he didn't realize that his actions were now out of sync with the team mind-set he really wanted. During staff meetings, he would single out individuals who had not achieved their targets, and become very accusatory as to why this happened. How did the others react? While they told me that they felt for their teammates, they wanted to stay out of the line of fire. If they came to the victim's aid, then they too might be singled out for blame for the challenges in their own areas. They could see very clearly the interdependencies that existed, and how they needed to work together to fix the problems; but the support from the team leader was not there to make this cross-collaboration happen.

Interestingly, when I shared this feedback with the team leader, he was not surprised. He knew it was going to be tough to change his behavior. He was committed to making it happen, however, because he had no other choice; not if he and his team were going to continue to be successful in an increasingly unfavorable marketplace. We also used the session to create some conflict norms, for which everyone on the team promised to hold themselves—and each other—accountable.

The leader clearly undertakes a critical role by establishing a firm foundation for personal and team accountability to take hold. Let's turn our attention to those times when the team is together, and the potential that meetings have for being a place where the team's commitment to accountability can truly shine. The leader can play an incredibly valuable part in keeping the team focused on crucial business issues.

Staff meetings can become can't-miss events if people believe that challenges and problems will be discussed and resolved, that decisions and commitments will be made, and that they will be upheld.

Bob was a team leader whom I encountered with an accountability problem. His people were not taking action on the tasks to which they had committed during their weekly staff meetings. Bob asked me to come observe their meeting and see if I could give them some advice on how to improve the team's functioning. The gathering began with a team member named Kathryn briefly reading through the action items from the prior meeting, and getting status updates from people as she reached their name on the list. There seemed to be a lot of hemming and hawing for most of the items. I could see what Bob meant when he said that people weren't sticking to their commitments; and I had a good idea why. More on that later; now on to new business.

There was actually very lively debate on several pressing issues. The team was floating around a lot of ideas for solutions to problems; however, it was hard for me to tell when anyone had actually *decided* anything, or assigned a corresponding obligation. There were some vague comments like, "Sue, that would be a good thing for you to think about following up on with the marketing department." The meeting ended, and I shared my perspectives with Kathryn (at Bob's request). I realized she had been taking notes on the ideas that were batted around, and she thought she was clear on who had been asked to do what. I told her I wasn't so clear; and I was in the room, too. I even wondered whether the leader was absolutely clear on when something had been assigned, and to whom it had been allocated.

I recommended some changes for the next staff meeting. First, team leader Bob—not Kathryn—should be getting the status update from each person, since he is the one to whom the team members report. They should be eyeballing *him* and trying to fluff their way through the answer, since Kathryn couldn't hold their feet to the fire like he could. I also suggested that she keep a running list of action items that arose from the discussions in a way that was visible for all to see. Either on a flip chart, or—since they had an LCD projector mounted in the ceiling—as a Word document to be updated and reviewed at the end of each discussion item (or at least at the end of the meeting). As I've stated before, there is something about seeing your name up there in bright lights with an action step and a due date beside it to make it *really real.* People seem to take a lot more interest in what is actually written up there when their name is listed beside it. I asked Kathryn to give me a call after the next meeting to tell me how things went.

The feedback that I received from her, after only two weeks using this new action planning approach, was wonderful to hear. Kathryn told me that Bob expressed some discomfort when she informed him that *he* would now be addressing the action items from the previous meeting. (I personally think this was because he hadn't clearly assigned accountability to specific team members, so holding them responsible would be equally difficult.) She encouraged him, though, by saying that the first time would likely be very difficult and uncomfortable for *everyone* in the room, but that it would only take one time before people would get the message that he meant it. And she was right! They had captured the assignments real time during the meeting, and then Bob made his way through the list and asked directly for explanations on why things had not been completed. Although this was uneasy for everyone, the message was unmistakable: People were expected to fulfill their commitments, and lame excuses would not be allowed anymore. The accountability level for the whole team, including the leader, had been taken up several levels. Kathryn also told me that several of the team members had instituted a similar procedure for their own staff meetings, since it had worked so well with the initial group.

One other area of accountability that I want to discuss briefly is the need to take responsibility for team decisions. When you complete a discussion, is there a clear outcome or next step that is understood by all? When two or more members take a conversation off-line, how will the team know if the issue is ever resolved, or learn the results and rationale for any decisions made? Those members need to discuss in detail the decision's impact, and how they can support its execution, with the rest of team.

There must also be a mechanism in place for tracking the effectiveness of the decisions that have been made. What can we learn from those situations when a decision wasn't implemented with excellence? Was it the wrong decision? Did the team make faulty assumptions? Did we not have true commitment? Were there unforeseen circumstances? Only by taking the time to conduct this after-action review will the team be able to improve its hit rate and truly raise the bar on its level of effectiveness, and become comfortable revisiting and revising decisions based on new information.

In addition to holding themselves accountable for improving decisions and execution thereof, I recommend that teams also hold themselves accountable for improving their overall meeting effectiveness. This can be as simple as conducting a five minute plus/delta evaluation—what worked well in this meeting versus what can be improved upon for the next one. Pick a few of the most critical items to work on for the next meeting; these will be the ones for which people feel a little bit of improvement will have the greatest impact. You can conduct a more formal assessment in which to track changes over a period of time (if your team is really into data). Doing this in real time gives everyone a chance to offer suggestions for how to improve the next time; therefore it is not just the team leader's responsibility to fix it, it is everyone's.

So, how would you describe the accountability level for your team? How successful are your team members at upholding their commitments? Do individuals realize and own up to how they may be contributing to the problem? I recommend that as the leader, you share with the team the significance of holding oneself and each other accountable. Assure them that you've established a safe environment in which everyone can comfortably share their honest opinions on this subject, and be sure to stay true to your word. Then, conduct this accountability assessment: ask team members to write down where they would rank their team on accountability—Above Average, Average, or Below Average—and why. Go around the table and ask each person to share what they wrote down. Be sure to reveal your own thoughts last, so as not to influence others' responses. If you're not sure if people will be truly candid, then give them a three-by-five card and a black pen and ask them to submit their evaluation and comments that way.

Once you've had a chance to analyze their responses, try to pinpoint some common themes for why the team received the rating it did. If it was low, explore the barriers and challenges—both personally and organizationally—which keep us from being models of personal responsibility and hinder our ability to hold our team accountable for our actions. Use the information you've gleaned to decide on the top three areas where you want to make improvements, and conduct a brainstorming session for how to improve in each area. Reach consensus on what you will actually do, and specifically assign tasks for each team member to carry out over the next 30 days to improve accountability. And while you're at it, determine how the team will hold itself accountable for actually completing these chosen assignments and course correct as needed.

So there you have it: a framework and process for driving accountability at all levels—personal, leader, and team. What do you think are the positive outcomes of greater accountability in all of these areas? Perhaps the most rewarding is a sense of direction and empowerment—no more victim mentality or feeling that we are controlled by the external circumstances and actions of the outside world. Everyone is called to step up to the plate and perform at a higher level. There is a renewed sense of collaboration and commitment to keeping your word to your teammates, and the leader reinforces this behavior at every opportunity. The team's standards are high, and everyone knows what it takes to be a true contributor to the team's success. The words you say are not nearly as important as the actions you take. Your team becomes a role model for what a high standard of accountability looks like, and takes advantage of the tremendously powerful impact this can have on business relationships ... and results.

Part V

Sparking Creativity

Chapter Fifteen

The Firefly Chase Begins

Fireflies and glow sticks create light in the same way—through a process called *chemiluminescence*. When you first bend your glow stick, two chemicals mix and release light as a result. Similarly, fireflies light up because they contain an organic compound in their abdomens called *luciferin*. Air rushes into their abdomen and reacts with this chemical, prompting magic to happen: they begin to glow. Scientists have been conducting research for years to discover how fireflies regulate the airflow, causing the flashing pattern that mesmerizes children and adults alike.

What an incredible metaphor for what occurs in organizations. We all have the power within us to light up. The drive starts within our gut and is fueled by elements, or airflow, outside of us. We can then decide, or regulate, how we want to use this external influence to let our light shine. Sometimes a new manager, external threat, or project can be like a breath of fresh air that starts a chain reaction and causes people to begin to glow with possibility. If we play our cards right, we can intentionally trigger that reaction when people come together, with a compelling goal, new blood, a critical problem to solve—something to jump start the team. I believe it, because I have seen it happen; people can truly *glow* with energy when they get to use their brain and creative talents to work together to solve the most difficult problems, or capitalize on the most exciting opportunities facing the team and the business.

Some of the teams I work with are stuck in a rut. If they have a strong Blue/Green (Analyzer/Organizer) HBDI tilt, then their problem solving might look like this: see and solve the problem in Blue, implement the solution in Green. From Blue to Green again—problem solved. From Blue to Green again—same problem solved again. This is what can happen when a team is fixated on resolving the immediate problem, and refuses to go Yellow to look at the bigger picture. They can't seem to consider that perhaps the dilemma they are solving is just a symptom of a much bigger issue that is impacting, and being impacted by, forces outside their imme-diate influence and control. This more widespread problem is not as easy to see, or therefore, to fix.

In this chapter, I will share my approach to spurring the creativity of the team in order to improve products, processes, and business performance—often the very challenges and opportunities with which they struggle on a daily basis. You might even think of this as *everyday creativity*—it's no big deal, this is just the way we work. No longer is creativity solely within the purview of the research and development, market-ing, or design departments. The best companies realize that the drive for imagination and innovation needs to permeate throughout the organization. This is where the true competi-tive advantage lies; and creativity is not restricted to large-scale product advances, or new marketing approaches. It can be found in improved work processes and new execution initiatives. This enlightened view makes the notion of being creative much more accessible to every team and every leader; bringing ingenuity actually becomes an expected part of the process for getting work done.

This is true in the good times of a company and, I like to think, especially true during the tough times. Although a top leader's natural instinct might be to exert greater control over the organization in a downturn and keep decision-making authority at the highest levels, the research in fact shows that groups make *better* decisions than individuals. Thus, the superior approach is to engage the minds of diverse members of the team and focus those creative energies on the critical problems of the day. The bonds that can be formed in a crisis have the potential to be incredibly powerful, and often enrich the team once the immediate difficulty has passed. In this chapter, I will describe the leader's critical role in establishing an environment that's conducive to this kind of work; and I will take you step-by-step through a straightforward, creative, problem-solving process.

As the leader, you play a very powerful role in demonstrating the extent to which problem solving and opportunity finding is the team's responsibility. In fact, you need to let them know that in your mind, this is part of what you are *paying* them to do; and then you need to support that statement by ensuring that there is time clearly set aside on people's busy calendars to engage in this activity. Management consulting firm BlessingWhite, Inc. recently conducted a survey in which 40 percent of respondents claimed that their managers *never* encouraged them to look for new solutions or to take risks, with 34 percent saying that they were *rarely* encouraged. An issue that correlates strongly with this trend is managers' tendency to tell their employees something like, "Don't bring me problems, bring me solutions!" While avoiding these complaints might temporarily improve your mood, you are potentially eliminating the opportunity to address problems that make your employees' work more difficult than it needs to be; and you're closing your eyes (and everyone else's) to issues negatively impacting your customers or other departments. What a lost opportunity for managers, especially when you examine recent research on the way our brains work. According to these studies, managers should be taking an interest in and celebrating those employees who desire to improve the performance of the business, even if it is initially presented as a problem to solve and not a solution served up on a platter to the manager. *HR Magazine* published an article that explored a new field of study which joins psychology (the study of the human mind and behavior) and neuroscience (the physiological study of the brain) to shed light on the brain's role in human nature and behavior. New MRI equipment and other tools and techniques are allowing researchers to study what happens in the brain during learning, engagement, motivation, and social interaction.

One scholar in the field, Dr. Ellen Weber, PhD, director of the MITA International Brain Based Center in Pittsford NY, described the phenomenon in this way:

> If a manager shows interest in employees, supports them and praises them genuinely, he "squirts" a chemical called serotonin into their brains. Serotonin opens employees' minds to ideas, and creates desires to get to know managers better and to support whatever the managers need done.
>
> If you diminish me, you "squirt" cortisol into my brain that shuts it down and closes it off to new ideas and my willingness to help you.... Because of brain-imaging technologies, we know that we use only 3 percent to 5 percent of our brains. If you send me to your staff meeting and sit me there and talk to me, I use 3 percent of my brain, and that is the reason I hate being there and why I'm disengaged. However, if you stir up my environment meaning-fully ... I will use 90 percent of my brain.

This is exactly what I am encouraging leaders to do—engage the team in a meaningful way, either during staff meetings or during a completely separate session dedicated to solving the team's most impactful business problems. This serves the dual purpose of encouraging the team to concentrate on the most important things, rather than joining in a flurry of activity or allowing internal negative backbiting to get the best of the team. My work with teams has shown me that they really want more of this kind of thinking, not report outs, in the times they come together. As problems or concerns arise during staff meetings, this is a great way to deal with them— "Let's focus on that issue in our next team problem-solving session." Employees feel as though they're being heard; they know action will be taken; and they are a part of the solution, instead of just complaining about the problem. In fact, neuroscientists have found that the brain doesn't build connections when told what to do; it only changes patterns when we're involved in the process. Thus, involvement literally equals changed mind-sets.

So you believe in the value of engaging employees in solving the critical business problems; and you take time to address these as a team. If possible, have a placeholder in your regular team meeting for identifying problems that need attention at a future, separate session. I don't recommend that you deal with them at the time of the meeting; you will merely take away from the original purpose. However, asking people to keep an eye out for areas of improvement on a regular basis is a great way to keep them engaged in the discovery process.

If you can't cover this issue during a separate session and it needs to be incorporated into a regular team meeting, then only choose one problem to discuss and make sure you allow enough time on the agenda to really get into it. And don't make it the last agenda item, because you might never get to it; or by the time that you do, the energy level has been sapped by dealing with the more mundane, but urgent issues and people are just ready to get out of there. If you can create separate, focused, creative, problem-solving sessions, then I recommend you move to a different location from your regular staff meeting. A different view out the window can trigger a different view from your mind's eye.

Now that you have made it clear that thinking with creativity is a priority—and have demonstrated this by setting aside specific time to be creative—how do you make sure that *your* behavior during the session doesn't put a damper on your teammates' desire to offer their ideas? People can feel very vulnerable sharing original thoughts; in fact, many consider the risk of speaking up to outweigh any possible benefits. "When in doubt, keep your mouth shut," says that little voice in their head. I worked with leadership teams whose members' only introduced issues at the weekly staff meeting that they knew had already been resolved. Bringing something new to everyone's attention was simply perceived as too risky. In addition, they were worried that their colleagues would think that they were throwing someone under the bus or blindsiding them if they hadn't already shared—and resolved—any problems with others *outside* of the meeting. Everyone except the leader knew implicitly that it was better just to keep quiet.

So what's a leader to do? You need to somehow convey to your team the value of speaking up. You have to make it clear that you don't mind having your ideas challenged, and will not punish those who step forward with different opinions, even on those subjects nearest to your heart. I also recommend that everyone set a ground rule to "Speak so you can be heard." This simply means addressing others with respect, so as not to incite any unnecessary, defensive reactions that might shut an open mind. You can also publicly acknowledge those employees who have volunteered innovative ideas, or cite times that your mind was changed by a member of the team; however, try to do this without playing favorites.

Deciding what problems to tackle first can be an issue in and of itself. I recommend that you select early on the ones that are low-hanging fruit type of problems; in other words, those that are most familiar and annoying to employees and may require focused effort, but that don't require much money or a long planning cycle. Therefore, begin with the problems that will garner a high return on your investment of limited time and effort. The team needs to solve a few problems early and implement the solutions before tackling the toughest and longest-standing issues. Instead of the team leader deciding which topics to address, I recommend that people bring one problem to resolve from their own area, as well as one that crosses functional team areas. Another place to find potential problems to solve is the team dashboard of results. Where is the team falling short of the target? Where are we not hitting our numbers or goals? This is a great way to make the session very meaningful and engaging for everyone.

On the other hand, one of the first problems you might want to tackle is to identify ways to promote greater creativity. It's a good idea to send out information in advance of the session to get everyone's creative juices flowing and build up excitement for what they will be working on as a team before they even arrive. This can also be a great way to make sure that everyone has at least a foundational knowledge base to be able to actively engage in the discussion. Be careful that you don't slant the discussion or the search for solutions by what you select to share in advance. If there is a significant chance that this will happen, I recommend not sending out anything prior to the session.

People will feel more engaged if they get the chance to *select* the problems they'll be working on versus receiving these issues as an assignment. I call this voting with your feet when working with a group. Choosing the problems in advance, then allowing each team member to select one that especially resonates with them is a great way to engage them. And don't assume that everyone who works on a problem needs to fully understand the issue's entire background to be effective. In fact, I sometimes find the ignorant ones—those without preconceived notions about what will and won't work, who aren't fully versed on how things work *now* or the challenges and barriers currently at play—make some of the best members of a problem-solving team.

The problem-solving or opportunity-finding process should be kept fairly simple. That makes it easier to remember, and easier to use. In a nutshell:

1. Begin with a very clear, specific *problem statement.*
2. Briefly *discuss* to make sure there's *common understanding.*
3. Search for *solutions.*
4. *Evaluate* the ideas.
5. *Implement* the chosen alternative.
6. *Assess the results* and course correct as needed.
7. *Learn* from the process, and *apply* to next problem.

The first step is to reach agreement on the problem statement and write it on the flip chart. You would not believe how important it is to *write this down for all to see.* It is like a guiding light that should be used to remind everyone of the actual problem you are trying to solve, especially when you get into the idea generation stage. The HBDI Blue (Analyzer) quadrant people often show a real knack for helping the team create a problem statement. It works well to say to everyone, "Okay, let's 'go Blue' and formulate a really clear problem statement." Make sure that the problem is small enough to solve. I like to say "The smaller the focus, the better the brainstorming." You might think the reverse is true—"Let's keep it wide open so that we can get a vast array of ideas." I assure you that when the field is too wide, this actually hampers good problem solving. Imagine the problem statement, "How can we improve our marketing programs?" There could be any number of directions that the ideas could evolve; so many in fact, that you might get stuck trying to figure out which way to direct your thinking. If you instead focus this particular problem-solving session on, "How can we increase the number of repeat customers to our website?" then you can actually (and perhaps counterintuitively) generate better and more relevant solutions.

The second step is to take a few minutes to openly discuss and gain a common understanding of the problem. This will dissuade team members from trying to solve it too quickly, before they even know what the issue really is. It also can head off needless friction. There's actually a story that proves this point beautifully, one that you have likely heard before about the three blind men who touched an elephant to learn what it was like. Each man touches a different part of the animal, and then reaches a conclusion on what they felt. When they compare notes, they learn that they are in total disagreement. One, having only touched the squirming trunk, describes the elephant as being like a snake. The second, having touched just the swinging tail, says no, it is like a piece of rope. The third blind man, having only felt the leg of the great animal, says it is truly like a tree. They begin to argue vehemently, each certain of the correctness of their answer.

The moral of the story is obvious: There may be some truth to what others say, and sometimes we can see that truth, but only if we listen to them and hear things from their perspective. Be tolerant toward others and realize that although none of you knows the *whole* truth, combining your unique experiences might bring you closer to it. Begin with a curious mindset and seek to learn what they know. Doing so will allow you to build a sense of collaboration and mutual purpose on solving the problem you now all more fully understand. How many times have you been in a meeting and experienced this same needless conflict, debating over who has the correct version of the problem, when in fact all may be true and are simply relevant based on each person's unique experiences?

So how do you get people to openly share their perspectives on the problem? I recommend you ask them to discuss the following questions for about 10 to 15 minutes, and jot down the highlights of their conversation.

- Why do you think that this is an issue at our company/on our team?
- What are the symptoms of the issue?
- How do we know it is a problem?

- Why is it important to solve this problem?
- How is it impacting us as an organization?
- If this problem ceased to exist, what would be different?

Ask that they really restrain themselves and not jump into brainstorming solutions until the next step. I warn you, this is hard not to do. But I assure you that taking this extra step to further develop and understand the problem is well worth the investment of this little bit of time. In fact, it often results in the team's decision to change the problem statement to make it more relevant and actionable.

Now we come to step three, and what people traditionally (and erroneously!) think of as the *first* step in a problem-solving session—the search for solutions. Everyone is familiar with brainstorming, and that is part of the problem. There are a lot of people who are not doing it well. The biggest mistake I see is that "he who holds the marker, becomes judge and jury" for what gets written on the flip chart as a good idea. Overly controlling people have a very difficult time accepting ideas that they think are just not doable, or too far out there. You can solve this persistent problem in a number of ways. First, remind everyone of these very simple but effective (if followed!) ground rules for great brainstorming (you can even post them on a flip chart, if it helps):

- No discussion or evaluating of ideas until later
- All ideas, even absurd or impractical, are welcome
- Quantity of ideas is the major objective, since it leads to quality
- Build on ideas of others
- Everyone participates; don't hold back

Second, you can give everyone the opportunity to think individually about the problem and then capture their own ideas on individual sticky note pads (one idea per note). This eliminates the oft-detested role of reluctant flip chart scribe. In addition, even if the team idea writer were inclined to capture all of the ideas, the typical person can't write fast enough; something that slows down the creative energy in the room. The negative component of this solution is that it is harder for people to build on each other's ideas in real time. You can, however, overcome this issue—somewhat—by allowing everyone to post their sticky notes on the wall, and then providing time to review and add new ideas that are prompted from these. I will share two other tools—mind mapping and brainwriting—with you in the next chapter. I use these constantly with teams for brainstorming a wide variety of solutions.

The next step in the creative problem-solving process is to evaluate the ideas and select the top solutions to recommend for implementation. I always suggest that teams take at least a 10-minute break between idea generation and evaluation. It's even better if you can take a break of a few days, for two reasons. First, a delay keeps you from choosing an easy, recognizable solution. It causes you to stop action and explore the options further. Second, it is difficult for most people to generate their best ideas on the spot within the X number of minutes allotted to this brainstorming session, which becomes especially true if no one sent out information in advance to stoke creative juices. If you ask the members of your team when they got their best ideas, they will likely say that it was *not* under the pressure of the buzzer. Most people's (especially those high in the Yellow risk-taking, strategizer quadrant) best ideas show up overnight, in the shower, or driving in to work. It is a myth that pressure enhances creativity.

But what if the team doesn't have time for a longer break of a couple of days? There needs to at least be a few minutes break before people start telling you that your baby (the idea you just generated) is ugly. I will share some simple approaches here, and then discuss more involved evaluation tools (i.e., impact vs. effort grid; decision matrix) in the next chapter. The important thing is to have clear criteria upon which all can agree and understand for making the evaluation, and your team needs to identify these *before* you start discussing the ideas. This makes it much more objective when some ideas are not selected for implementation (or at least for execution at this time). After the decision criteria are clear to the participants, each person selects their top three to five ideas and writes down their rationale for choosing them. Conduct a round-robin to let everyone hear the top choices and corresponding rationale, and capture these ideas on a flip chart.

Once all of the top ideas are listed on a flip chart, give each person three to five sticky dots (or more dots per person for more choices). Numbering the ideas and asking each person to write the number of their choice on the dot itself before they go place it on the list is a simple way to prevent groupthink. You know what I mean—when people get up to place their dots, and change their mind to go with the herd. If the voting is close, then the team should spend the necessary time discussing the various alternatives to see if they can combine them to develop stronger solutions that can satisfy all parties.

This is a great time to remind everyone to keep a both/and mind-set versus either/or. You can ask members of the team to actually make the case for the benefits of the idea they don't support, which is a wonderful way of helping them to see the strengths of the other idea, and thus making it easier to build upon or improve. It can also be very beneficial to get the input and feedback from the broader group if there were several problem-solving teams working concurrently. It's also worthwhile to consider using the more elaborate evaluation tools presented in the next chapter. Whatever the final choices may be, try to be as clear and specific as possible about the solution. You can even use examples if that would help to clarify what is meant.

The team leader and those who have strong preferences in the HBDI Red interpersonal quadrant have a critical role to play throughout the creative problem-solving process. They need to make sure that everyone is staying engaged along the way and promoting an open environment. You might even want to call for a process check to ask people how things are progressing from their perspective—are they feeling engaged? Is everyone remaining receptive and actively listening to each other's ideas? This puts everyone in a Red quadrant mind-set at the same time. It's better to know in the midst of the session if some are not feeling engaged than to find out later when it comes time to execute the ideas that they have no desire to commit to the chosen solutions. Everyone's voice must continue to be heard in order for the best ideas to continue to come forward. Losing one team member's participation means losing their viewpoint. Make it safe for them to contribute their ideas. Keep the conflict productive, and remember—creative abrasion. Discourage people from making such creativity killer statements as: "That will never work." "We've tried that before, and it didn't work." "That's a good idea, but ..."

Remember to seek the third way, not only your way or my way. How do you make that happen? Ask people to take on the role of another key stakeholder (such as a key customer or the CEO) and brainstorm ideas from that perspective. Explore alternative scenarios, and ask questions like, "If this works as planned, what do you see as the end result?" or "What is the worst thing that could happen if we tried it?" Make implicit assumptions explicit. Ask people to restate what they understand other positions to be. Remember to balance advocacy (arguing for your own position) with inquiry (seeking to understand another's).

Once you've completed the evaluation of all of the ideas, the final step is to reach an agreement—as a team—on those critical few ideas that will actually be implemented. Upon selecting these ideas, let those with strong preferences in the HBDI analytical Blue quadrant help everyone to test these solutions to make sure they will solve the original problem. Then allow those with the high Green organized preferences to lead the charge by engaging the team in the development of action steps for executing these ideas by asking questions (such as the ones following). Beware—you might get some groaning from the high Yellows who love the creative brainstorming part but not the detailed planning; remind them that the great ideas we just developed won't get fully executed if we don't do the hard planning work now.

- What does success look like at the end of full implementation for each idea?
- Where are we currently with this problem?
- What are the major steps to get from current to future state?
- Who needs to be accountable for each one?
- What are the due dates?

It's best if you create these timelines and major milestones while the team is still present at the session. I also like to keep the planning timeframe short—about 90 days. That is about as far into the future as most teams can see. (One exception to this is for very large-scale change initiatives.) You don't need to outline each detailed activity step at this time; that is up to the individual to create a more complete project plan later. But do spend at least a few minutes troubleshooting the plan by asking such questions as:

- What are the most difficult, complex, or sensitive aspects of our plan?
- What organizational or technical blocks and barriers could we run into?
- Have we incorporated some good change management principles into our plan?

During the large-group debrief, ask each solution implementation subteam to walk through each of the major steps, while the others listen for interdependencies, gaps, and redundancies. They can also help the team to stress test or troubleshoot the plan. I warn you that by this stage most teams are very excited and want to plan very aggressively by choosing many ideas, short time frames, and front-loading them for the first 30 days. Help them to temper their fervor with reality testing, but not enthusiasm busting. This public announcement of the team's intentions is a great way to build commitment to the plan and to help each hold the other accountable for living up to their deadlines.

Last, reach agreement on how to check progress and course correct. These progress reports should include the activities that have been implemented, the results achieved, and any remaining items with corresponding expected completion dates. The leader and the team need to take a positive, action-learning approach to dealing with failure. Were the dates too aggressive? Did we meet unexpected obstacles? Should we revisit some of the ideas that didn't make the cut to see if they might work instead? The team needs the leader's support the most at times like this. Remember to celebrate the successes and be tolerant of intelligent mistakes, but not delays or errors due to such things as a lack of collaboration or a lack of commitment to execution. Keep the creative spark alive and it will light a fire under future problem-solving sessions!

Chapter Sixteen

How Could You Forget the Toys?

I entered the room in the National Building Museum in Washington, DC, the setting for this year's committee meeting to select the winners of this company's special award for excellence. Although it was my third year working with the committee, it was the first time it was being held out of town. As I was getting set up to facilitate the two-day session, some of the participants began to arrive. I had worked with the majority of them on several occasions before. They began to glance around with a look of expectancy on their faces. Finally, one of them asked me point blank, "Where are the toys?"

You see, my clients have come to know me for bringing really great, engaging toys to the meetings I facilitate. I find it keeps participants' hands busy, while surprisingly releasing distracting nervous energy and allowing their minds to remain engaged in their work. The toys are my way of reminding them to keep their minds open and to feel free to explore, just as we did as children. Entering a room to see the fun props all laid out incites a mind-set shift, and the realization that this is not going to be a boring meeting.

So, back to the room in DC. Since I had to fly in, I had not brought these toys with me on the plane, and I had a revolt on my hands as a result. The participants wanted their toys. Thankfully, the museum had a great toy shop in the lobby that would be opening just in time for our break. I promised the committee I would get some great ones in their hands very soon—and it was a toy paradise! These are still some of the participants' favorite toys today.

Who knew something as simple as toys at a meeting could help to create such a different environment? And what, you might wonder, makes for a great toy? Well, it's something interesting enough to engage someone's hands, but not their minds. It can't be so fascinating or noisy that it distracts them or their neighbor. If thrown, which often happens (almost always in jest), it should not injure anyone or anything. Also, it will not explode if, in the heat of the moment, someone squeezes it just a little too tightly. (I have learned this the hard way. Let's just say I don't bring the toys that are sheaths of plastic filled with fluid anymore—there's a boardroom in Atlanta that is a little worse off because of one of my toys!). The ironic part is that my groups often ask for permission to get to play with the toys. They think that they are there for a specific activity to be done later on. The smile that comes out on their faces when I tell them to go ahead and play with them now is terrific. I even need to remind some groups to use them, and to use their creativity, or they (and the toys) will just sit there. Other groups need to be reminded to share their toys nicely; I even have to call for a toy rotation before they get too attached to them.

The point of all of this is that toys help me to create an environment that people want to be a part of. I have facilitated all types of meetings, and the more dreaded or awkward the meeting topic, the more—and better—toys needed. For example, strategic planning is not usually seen as a great venue for creativity, yet I have had passersby want to join my strategic planning sessions just to get to play with the toys alone. I recently attended a conference center to facilitate a strategic planning session for a leadership team for a hospital. This group of doctors and administrators was not used to having fun on the job, much less thinking of strategic planning as fun, so I was going for the shock value. The meeting was held in a rounded room with two separate entrances. I saw people slow down as they looked in through one of the doors and saw toys, colored markers, and sticky notes on the tables. By the time they reached the second door, they were noticeably intrigued. One group of three women even came in and asked what kind of meeting this was. In fact, one jokingly asked if she could join us and skip the meeting she was supposed to attend!

Think of how this might apply to your own team. Are you holding a creative problem-solving session or team meeting that people will want to attend? What small thing could you or others in the group do to make it more exciting and boost the creativity level? Toys are just one way to create a light, fun, and engaging environment that will bring out everyone's best thinking. And oh, the magic of a big whiteboard! It was such a gift when I worked at Coke to have one in my office. It never ceases to amaze me how this tool can transform one's office into a gathering place for brainstorming and camaraderie. One of the first moves I made when I changed jobs was to put a whiteboard in my office. I love clearing off old things and truly starting with a blank slate. It's the reason why I called my blog The Whiteboard—because I wanted it to become a virtual gathering place for people to contribute their ideas and thoughts in a welcoming, free-flowing kind of environment. And you don't need one of the new fancy ones that are computerized and interactive, or allow you to print out what is written on them. Any simple board where you can post and erase items will do.

I remember how exciting it was to gather in my office (or *anyone's* office) to whiteboard a problem. There is such freedom in the whiteboard; it is so forgiving of mistakes, much more so than even a flip chart. I have seen teams of people circle around one, each with marker in hand, contributing their perspective to the discussion. Whiteboards also seem to invite more collaboration than one person at a flip chart or capturing everything on a laptop does. For your next problem-solving session, find a room with a whiteboard and bring some new dry erase markers with you. You won't believe the engagement you just might kick off!

Once you've established an environment that is conducive to creativity, you can use one of two tools that I use extensively with teams to help them generate a great deal of ideas in a short period. The Mind Map is geared toward freeing up the left-brain thinkers; and Brainwriting is designed to give some structure and focus to right-brain thinkers.

I most often use mind mapping as an individual brain-storming method to encourage all group members to think freely about the same problem at the same time without fear of interruptions, distractions, or the domination by some members of the group. Many of us are used to making lists of all of the things that need to be done, which is a very left-brained approach, and potentially very constricting when it comes to devising new ideas and solutions to a problem. I can personally attest to using mind mapping with great success on a wide range of issues, like deciding what to discuss during a facilitation training session, and what material to include in one of these chapters. I even use it when I am feeling overwhelmed with too much to do and anxious about how to get it all done. I promise you there is something very freeing and uplifting when you have all of these issues, distractions, tasks out of your head and on the page in front of you and you can then begin to tackle them.

So how does mind mapping work? Get out a blank piece of paper and turn it landscape style (horizontally) in front of you. I know the idea of the blank page can be a little scary; but trust me, this tool works. Write the problem statement in the center of the page and draw a circle around it. This is your central theme. Then, let your mind run free. (I often recommend to participants that when trying this out at home for the first time, a glass of your favorite wine and some new age music can really help put you in the mood!) As an idea occurs to you, draw a line outward from the center circle, write the thought at the end of the line, and draw another circle around it. Does a related idea come out of that one? Simply draw a line from your new circle and write the idea at the end of that line. Got a new train of thought? Pick another spot on the page, jot down your idea, draw a circle around it, and connect with a line to the central theme. Simply jot down ideas as they come to you. Don't let that analytical logical side of your brain take over—no editing or judging allowed. Keep it free flowing and right-brain-oriented.

Remain relaxed, because there is no right or wrong way to do this. That is the beauty of this tool. Think of it as emptying your brain of all ideas related to the focused problem statement in front of you. Some mind mapping experts (and yes, they and their software tools are out there to help you, if you need them!) encourage you to use colors, drawings, symbols, and other visual techniques. I personally prefer the speed and simplicity of a regular pencil. Once I feel that I have truly captured all of the ideas on the page, I can then step back and let my left brain go to work. What interrelationships do I see? Are there some patterns that I hadn't noticed before? Do some ideas rise above the rest as being more creative, actionable, likely to solve the issue? Have fun with it, and let your natural creative instincts take over. I promise you they are there just waiting to be released—almost like fireflies from the jar!

The second idea-generating tool that I use is brainwriting. This process is ideally suited for allowing each person to view the problem from their own unique perspective, and then to encourage them to build on and improve the ideas of others. It can also be very effective when there is a concern that one or more people might dominate the problem-solving session, or that some may be fearful of sharing their ideas in a large group brainstorming session. The anonymity of the ideas and the emphasis on stretching the ideas further and further increases the odds of coming up with … well, odd and potentially very novel solutions.

Let me walk you through how this exercise works, and you will see what I mean:

1. The problem-solving team—ideally, four to six people—is seated around a table, and each receives a blank sheet of paper.

2. Everyone writes the agreed-upon problem statement at the top of the paper, and then draws three columns on it. If a team gets stuck on how to write a good specific problem statement, I give them sentence prompts like, *How can we improve X? How do we ensure that … ?*

3. Give the team two minutes to write (legibly!) three ideas—one per column—for addressing the problem. Someone needs to be accountable for setting the timer.

4. At the end of two minutes, the timekeeper asks everyone to draw a line under their ideas across the whole page, and then pass the paper to the person on their left.

5. Set the timer for three minutes this time, giving each team member the chance to read through the ideas and

piggyback on the original solutions by writing new ones under the original suggestions.

6. This process of writing in ideas continues for as many times as there are people around the table, with each instance allowing a little more time (a maximum of five to six minutes per round) since the addition of ideas makes it progressively harder to come up with new solutions. (Just in case you are asked—I do allow people to enter a completely new idea instead of building upon one, if they truly are stuck. But make this a last resort versus a first choice.)

7. There are several choices for next steps at this point. One is to pass the paper one more time (so people aren't evaluating their own ideas that they just wrote down). Then have everyone read through the entire list of suggestions and select the best ones based on some previously agreed-upon criteria. (See the next section on using a Decision Matrix for how to select criteria and use them for evaluation.) Another option is to read all of the suggestions aloud, record them on a flip chart, and discuss them openly. While this might be the most equitable approach (and ensures that no ideas are improperly screened out by just one person), it could prove to be a very laborious process to actually have to get through. A third possibility is to post the sheets on the wall or pass them around the table such that each person could read all of the ideas and write in their initials beside the ones they think are most likely to solve the original problem statement. Better yet, let them see if they can combine ideas from one or more pages to come up with an exponentially better idea. Remember, don't be ruled by the tyranny of the "or." Search for solutions that incorporate "both/and," not "either/or."

I always recommend that clients hang on to these sheets for a while after the session. You never can tell when someone might get an inspiration overnight or in the shower. They might need a reminder of the idea they saw that prompted their creative thinking.

Now, how do you evaluate all of these ideas and select the ones that you want to action plan? *The* tool that I literally use all of the time with my clients is the Impact versus Effort Grid. It is very easy to use right away since there is no need to create criteria (unlike the decision matrix) and the grid has already been designed. It is also perfectly suited to evaluate a large number of ideas in a small amount of time, and it can be easy to determine fairly quickly what the highest priority ideas that should be moved forward into the action-planning phase are.

The other evaluation option I mentioned previously is the Decision Matrix. While I don't use this one nearly as much, it is especially ideal for more complex decisions, especially if you incorporate a weighting of the criteria. It also allows you to directly compare all of the ideas against more rigorous and standardized measures. Furthermore, the rationale for the decisions is a great deal more transparent with this matrix comprised of multiple criteria versus the impact/effort grid with only two. Both of these tools bring greater objectivity and thoroughness to the process than a simple sticky dot vote does, especially since it involves the entire group in the decision-making process as opposed to just majority rule ("The idea with the most dots wins!"). Using them—at the outset or as a back-up plan—can also ease tensions when strong opinions combined with strong-willed individuals make reaching consensus on the top ideas more and more unlikely.

"If you can create a two-by-two matrix, then you, too can be a consultant!" This is how I usually introduce the Impact/Effort Grid, because that is what this tool looks like. (See Figure 16.1.) That's right—you simply draw a large square over the whole surface of a flip chart, then draw intersecting lines to divide it into four equal quadrants. Along the horizontal axis at the top of the square, write the word *EFFORT*, and then write in *Easy* on the right side, *Difficult* on the left side. Along the vertical axis, write *IMPACT*, and then write in *Major* at the top, *Minor* at the bottom.

This is what those four boxes mean, and how you should deal with the ideas that fall into each one:

- **(1) Easy Effort/Major Impact.** The best of all worlds! Create a quick project plan, assign some accountabilities, and get started right away.

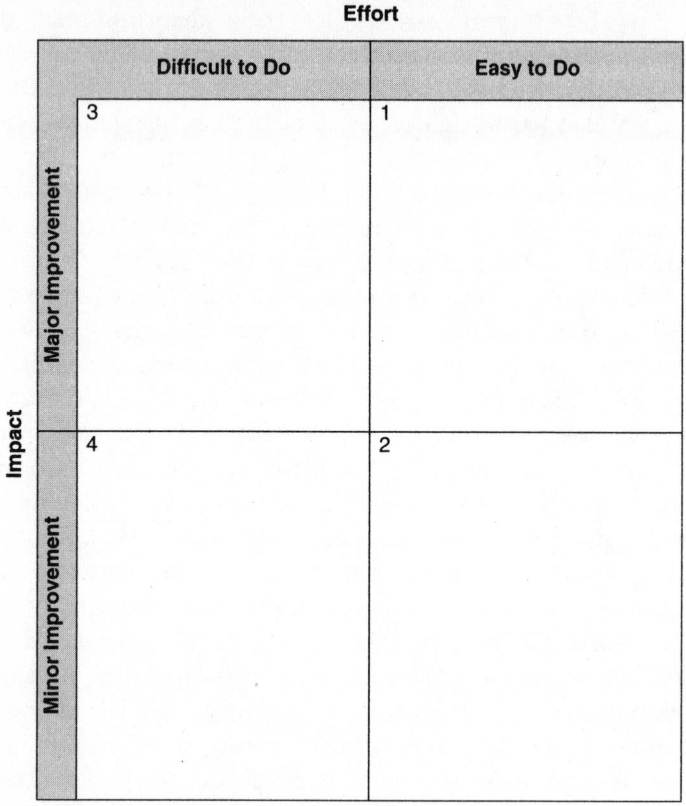

Effort

	Difficult to Do	Easy to Do
Major Improvement	3	1
Minor Improvement	4	2

(Left axis label: **Impact**)

Figure 16.1. Impact Versus Effort Grid

- **(2) Easy Effort/Minor Impact.** It's up to you and your team whether to execute on this idea or not. If you need more quick wins than you can get from the one above (Easy Effort/Major Impact), you might want to build some of these ideas into the plan, especially if people have the capacity to take them on.

- **(3) Difficult Effort/Major Impact.** These ideas will need detailed action planning, so I recommend waiting to fully execute on them until the ideas above are exhausted. One caveat is that if there are not enough great ideas in the first two boxes, then you might need to get to work on these. Also, if you strongly believe that you will eventually implement these ideas, and some require a lot of up-front planning before full implementation would be possible, then you might need to get started sooner rather than later.

- **(4) Difficult Effort/Minor Impact.** Who would want to do these? Discard!

I think this process works best when all of the ideas that need to be evaluated are already written on sticky notes. This is therefore the perfect next step from a brainstorming session when each person wrote down their ideas on individual sticky notes. I would suggest that you ask a neutral party to conduct the discussion and posting of each idea in whichever quadrant the team feels is most reflective of that idea's impact and effort to execute. The next best option is to mix up all of the ideas and divide them equally among the participants, with each person leading the discussion and placement on the flip chart for the notes they are holding. What you *don't* want to have is someone with an agenda leading the discussion and forcing consensus on what *they* feel is the right box for each idea. That's almost as bad as having each person lead the discussion for their own ideas they just worked so hard to create. Who wants to put your own baby in that dreaded fourth box?

The easiest approach is to use sticky notes. This allows everyone greater flexibility to move ideas as people begin to get more consistent, and sometimes harsher or more lenient, in their assessment of impact and effort. A less attractive approach is to write and number all of the ideas on a flip chart, and then write the numbers in the agreed-upon box after discussion. Unless you happen to have some whiteout handy, this can begin to look pretty messy as the team refines their opinions about what warrants placing an idea in each box. It can also be difficult to remember what each number stands for, thereby forcing people to keep going back and forth between the list of ideas flip chart and the impact/effort flip chart and lose their flow of thought.

Two other words of caution: First, some people will be tempted to start combining ideas, saying, "Well, they're pretty much the same thing." They may like order, fewer choices, and less work. Any collapsing of ideas needs to be done very carefully. Again, this works best with sticky notes (if everyone agrees) by placing the notes for two ideas that are truly the same directly on top of each other. This creates a great visual effect as well; you can really start to see some of the more frequently mentioned ideas much more easily.

It is perfectly acceptable to tailor the criteria that you are using to your own needs or situation. You could replace impact/effort with important/urgent, cost/value, or two other measures of your own choosing. It is very important to spend a few minutes up front, before any idea placement decisions are made, making sure that everyone has a clear idea about what these standards mean. For example, I explain to participants that *impact* refers to what achieving this goal or solving this problem would mean to the team, department, or overall organization. When determining the *effort* required to successfully implement an idea, the problem-solving team should consider everything from dollars spent on new technology to dollars spent on allocation of people resources, from changes in individual human behaviors to changes in the entire culture of the organization. Agreeing upon the criteria's meaning early, before the discussions even begin, will enable you to avoid a lot of needless, unproductive debate later on.

Now let's shift our focus to our last tool of this chapter— the Decision Matrix. As a reminder, this is another tool that your team can use to evaluate and prioritize a list of options. It's a better choice than the Impact/Effort Grid when the alternative solutions are more complex; in this situation, criteria are more numerous, and greater depth of knowledge and judgment may be involved. In addition, this tool can be especially helpful when you are attempting to narrow the choices to only one option. The process works like this:

1. As a group, brainstorm a list of the most relevant criteria for selecting ideas to move into the action-planning phase. Give everyone a few moments to jot down a couple on their own before opening it up to the large group. Then ask them to determine the rank order of their list. Next, conduct a round-robin, asking each person to share their number one criterion—the one they think might be on several people's list. Write each person's number one on the flip chart and ask for a show of hands for others who had similar ideas,

capturing any alternative wording they might have used. Proceed on to each of the other members in the same manner, asking for their number one choice, show of hands, alternative wording, and so on. Some examples of such criteria include:

- Ease of implementation
- Cost to implement (can include money and time)
- Management and/or team support
- Cost/benefit relationship
- Technologically superior
- Time required
- Availability and extent of resources required
- Extent of training involved
- Potential negative consequences
- Return on investment of time and money
- Potential effects on key stakeholders (customers, suppliers, other departments)

2. Discuss and refine the list of criteria; identify any criteria that must be included or excluded and why. Reduce the list to those that the team believes are *most important* for reaching the right solution. Ideally, I would not recommend that you use more than five to seven criteria, since there tends to be overlap among them when you start adding more than this number. Also, the more you add, the more it becomes nice to have versus need to have. While voting with sticky dots can be used, first see if you can reach agreement the old-fashioned way—by talking it through. In the end, make sure everyone is very clear on what each criterion means.

3. The team then needs to decide whether each idea will be assessed against these criteria using a rating scale, a simple Yes/No, or a check mark to indicate the presence or absence of that item for this particular idea. This will obviously impact the wording of the criteria themselves. For example, *Low Cost to Implement* can be answered with a simple Yes/No or a check mark, while *Cost to Implement* needs to be rated on a scale. This scale could

be as simple as Low, Medium, or High; or you might choose to assign a numerical rating, with the highest number consistently representing best score. Make sure that everyone can verbalize the differences between each of the levels for each of the criterion.

4. The next step involves deciding whether the criteria should be weighted to show the relative importance of each in the final decision. (You can see now what I mean about the beautiful simplicity of our two-by-two impact/effort grid with its criteria already laid out, and why I use it all the time instead of this matrix!) Here are several approaches you can take to assigning these weightings:

   • Have a general group discussion as to whether any-one believes that some criteria should carry more weight in the decision-making process than others, and why they feel that way. Assign the weights so that items of less importance have a lower number, and those of greater importance have a higher num-ber. And keep in mind that the same weight can be applied to more than one criterion.

   • There are some experts who recommend testing the weighting decisions by turning them into sentences, such as, "If I understand the decision we just made correctly, then we are saying that it is three times more important that we choose the least cost solu-tion over one that has a higher return on invest-ment." If something doesn't ring true with the team, fix it now before you actually start applying these weights to real solution options.

   • Another simpler and therefore less refined alterna-tive is to discuss and reach agreement on how to distribute 10 points across the chosen criteria.

5. Once you've identified the criteria and made a decision on how to score and rate each one, write this informa-tion along the top of the flip chart or the sheet of paper. (Some groups even go so far as to enter all of this information into a spreadsheet. Check it out—there are lots of templates for this online.)

6. Then list all of the ideas in a single column down the left side of the page.

7. In most situations, the group discusses each idea and reaches an agreement on how to rate it on that particular criterion. Other approaches advocate rating each option or idea on the same criterion at the same time. In this way, the team is better able to compare the various options relative to each other against the same criterion.

   It can actually be very beneficial, especially in the beginning of the process, for each individual to come up with a rating independently and then to compare scores. This allows each team member to feel more responsible for and take greater due diligence with their initial rating and the rationale for that rating. Sharing these ratings and rationale across the team can create a significant learning experience, if everyone keeps an open mind that their initial perception might not represent the whole story.

8. If it is likely that a dominant personality may over-shadow the will of the people, then you could have each individual anonymously complete their own score sheet. Then tally each of these to arrive at an average. Since the average could significantly misconstrue the true ratings, you would likely want to also track the median score for each one and revisit the items with a sizeable difference between these two measures.

9. Once all of the ratings, check marks, or Yes/Nos have been tallied, and the weightings (if used) appropriately applied (i.e., multiply each option's rating by the weight of that particular criterion), then you can see those ideas or solutions the group thinks have the greatest likelihood for success. It is not necessary for the score to stand as it is, if the team feels that it can benefit from a discussion of the relative scores.

I recommend that once the assessment and tally is completed, you allow everyone to review the information silently first and jot down their thoughts about those results with which they strongly disagree. Conduct a large group debriefing to see if you can address and resolve these key points of disagreement or concern. See if reinforcing a both/and mind-set to take the best parts of several alternatives helps to shore up some solutions that might have scored high overall, but might be missing some critical pieces that other solutions scored more favorably on.

If you are still having a tough time reaching a decision as to which idea/solution to move forward into the implementation phase, then you might want to consider taking on another person's perspective—such as the CEO or the customer—and see how that lens might impact the ratings these ideas receive (and perhaps even the criteria and/or the weighting that were used).

Finally, if all team members are not in full agreement, recommend a definition of consensus that can be fairly used for making the final decision, such as "I can live with that and support it" or "I believe this is the best decision for the organization at this time, and I will support it."

Just as fireflies flash in patterns that are recognizable to other fireflies, we also can see when someone is on fire with a new idea, a new project, a new job; and it is contagious to others. If the light is strong enough, then we become part of this glow. Remember how creative we were when we were capturing fireflies as children? It was fun to discover new ways to catch them, what to keep them in, and how to keep them from getting out. We felt a greater sense of freedom as children, especially on those warm summer nights when anything felt possible. I urge you to reconnect with that magical, creative time—even when you are addressing some of the most challenging problems of the team and the business. The more your mind is open to seeing the creative talents of your teammates, the exciting opportunities for improvement, and the new ways of solving problems, the more effective, collaborative, and engaging the work of your team will be.

Chapter Seventeen

This Place Is a Zoo!

When was the last time your team gathered for a purpose other than a regular staff meeting or a budget review? Have you ever gone off-site for a really engaging, exciting, team-building event? No, I'm not talking about ropes courses or blindly falling into your teammates arms and trusting them to catch you. I'm talking about those excursions that truly create lifelong lessons and connections that you can immediately apply to improve your performance as a team and a business unit. There are many unique and effective ways in which I have seen teams boost their ability to work together—and tap into each member's creative talents. I will share with you a few of these experiences that were quite meaningful to me; experiences in which I hope you will find meaning and potential activities for your own team, as well.

Let me start off by telling you about one that I can still vividly recall, even though it occurred over ten years ago. I remember arriving in San Francisco for the fiscal-year kick off of one of the largest divisions of a Fortune 500 consumer products company. After the usual PowerPoint presentations, things really got exciting. We were divided up into cross-functional groups, with each assigned to visit a different setting to observe how unique teams function. One team went to a jazz club, another to an emergency room, and another to a fire station. And my team went to the San Francisco zoo.

Our challenge was to go and observe how the team worked together, and to bring what we learned back to the group at large. We were to observe aspects such as how each member fulfilled their individual roles, how they collaborated to get the work done, how they prioritized the work, and what could we apply to our own teams. What I discovered is that the teams did not all function the same way. It's an obvious concept when you stop to think about it, yet we don't always consider the team's *purpose* when we picture high-performing teams. We often try to create a one-size-fits-all model for team effectiveness—something that can kill the creativity and vitality of a unique team.

I remember the jazz team's findings the most lucidly. It was important for the jazz quartet to feel complete freedom to riff off each other. When they were most relaxed, they were most creative. They needed complete trust in the skills and intent of the other members. Once they knew each other and their talents well enough, they could truly jam and play off each other. Even though each person was incredibly talented in their own right, they would willingly and happily give up being the lead to let another step briefly into the limelight, allowing the group to then play off that new path that the star took. But they always synced up on their goal, not only for their own enjoyment, but also to make beautiful, powerful music together. It reminded me of a very moving James Thurber quote: "There are two kinds of light—the glow that illuminates, and the glare that obscures." Those who glared would not long be welcome in a jazz quartet.

But what of the other groups' findings about *their* unique teams? The firehouse team spent a lot of time preparing for emergencies. Close quarters and constant contact 24/7 for days at a time; these conditions demanded that everyone get over small petty conflicts. In fact, their lives depended on it. And what about the emergency room? Their work was the embodiment of seamless integration. Everyone clearly knew their role and how it contributed to the greater good—saving the patient. Crisis caused complete collaboration.

And what about my own trip to the zoo? I learned that there was a clear, twofold sense of mission. They needed to please the crowds—letting them get as close to the animals as possible—while also protecting the animals (many of which were endangered) and the humans from each other. You can't always give the customer what they want exactly the way they want it; but this perceived limitation had actually sparked real creativity in the way the barriers were designed. These team members had a thorough and intimate knowledge of their product's capabilities and their customers' needs. They had to communicate continually and clearly—how the animals were behaving, if there were any signs of disease or distress, when to call in experts, and so on. Aside from the actual lessons we could potentially apply to our real teams back on the job, it was a wonderful way for me, as a new employee, to get excited about the drive for creativity and collaboration that was apparent in this company.

We took a few other field trips that also had an impact on me, such as our organization effectiveness team's visit to a plane-manufacturing plant. There was something so grand in scope when you saw that plane being built piece by piece as it moved down the long assembly line; and you learned how this group worked together to resolve problems as they arose on this journey. I remember touring an automobile-manufacturing plant and seeing the cords hanging down along the manufacturing line. The ultimate symbol of trust and accountability—waiting there to be pulled by any employee who saw a problem—and decided there was an immediate need to stop production.

Field trips like the 360-degree landscape excursion affected me positively as well. For this expedition, over 100 members of the sales and marketing teams went out into the marketplace to see how our products were displayed, and how the consumers interacted with them. Each subteam went to a different type of delivery channel—grocery store, convenience store, restaurant, and so on. Each team had a series of questions to ask and things to look for and learn about the product. The power of being off and learning together, and the new insights they shared when they returned ... all of a sudden you were bonded like never before.

And how would you like to go sailing ... in January ... with strong winds, clouds, and 30-degree temperatures? No? Well, the team I was working with was none too excited about the prospect, either. Yet when the adventure was over, they felt they had truly beaten the odds and they were emboldened to take on their competitors with new energy and confidence. So how did we arrive at this positive end? Perseverance! I had collaborated on team events with a local sailing captain for a number of years, but never under these severe conditions. We typically send out prereading to all the participants to truly familiarize them with how to sail a 30-foot yacht. Terminology, sailing theory, crew assignments are all covered, and expected to be read. This actually becomes part of our debriefing after it is all over—how a cavalier preparation for sailing into these unchartered waters might signal a lack of preparation on other critical, business-related ventures.

After a dockside orientation to review the prework, it is time for crew assignments. I almost always design this activity for cross-functional teams, since the last thing I need for most of these executives is to make them even *more* competitive within their department silos. I really like to tie in the HBDI as well by forming cross-functional, whole-brained teams. It is a great reminder of how people see events, think, and communicate differently. Once on board, they receive hands-on instruction from their assigned (real-life) sailboat captain. They learn how to function as a team in all of the crew positions. Assignments are rotated as each team faces a series of unique challenges requiring problem solving, successful navigation, and sailing skills to reach destinations. And the grand finale is "Blackbeard's Regatta," when each team gets the opportunity to apply everything they have learned—about sailing and collaboratively working together—as they make their way to shore, beautiful sails full tilt to the wind.

Well, usually that's the way it's supposed to work. I had been debating all morning with the team leader on whether we should scrap the whole thing, due to the harsh weather and rough seas. However, this person really liked the metaphor before us: tackling and overcoming tough sailing conditions equivalent to the difficult and unfavorable circumstances in their marketplace. And by the time they had successfully completed every challenge we threw at them and collectively and collaboratively sailed for shore, they really did feel (and rightfully so) like they had conquered tremendous odds—30-degree weather in January, wind blowing, never having sailed before. They were so pumped to take on any market challenge that would be thrown at them. And their team leader was extremely proud of what they accomplished, and let them very clearly know how he felt. To this day, this is the most powerful sailing outing I have experienced with any team.

"We don't have time for this!" That's what one EVP heard upon suggesting that his team go off-site for a one-day team-building activity with their 16 senior executives. But they made time, and they used the Olympics as their theme to participate in an assortment of physical, mental, indoor, and outdoor events. This was purposely differentiated from those executive golf team-building outings, where the same people who always hang out together still hang out together on the course. Events like that separate out the haves (as in have the golf skill) from the have nots (better sign up for that massage or walking tour now). No, no; in this case, four cross-functional teams together found the various competitive events to be fun and challenging—ultimately leading to a deeper understanding and appreciation of one another. Here is how one participant summed it up: "Some people were hesitant about this session, because they didn't think they could break away from the office for a day to 'play games.' But by the end of the Olympics, they were having such a good time it was actually hard to leave. We were all reminded of the power of teamwork. People were engaged, and the different environment caused us to see each other in a new light. Morale and communications have really increased."

So—what do you, as a leader, do when everyone says they are too busy to join in the firefly hunt, leaving group problems to remain unresolved? It is hard to take time—correct that, *make* time—to be away from your daily tasks for the purpose of enhancing your collaboration, creativity, and cohesiveness as a team. But I promise you that the payoff will be the long-term vitality and effectiveness of this group of people. As the preceding Olympics team discovered, the results last way beyond game day. If you are only getting together as a team during regular staff meetings, then you are really missing out on the many other powerful ways to bond together as a team.

I'd like to share some of the concrete, doable steps that I have either read about or personally seen work, created to carve out time on the team's calendar for higher value-added activities. On the easy end of the continuum (in terms of not a whole lot of up-front planning being necessary) are such ideas as a team declaration of a moratorium on meetings for just one day out of the workweek. This has the unintended (but happily foreseeable) consequence of causing people to be much more invested in making the meetings they *do* attend on the other days much more impactful. Heck, why stop there? Why not declare a ban on all habitually pointless meetings? How do you know a meeting will not be worth your investment of time? No one, including the meeting leader, knows what the critical meeting deliverables are. There is never a well-thought-out agenda for the meeting, much less one sent out in advance so participants can prepare to, well . . . participate. We never have everyone there, since this meeting is not seen as a can't miss event, so the same discussions happen over and over again . . . and decisions get delayed . . . and delayed . . . until just maybe the problem resolves itself.

Sound like meeting hell? Well, in addition to implementing the ban on meetings for at least one day of the week, you could also try making the meetings you *do* attend more effective using the above-mentioned tips. And you could try replacing an unnecessary meeting with a brief phone call or one-on-one conversation, an e-mail exchange, or posting a document on a shared drive for people to add their comments and questions.

Hopefully, these suggestions will prompt you to find the elusive excess time on people's calendars that is needed to engage in quality team-building events. Perhaps you have even canceled the worst offenders of habitual meeting madness. How about engaging your team in picking one of the events above to try out? Better yet, release their creative talents and allow *them* to design one that will truly engage them, and result in newfound collaboration and ideas to apply to your toughest business challenges and your most exciting business opportunities!

Chapter Eighteen

When Sparks Collide–Dealing with Interteam Conflict

Let's just assume for a moment that your team has been working very hard on improving the creativity and collaboration among one another, and that you have found great success through your efforts. Now, you could really be effective if it weren't for that other team, department, or business unit messing things up. Why can't they get their act together? It sure would be easier if you didn't have to interact with them at all. But that's not possible, is it? So what can you do?

I find this situation so often in organizations with whom I work. There is a lot of very unproductive conflict at the edges, where the work of your team bleeds over into the work of other teams. And with the increase in matrix organizations— where the line blurs between the projects for which *your* group is responsible versus mine—this situation will only be on the rise. Therefore, I want to share some typical examples of interteam conflict that I have found in my client organizations, and what we did to resolve it.

"Understand, Kimberly, this meeting better not fail." With those fateful words (and even said with Ed's smooth Southern drawl, there was no mistaking how serious he was), I heard one of the executives on the IT team give me my marching orders. I was there with Ed and his boss, George, planning a session that would bring together the 50 senior most leaders of the IT organization for a large financial services company; something that Ed told me, in no uncertain terms, had never been done before. That was how dire their situation was. One of the IT business goals for this fiscal year was to "Leverage Technology as a Strategic Business Tool." The infighting among the departments had reached such intolerable levels that it was severely jeopardizing the success of several very large, costly IT projects that the business desperately needed in order to remain competitive. They were willing to try anything . . . but *I* had better be very darn sure it was going to work. As George himself had said in the session invite notice sent to the participants: "I believe that teamwork is one of the most critical elements for success in meeting the needs of our lines of business and our customers."

We needed to know the extent of the problem, so we sent the attendees prework assessments wherein we asked them to measure the current level of team effectiveness and the alignment of the strategic priorities across the entire IT organization. The IT team as a whole was only rated "very effective" 6 percent of the time versus 34 percent for the team of which each participant was a member versus 57 percent for the team they managed. When we looked at the comments to help us interpret these results, we read overwhelmingly about the lack of coordination, cooperation, and communication *between* teams—and how this was adversely impacting the ability for IT to optimally perform.

There were two key sections of the session agenda that I believe were especially effective in positively impacting the perceptions that came out of this gathering. On the first day of this two-day meeting, I conducted the HBDI Diversity card exercise to help the team learn more about each other and see their colleagues as whole people—not just an IT box on an org chart, or someone who sits in the cube across the way. This would also improve their ability to value and then capitalize on the different thinking styles that existed within the team. We had just completed trading out the cards so that each person had their best most-like-me hand. It was now the moment of truth: time to divide team members up into the quadrants of their *most preferred* card. I called on all the people who had Blue as their top card to come to their quadrant's assigned space in the room. With Blue being the quadrant for analytical, logical thinkers, as you might imagine with a strong technically focused IT group, there was a lot of movement to this spot. I got out of the way in a hurry.

Next came the call for those with Green cards to move to their corner, which being the kind of people they are, they did in a very organized, orderly manner. As I typically do, I then moved to the next quadrant's spot ... Red, the interpersonal quadrant. "Now, all of you who have Red as your *most like you* card, please come join me in this corner." Something occurred at that moment that never had before with a group this large ... no one moved! That's right—out of a group of 50 people, no one had selected a Red card as most like them. My usual experience has been that any time there were at least 10 people in the room, I expected to find a whole brain present; in other words, each color represented. It was clear to me that even if someone on the team had a strong Red tint (so to speak), they sure wouldn't want to let anyone in this room know it—much less use it to help resolve the interdepartmental conflicts. Until the team could show that they valued Red's (or any quadrant's) thinking, it would remain underground.

Did you know that fireflies undergo a process called *overwintering*? In other words, they survive the harsh conditions of winter and very dry conditions of drought by burrowing underground or finding protection under the bark of a tree. They almost completely cease activity, only to emerge in the spring when the conditions for their survival are more favorable. Amazing, isn't it, how much this resembles what happens to those with a thinking style that other members of the team might not value as much as they should? If our team's environment feels like winter or drought, then we, too, may take our different perspectives, unique talents, and creative ideas underground. It will require the emergence of spring—be it a new leader, a team setting that calls for change, or a critical business crisis—for us to take the risk of exposing ourselves to these harsh conditions. Monarch butterflies may migrate to a new, more favorable climate (or *company*), but the firefly holds out hope that it can wait it out until it's truly time for them to shine.

And thus it was for this group of IT leaders in a financial services organization. Was this group going to value Red thinking? This was exactly the kind of perspective that they needed to be able to address the high-conflict situation they were facing, but would they see it before our two-day session ended? Would they take building the effectiveness of the IT *team* just as seriously as they would solving a technical problem that was standing in the way of their success? I knew that interpersonal strife and conflict were just as strong a barrier as any hardware or software issue. Would they discover this too?

Our first exercise after lunch on that first day was to gain clarity on the role of each department within IT. I opened this segment by explaining that good teams know what is important to the other teams with whom they share interdependencies, and that this next exercise was going to help us learn more about the critical drivers for each of the other departments. Each team was asked to identify—within their own department and for each of the other three departments— what they believed to be the top five priorities and why. After they had this discussion and documented the results with their own department, they were then to disperse and form cross-department teams to compare results.

The atmosphere was electric when they went into these second groups of teams. You could hear people voicing new appreciation for the other departments' demands. People were talking animatedly face-to-face, often never having corresponded before today except via e-mail. As Ed walked among the groups, saw the similarities in each other's priorities, and heard the productive dialogue going on, he asked me, "So what's the problem?" You see, the interdepartmental problems they had identified weren't personality based, but were rather solvable structural issues. However, the group's lack of presence and appreciation for all things Red had kept them from facing these issues in an effective way. This often happens at this point in a really productive interteam conflict situation. They have become so used to making the other department out to be the problem for so long that they can achieve very significant breakthroughs just by beginning the dialogue between factions. Once they do so, they become aware of topics upon which they can agree, by really listening to others and realizing they are all working toward the same goal.

We played another card game at the group dinner later that evening that I like to use with big groups like this—poker! I use this fairly often as an evening icebreaker, because many of the groups I work with involve men who have a lot of poker experience under their belt. In my brand of poker, I hand each person a single playing card when he or she arrives at the restaurant and tell them: "Go make your best five-card poker hand." This is a great way to break up cliques of people who normally hang out with each other, and to make everyone feel very welcome as soon as they arrive. As a matter of fact, if the prizes they are playing for are really good, the new arrivals get mobbed by those looking for one last card to make a really high-scoring poker hand. When all these IT people were later seated with their new best poker-hand buddies, laughing and talking easily among themselves, Ed's eyes surveyed the crowd. He raised his beer glass in a toast to me and declared, "I never would have thought I would see this sight. You did good."

Epilogue: Two weeks after this session, a small box was delivered to my office. I couldn't help but smile as I opened it and lifted out a small *red* M&M, complete with a smiling face, arms, and legs. This one had the IT company's logo on the back and the name *Seymour Red* emblazoned across the front. The note simply said, "Everyone got one of these. We thought you should, too. Thanks, Ed." I think they got the message—spring had emerged on this team.

Now that I have shared a success story with you, let me balance it out by telling you about a near disaster of my own making. I was undergoing interviews to see if I would be selected to facilitate a two-and-a-half day strategic planning session for a branch of the military. I kept passing muster with higher and higher levels, until I finally got the word that I had been selected. I began the hard work of designing the session in earnest, which meant that I was working very closely with the planning committee (a group of seven *core* members, mind you), but not the key decision makers. This was a different setup than I was used to. I normally spoke directly with the key stakeholder on the desired outcome of the session, and *then* began to design the process and content to achieve that end. Yet I took the planning committee at their word. Yes, we really needed to have (literally) 42 presentations on possible strategic initiatives—each one hoping to make the cut and get the funding. Basically, this was each presenter's opportunity to get in front of the most senior leadership and shine . . . and no one was willing to forego it. I kept asking the questions—Are you sure we need to have everyone present? Will they really be able to make the right decisions after only a four-minute presentation that includes Q&A? Can we look at other options? I was assured that everyone coming knew what they were getting into.

The small hotel room in which we gathered to hold the session was jammed with people. There were 18 highly decorated uniformed officers sitting at U-shaped tables, with 25 more people seated in chairs around the perimeter. As the child of a career officer myself, I was used to seeing a lot of brass, and this was a lot of brass—in very tight quarters. There were brief opening comments, and then I was on. I explained the process we would be using to determine the rank order of our top 10 strategic initiatives, and the criteria they should use to make the determination of what was strategic. I also distributed the handout they would be using to summarize their thoughts during each presentation. This was my attempt at keeping them engaged by requiring that they think and look for things during these 42 four-minute (almost three hours' worth) presentations.

We jumped right in and the first presenter distributed their handout about their initiative, talking as people passed along copies. After all, he only had four minutes. When this presenter's time was up, I asked everyone to please jot down their comments as to whether they thought this initiative met our criteria for strategic and why. I noticed a little discomfort among the participants; but there was no time for me to address it, since the next presenter was up. The next four minutes went by even faster than the first four. The tension and anger building in the room was palpable, and I knew this scenario wasn't working. I had to make a split-second decision—do I keep trying to ram this process down their throats or do I run the risk of changing it up—even though I had no idea how to make it better at that very moment. Would the planning committee think I was throwing them under the bus? What if they were right and this was the only way?

So I uttered the fateful words ... "How is this process working for you?" Now, it's not unusual for me to do such a process check, but *never* in the first 30 minutes! It was like the dam burst. *No one* was happy with the process. So I asked the five top leaders to join me out in the hall to discuss this and come back with a solution. Until then, everyone else was on break. Once we had the key leaders gathered, we created a rather easy solution. These top five leaders met with their direct reports and support staff for 30 minutes to review all the initiatives they submitted and determine which ones should be formally presented and/or consolidated, based on a specific set of criteria.

These were the lessons I learned—and I hope you, in turn, can gain something from my mistakes. Be crystal clear on what the key stakeholders want to achieve, and let *that* be your guiding light as you plan the content and process of the session. Don't let certain assumptions, especially unproven ones, cloud your better judgment. Always test them, especially if they are getting in the way of your success. Have the courage to say out loud what you feel in your gut—"Is this working for you?" Engage the creativity and different perspectives of others in solving the problem. Keep working at it—don't give up.

Do you have critical processes that cross the boundaries of department lines? If so, then you have a situation that is potentially rife with conflict. These processes can be sources of great tension in their everyday work world, because these are the places where departments rub against each other. It's where you will see the first signs of loss of trust, doubt about others' intentions, and attribution of bad attitudes or lack of competence to each other. I have seen these kinds of clashes arise in all kinds of industries—property management companies, financial services firms, and consumer product organizations, to name a few. There is a technique I like to use to ascertain and then address these, and it works like this. I bring together the two departments with the most heightened conflict—this discord has the most critically negative impact on the business. During the session, I break them into their respective department teams and ask them to discuss and flip chart their responses to these four questions:

1. What are we held accountable for?
2. What do we think the other team(s) is held accountable for?
3. What is our greatest conflict with them?
4. What do we think is their greatest conflict with us?

It is amazing how much the dialogue among the team and in the large group debriefing can help to shed light on where the key difficulties and misconceptions lie. Having the groups discuss what they believe the other team is accountable for will help you to walk a mile in their shoes, and develop a true appreciation for the tasks they regularly undertake. Additionally, acknowledgment of your own conflicts helps to deflect the natural defensiveness that would occur if others just told you outright. Many, many times these clashes revolve around broken processes—something that is actually good news, because it's something on which the groups can collaborate to improve and together put their creative talents to work.

Now, I will admit that I am a keep it simple kind of process improvement person. I never can remember, while constructing a process flow chart, when you use a triangle, a square, or a diamond. So my simple process improvement method looks more like this:

- **Step 1:** Identify the starting point in the process—that is, the trigger(s) that something needs to be launched or changed. Write them on a sticky note and put it at the beginning of the process flow.
- **Step 2:** Define what success looks like at the end of the process, write *that* on a sticky note, and place it at the end of the process flow.
- **Step 3:** Determine the 8 to 10 major steps involved in getting from the triggers to the ending point. We are expecting a high-level overview of the process, not deep detail. Write each of these major steps on a sticky note and place it on the process flow chart.

Sometimes just walking through the process steps helps all parties to realize where the problems lie. Is there a handoff that isn't going smoothly? Did either group lack clarity as to who needed to be involved in a key decision versus who was the final decision maker? Has there been duplication of activities or functions because of a breakdown in trust or communications? Are there key people who are unaware of, or simply not using important supporting processes and procedures? Why and how could they be revised to make them more useful? These are the natural discussions that will evolve if you don't overcomplicate the process, and use it instead as a vehicle for healthy, candid dialogue.

The heads of each department play a critical role throughout such a session. Too many times, I see team leaders fool themselves into thinking that the people in their organization don't know how they feel about the leader of another department, but that is almost never the case. While some may be more politically correct than others and don't directly bad-mouth their peers, the subtle message is just as damaging. So before I ever bring the actual departments together, I first arrange for the two leaders to meet to make sure they really want this session to be a success. How they kick off the session—not only their words, but the passion with which they speak them—will oftentimes set the stage for what will happen the rest of the day. Of course, the actions that follow their words had better be in sync, or they run the risk of losing not only the trust of the other department, but their credibility within their own team.

One other thing—this needs to *not* be a one-time activity. I would suggest that before you leave this session, everyone agree that they will come back together again in 60 days to check progress. This is a great way to hold everyone accountable for sticking to their commitments to each other, and it also clearly communicates to everyone that we aren't expecting quick fixes from one eight-hour meeting. It is hard to get everyone in the same room at the same time to deal with issues that cross departments. Putting a date on everyone's calendar for a follow-up sets the expectation that there will still be things to work through.

If collaboration between these two departments is mission critical—and if there is still significant room for improvement at the check-up meeting—then I recommend that you continue to hold regular gatherings between these departments, at least quarterly, and perhaps monthly or bimonthly. Make sure these meetings have a positive focus and that the agenda is filled with important topics. Go for some quick wins. I have seen interdepartmental relations improve dramatically through something as simple as an easy-to-use, up-to-date contact list that clarifies who is accountable for what, so that you clearly know whom to call when an issue arises. The frustration and wasted time that this prevents is well worth the small investment of someone's time to create it. Find opportunities for members of each of the departments to form ad hoc teams and work on critical business priorities of mutual interest. The more opportunities for them to collaborate successfully, the better.

In one of these future sessions, you might also want to create some norms for how the group can work together most effectively—rules of engagement, as it were. For example, I worked with one team to develop escalation rules for when and how an issue would be taken to higher levels in the organization. There had been conflict between the corporate and field units of a single function because issues that were not being resolved at the lower levels were bumped up for resolution to higher levels far too quickly. The complexity of the matrix structure, with a dual sense of allegiance to both the function and the business unit, hampered the effectiveness of these interdepartmental communications. Mistrust, anger, and resentment resulted, all because of a lack of agreement on the ground rules for escalating an issue. These were some of the escalation guidelines we developed:

- Make sure you have all the facts your boss will need to help solve the problem. If you don't, push back to get them prior to escalating.
- Indicate why you are escalating it. If it's informational only, put FYI in the subject line of the e-mail; if their involvement is needed, put ACTION NEEDED.
- If it's impacting the business or is a deliverable, escalate it. Don't use escalation to cover your back.

- Escalate when you think the issue will come to your management so they're not surprised.

- To best escalate, know the communication style of the person you are escalating to and utilize that knowledge to alter the communication for greater impact.

"What we've got here is a failure to communicate." *Cool Hand Luke* had it right; sometimes the conflict between departments is as simple as that. My first job out of graduate school was in HR for a hotel company. One of my first assignments was to serve as the HR liaison to the IT department, for we couldn't seem to communicate the information that we needed in a computer report in a way that they could understand it. I realize now that they were likely looking at it from the left side of the brain, and we were likely looking at from the right side—our big picture versus their need for detail. We made assumptions—wouldn't everyone expect an employee list to be sorted in alpha order? Not if you are in IT, apparently, and you are used to running all things employee-related based on their social security number. We didn't begin with a clear end in mind—what did we need to use the report *for?* Once we all had a common understanding of that, the IT department could then help us design it and get us the information we needed. My role was to help translate what we wanted into what that meant the report would look like.

I still see this problem today, when someone asks for a report to be run or for data to be gathered, but they don't slow down to tell the listener the Yellow, or how this information will be used. I think I was successful in this role because both departments trusted me to have their best interests at heart. I did not take sides. I knew that each group had good intentions. I showed respect for the competence of both parties, and helped them to work together to achieve their shared objectives.

On another occasion, I was working with the IT team of a telecommunications company. The firm was having a difficult time enlisting the support from the business units for the IT projects for which the team was responsible to keep on time and on budget. The team's leader informed me that he often asked his employees to send him their PowerPoint in advance of presenting them, so that he could coach them on how to improve it. This gave me an idea. As prework for the session, I asked each member to bring a recent presentation (that had not been refined from discussions with the leader). I also had them take the HBDI online before the session.

After debriefing their individual assessment results, I shared with them a communication technique based on the Whole Brain model and HBDI that I call *optimal flow*. (See Figure 18.1.) It outlines the ideal way to present information so that your message can be heard and have the intended impact, and it goes something like this:

- **Why**—Begin in the **Yellow** quadrant. Answers the why question—why are we here, why is this important. Give them a brief overview of the information you will be presenting. Wherever possible, connect this work to an overarching goal, a long-term strategy, or a broader positive impact on the organization.

HBDI's Whole Brain® Optimal Flow for Communication

Color	Quadrant	Question	Area
Yellow	D	Why	"Head"
Blue	A	What	"Head"
Red	C	Who	"Heart"
Green	B	How	"Feet"

Figure 18.1. HBDI Optimal Flow for Communication
© 1987–2009 Herrmann International. Adapted by K. Douglas. All rights reserved. The four-quadrant graphic and four colors are trademarks of Herrmann International and are reproduced in this text with permission.

- **What**—Next, move to **Blue**. Give them the relevant facts, the current status, how you will measure success, or trends analysis data.

- **Who**—Now that you have engaged their head, move to connect with their heart. Open the floor for questions. If you know what the impact on them personally or other key stakeholders will be, tell them. Remember everyone's favorite radio station, WIIFM: *What's in It for Me?*

- **How**—Only after you have engaged their head and their heart can you engage their feet. This is where you make it very clear what you need the listener to do when they leave here.

Now here is the real kicker. Even though you present this information in the order outlined above, *you create your message in the reverse order.* You begin with getting very clear in your own mind about what you want them to know, think, feel, and do differently after your presentation. Then you back up and ask yourself, "What would they need to know in order to accomplish that?" If you can't answer that question based on what you know about the audience, then this is the time to reach out to others who might know them better. Finally, ask yourself, "How does this link into something bigger and more important that they would care about?"

Back to my IT team members, who were trying to make presentations to nontechnical audiences. When they reviewed their past presentations, they had several big "Aha" moments. Some of them had been jumping right in by informing the listeners of the Blue facts, then moving straight to Green action planning—what the presenter wanted them to do about the facts—without making a strong case for *why* the listener should care. Some didn't give them the Yellow big picture—how these projects will help the organization to achieve some larger strategy or goal. Some only shared the Blue facts of the current status of the project, assuming that everyone could see what needed to be done about it and who needed to do it. And all of them missed the Red—how this impacts the listener personally, what support the IT presenter needed from them, what questions they had.

Not surprisingly, when they diagnosed their current PowerPoints, they realized how much their presentations reflected their own thinking and communication style versus reflecting what their listeners needed to hear. One reason that the leader was so good at reviewing their presentations and coaching them on how to improve it is because he was multidominant; he could view each topic through multiple lenses. Yet, without a leader like this pushing us, most of us—if left to our own devices—would much prefer to run our presentations by someone who is . . . well, just like us, thinking and communication style-wise! And so, you get what you'd expect . . . "It's beautiful. I wouldn't change a thing!"

Occasionally people ask me the question: "If I know that I am presenting to a bunch of people who think in Blue (finance, IT, and engineers are frequently named), do I really need to go through all four quadrants?" My answer is an unqualified *Yes*, for several reasons. First, you can't assume, based solely on a job title or department name, that you won't have a whole brain present. Believe me, in over 10 years of debriefing team HBDI profiles, you would be amazed at how much they aren't like what you think they might be. Second, although you might want to change up the amount of time you spend in each quadrant, the flow still makes sense as it is. Finally, it stretches your thinking to see the situation from all angles, and just might help you to truly have the greater influence you seek.

So, there you have it. How to make the sparks that fly when two departments with different goals, who might be competing for scarce resources, use that creative abrasion to light a fire that ignites an improved environment not only for these two departments, but also for others to follow in their footsteps. Isn't that the *real* calling of leadership?

Part VI

Sync–The Magic

Chapter Nineteen

There's Something Going On in My Backyard!

Imagine that it is 1577 and you are on an amazing adventure sailing around the world. As you near an Indonesian island, you behold a miraculous sight:

> Amongst these trees night by night, through the whole land, did shew themselves an infinite swarme of fierie wormes flying in the ayre, whose bodies . . . make such a shew and light, as if every twigge or tree had been a burning candle.

These are the words of Sir Francis Drake, and one of the earliest written accounts of the very rare, incredible, synchronous fireflies of Southeast Asia. That's right—synchronous. This particular species of firefly, the *Pteroptyx malaccae*, found in the mangrove forests of Malaysia and Thailand, has attracted millions of spectators since they were first discovered. Thousands upon thousands of fireflies all alight upon a tree, and slowly but surely, their flashes become perfectly attuned—all on, all off. Can you imagine such a sight?

Now, fast forward to 1992. It is late in the evening in early summer. You are bundled up with three generations of your family on the unlit porch of your Tennessee mountain cabin—as others have been doing for 40 years—waiting for and then watching the light show. But this time, something's different . . . *you see something differently . . . you do something different.*

> Discovery consists of seeing what everybody has seen and thinking what nobody has thought.
> —Albert Szent-Gyorgyi

Your name is Lynn Faust, and though you don't know it yet, you are about to make an amazing discovery. Having recently read an article by mathematician Steven Strogatz about those synchronous fireflies in Malaysia, you write to tell him what you have seen:

> I am sure you are aware of this, but just in case; there is a type of group synchrony lightning bug inside the Great Smoky Mountain National Park near Elkmont, Tennessee. These bugs "start up" in mid June at around 10 pm nightly. They exhibit 6 seconds of total darkness; then in perfect synchrony thousands light up 6 rapid times in a 3 second period before all going dark for 6 more seconds. . . . It is beautiful . . . like a waterfall of fireflies.

As Strogatz described it in his book *Sync*, "In her gracious and unassuming way, [Faust] was about to shatter a myth about synchronous fireflies that had lasted for decades." The myth—which had been uniformly accepted by all learned people in this field—stated that this kind of thing simply didn't happen outside Southeast Asia; and it certainly didn't happen in the United States (although there were many scientists studying fireflies and their behavior in this country as well). It took an amateur naturalist to shatter this myth and discover what scientists all over the world had agreed was not possible. Lynn Faust saw the phenomenon before her clearly, and even if she didn't know the importance of what she was seeing, she *believed* in it simply because she wasn't aware of what the experts had known to be true.

While Steven Strogatz might have been her initial point of contact, it was up to Jonathan Copeland, a neuroethologist at Georgia Southern University, to make the trip up to Elkmont to see what could not be. Copeland knew within ten minutes of his first sighting of these amazing creatures in that patch of

Tennessee woods that what he had traveled around the world to see and study was in a place that he *never* expected to find it— practically his own backyard. And each year, the numbers grow, all coming from the surrounding areas—thousands of magical fireflies, and thousands of witnesses to this miraculous sight.

An amazing story, indeed. But what, you're likely wondering, does it have to do with you and your team? How does this synchronous firefly spectacle connect to your business? Well, think of it this way: There is probably something positive going on somewhere in your organization that you could take to the next level. There might even be something that you stopped believing is possible for your team or company to achieve. There may be untapped pockets of greatness that exist all around you of which you may not even be aware. Or, like Lynn Faust, perhaps *you* think everyone sees what you see and they simply aren't doing anything about it. But they can't see it through your eyes, with your unique perspective and life experience.

What this story shows us is that a single person has a substantial amount of power to truly make a difference in an organization by first believing in something, and then taking action on it. You can be the one person who sees the possibilities out there, who can be one of the early adopters. Are you the one who will bring this message back to your team and your leader? Will you take action, in spite of all the known barriers and accepted truths that stand in your way?

There is an interesting difference between the synchronous fireflies of Southeast Asia and those of Elkmont, Tennessee. Those in Thailand and Malaysia perform in a lockstep, metronome-like manner. All on, all off. In Elkmont, however, it can instead take on the appearance of a wave of synchronized light, like a string of blinking Christmas tree lights. One firefly sparks another to begin to light, which in turn sparks another one to light. And like this one firefly, one person has to light the way and start the process. You can have a tremendous impact on your environment, because you can choose to see the possible. It begins with you—how powerful would it be if it didn't *stop* with you?

What if we could all learn how to synchronize our flashes so that we are all working together and complementing each other's light for a common good? What if we adopted a team-wide mind-set, a common commitment to an overall goal wherein each person played a unique and valuable role in the achievement of this vision of success? What if each team member wanted and believed in this so much that they were willing to suspend their disbelief of what was possible? What if every member of the group was willing to commit their discretionary effort to the cause?

If this were the case, then we might have a team, department, or company that looks very different from the one we have today. The call for greater creativity is indeed becoming a business necessity; the new economics of our world demand that we take that chance. As a matter of fact, there is an entirely new term associated with this concept called *innovation economics*. A recent *BusinessWeek* article asked the question: "Can America invent its way back? 'Innovation economics' shows how smart ideas can turn into jobs and growth—and keep the U.S. competitive." Some companies seem to think so. They have realized that a few choice departments or skunk works teams, in isolation of the rest of the organization, cannot be exclusively responsible for creativity or innovation; and they are taking active and aggressive measures to distribute that responsibility across their entire corporate environment. And the innovation landscape is changing as well; rather than being solely reserved for new physical products, it now includes new processes, services, means of entertainment and communication, and methods of collaboration. There are a few examples about which I've read that really strike a chord in this regard, ideas that you can potentially implement wholesale, or adapt to fit your culture and current capacity. It can begin with you and your team . . . and then spread, as one firefly's light sparks another.

Google. Before you groan and say, "Not *them* again," let me give you some interesting facts. You have likely heard about the fact that they allow their employees to spend 20 percent of their time working on a project that makes their light shine, so to speak. Any time I mention this to a company as one way to spur creativity, I hear responses like, "We could never do that here . . . senior management would never go for it." Well, maybe they would if they realized the value that such a program could bring to the bottom line. Although Google may have implemented this strategy in order to attract and retain the best and the brightest, they very well could *still* be doing it because it gets results. In fact, a recent article in *Harvard Business Review* shared the profound results of Google's analysis of the source of its innovations: "Its founders tracked the progress of ideas that they had backed versus ideas that had been executed in the ranks without support from above, and discovered a higher success rate in the latter category." One has to ask, were the ideas actually better, or was the commitment to champion them greater? And does it really matter? The result is clear—there is money to be made in spreading the accountability for innovation across the depth and breadth of the organization. No longer is it solely the province of R&D, marketing, or design and engineering. That just doesn't make good business sense.

It undoubtedly takes a dedicated leader to drive this kind of initiative throughout an entire organization; not all companies are as liberally minded about their employees' time as Google is. But you don't have to mimic Google's program word for word. Think about how *you* could adopt the concept to your team or department. Maybe you can't sacrifice one-fifth of your employees' time, but how about one hour of team time a week devoted to a truly innovative brainstorming session? While there might not be immediately usable outcomes, there is unmistakable value in keeping those creative juices flowing in a collaboration-building environment and keeping people engaged in the excitement of their work.

Let's say that you have figured out a way to make time for innovation. What comes next? You need to expose your people to a diversity of thinking styles and perspectives and make innovation a team sport. Procter & Gamble CEO A. G. Lafley has a name for this: *open innovation* and boldly stated in a recent *strategy + business* article: "The kinds of innovation needed at Procter & Gamble must be realized through teams." While he acknowledges that the initial idea for a new product may come from a single individual, it will take a collective effort to make a successful journey through prototyping and launch.

I firmly believe this to be true. One person with a bright idea is like one person watching fireflies in a backyard. They may be amazed, but if they don't tell others so that they too can partake in the wonder and catch the excitement, then it only remains with them. You must engage others to have an

226 SYNC—THE MAGIC

impact; you have to make this something they want to do for themselves. And that, in essence, is the point of this book. Not only will a diverse team with an open environment come up with better ideas, but also it will likely be the only way that these ideas ever reach their full potential and positively influence the business.

Lafley goes on to write that, "Our experience suggests that many of the failures of innovation are social failures . . . Often the root cause is poor social interaction; the right people simply don't engage in productive dialogue frequently enough." This can happen both within a single team and across several, and it's why I included the previous chapter that focused on resolving interteam conflict. For the truly big innovations, you will have to move outside the confines of your own team or department. You will have to spark excitement for this new idea, process, or invention in other critically relevant parts of the organization.

And what is your reward? Lafley sees the benefits clearly. When he took over as P&G CEO in 2000, only one of every six new product introductions had a return on their investment. Today, that number has shifted dramatically, as *half* of their new products succeed. This kind of rapid success is highly unusual in *any* industry, much less one as mature as household and personal care products. To what does Lafley attribute that dramatic turnaround?

> Once people have succeeded at innovation, you can see the energy in the company changing. People routinely say, "We can do this. This is feasible." Building this sort of capability often has the rhythm of, say, skilled basketball practice: a group of people who gradually learn seamless teamwork, reading one another's intentions and learning to complement other team members, ultimately creating their own characteristic, effective, and uncopyable style of successful play.

So what do you do when everyone has gathered and the fireflies (aka creativity) don't show up? You seek inspiration elsewhere. You look outside for new thinking, not necessarily to replace the internal ideas, but to spur them on to new heights. Remember the team excursions I talked about in Chapter 17? Well, I'm talking about something like that . . .

but on steroids; something that allows you to expose people to resources outside the four walls of your business.

For example, award-winning consultancy firm IDEO has become well known for their very creative, cross-discipline approach to developing their designs. In addition to more typical engineers and marketers, they also employ anthropologists and ethnographers whose role it is to get inside the heads of their targeted consumers (figuratively) by going to their homes and places where they shop (literally). By directly and thoroughly observing customers as they go about their daily lives, these researchers can discover their known—and even unstated—desires and needs.

But let's say that you can't afford to hire IDEO to go live with your customers for a while to better understand their needs. How can you apply this concept to your team or department? Ask yourselves who the consumers of your product are. You might hear people refer to it in terms of your customer and end user (your customer's customer). How much do you know—I mean really, intimately *know*— about what your customers, especially the internal ones, expect and need from your team . . . and what *their* customers expect and need from *them*? What are you doing to proactively seek out their input? Some of the best companies are making innovation a two-way learning experience.

I am currently working with an automobile parts manufacturing company. Their customer now expects zero defects—can you imagine that? *Zero* defects? Do you know why? Because their customer's customer—the person forking over the big money for the car containing these parts— expects *zero defects*. Customers' expectations rise, and you have to keep up. Do you and the members of your team know what your customers are now expecting of you in terms of innovation, quality, and effectiveness? Do you know how well you are currently meeting those expectations? Many times, there is no better inspiration for innovation than the burning platform for change brought about by this new awareness.

Let's consider your internal customers or users of your products for a moment. If you are in HR, you might conduct a field study with a manager the next time they use the online performance management tool. Or, if you are in Finance, maybe you observe how user friendly the new budgeting tool is. These criteria don't have to be pass/fail; you can think of them as the market research phase for any company's new product development. The focus is on learning and improving. Don't label products as final until they are field tested and refined; instead, think of them as prototypes. That's what the real designers do. Run small pilot studies. Succeed, fail, and learn.

Speaking of failure, there is at least one very successful, creative company that has taken steps to lessen the chance and the negative impact of failure—both on the business results and the establishment and maintenance of an innovation culture. Ed Catmull, co-founder of Pixar and the president of Pixar and Disney Animation Studios, described his company's approach in his September 2008 *Harvard Business Review* article. By his own admission, this process was not always effective, but they learned and improved.

> Of great importance—and something that sets us apart from other studios—is the way people at all levels support one another. Everyone is fully invested in helping everyone else turn out the best work. They really do feel that it's all for one and one for all. Nothing exemplifies this more than our creative brain trust and our daily review process.

Catmull went on to explain each of these in greater detail in this article. In summary, the brain trust is a group of nine senior leaders plus others who are invited in when needed, who can be called upon to provide advice and counsel when a project leader needs assistance on a current work in progress. So what makes these discussion sessions work? They are relatively short—only two hours. Everyone stays focused on the very clear goal—*make the movie better*—which is important when passions rise. Egos are checked at the door. There is mutual trust and respect among all participants before you ever even step foot in the room, all of which allows for very candid dialogue. Attendees see the meeting as peers giving feedback to one another. The brain trust has no authority, and that is a crucial element of its success. People are free to give their best opinion as an expert in the area, not the one accountable for deciding on the action to take or implementing that decision. What to use and what to ignore is up to the director of the project. Through improvements that are made along the way, Catmull now describes this as "a community of master filmmakers who come together when needed to help each other."

If the creative brain trust is Pixar's approach to dealing with significant challenges, then the dailies is their method for giving and getting constant—every day, in fact—feedback in a positive way on work in progress. And they have found that the in progress part is critical to the success of this procedure. The more that people were inclined to only share work that they considered good, the longer the delay in receiving very important team feedback—feedback that could ensure alignment with the director's vision for the movie along the way versus a surprise at the end. Convincing these very creative people to show work in progress to their peers took some doing; yet they discovered that it *enhanced*, rather than diminished, the creativity of their work. Additionally, it became an incredibly powerful experience, one that allowed everyone to learn from and become inspired by the work of others.

What if your team thought of themselves as the creative brain trust? I have long recommended that staff meetings be touted as a meeting of your board of advisors, where people freely solicit and give advice on how to deal with a problem or challenge they are facing. However, I really like this term instead—*a creative brain trust*. What would it take to instill this safe environment and encourage everyone on your team to overcome their natural fear and concern for sharing the vulnerabilities and problems that they don't know the answers to? The leader must model the way. What could you adapt from the daily review process? Are there ongoing projects that could benefit from receiving constant feedback (framed in a way that it could be received and heard)? Are you brave enough to ask yourself, "What would you attempt to do if you knew you could not fail?"

We near the end of this book and the end of our journey together at the same place we began—with a focus on the individual. In this chapter, we have discussed the power that one person has to truly see something different and then use this to *make* a difference. It can be anyone—someone who is a recognized expert or a person in authority, or just someone who has a passing interest and takes action. Are you that person? Do you see possibilities for excellence in your team and your work environment? What could you do to help others to see what you see? What revolution might you start today because you believed that things could be different?

In the next chapter, we'll talk about the important role of the leader in taking the concept of this one shining light, and using it to create a compelling case for change; one that just might trigger a synchrony of light . . . like a waterfall of fireflies.

Chapter Twenty

Change Is Not a Four-Letter Word!

There is a story that I occasionally tell to leadership teams about an executive who took his best performer out on the mountaintop and said to him, "Do you see that mansion in the distance? Do you see the four-car garage . . . the swimming pool . . . the tennis courts? Well, if you work very, very hard, one day that will all be . . . *mine!*" The response to this story is usually laughter at first, and then the flash of recognition—"That's what we've been doing, isn't it?" I have met so many executives in my work who try to sell *their* vision to employees. The approach that you *should* be taking, however, is attempting to inspire them to care as much about this picture of success as you do and vividly seeing how they can directly contribute to the results of the team, department, and company.

I truly hope that if you have read this book all the way through to this point, then you are on fire, so to speak, to instill a creative, collaborative culture on your team—one where everyone is actively engaged in driving the objectives of the business. Change must take place for any new strategic direction to be fully executed. If this vision for the future remains solely your own and not that of your teammates, then it cannot possibly be fully accomplished. As Peter Senge so simply stated it: "People don't resist change. They resist being changed!"

I can personally attest to the truth of this statement, and would like to share the following story with you as a cautionary tale. For seven years, I was a consultant with a global management consulting firm called the Hay Group. My role was to collaborate with the leaders of an organization in determining their total reward strategy, and then manage the project to implement the changes to their compensation, benefits, and performance management programs. It involved a lot of change—*for them.* When Coke (one of my clients at Hay) hired me to join their newly developing Organization Effectiveness team, I was very excited about being able to see firsthand the impact of our internal consulting projects for our business unit clients. What I was *not* prepared for was how I was going to feel about being on the inside. I discovered that I liked being the chang*er* a lot more than being the chang*ee*! At Hay, I knew what the strategy was and why the changes were being made. Heck, I had written the script for it! It was much harder being the victim, or the recipient, of changes that someone much higher up than me had decided upon. And I was in the role of change agent!

This was a very hard thing for me to acknowledge, even to myself. I had always thought of myself as someone who was very comfortable with ambiguity; but I guess this wasn't the case when it began impacting my very livelihood and daily work existence. Maybe I was just comfortable with *other* people's ambiguity or uncertainty. But it was a tremendous learning experience for me. The frequency and pace of change in today's world is rapid and constant.

You tend to have a very different perspective from the top—directing the change happening to those below you—than when you are the person to whom this change is being made. I like to use the following metaphor to describe this feeling to leaders. Imagine you are sitting atop a rain cloud. When you look down to the ground below you, you see that there is structure and order to the pattern of the raindrops. Now reverse roles. You are on the ground and the rain (the multitude of simultaneous change initiatives) is just pelting you from up above. You have no control over it. There doesn't seem to be any pattern to it. It just keeps coming with no end in sight. Your role as the leader is to make sense of the rain for your employees. Help them to see your perspective and perceive how these seemingly disparate projects and initiatives all fit under the large umbrella of a critical new strategic direction. Without this common understanding, you lose the power of their coordinated, focused efforts.

There is no visible leader among the fireflies, even when they are synchronizing their flashes. This baffles scientists— they can't understand how such an amazing feat can happen without a queen bee or some other similar leader orchestrating it. But there simply isn't; just as there is no room for command and control in today's fast-paced environment. The leader of today, while not invisible, is not obvious and showy in his leadership. I don't even like the notion of empowering your team, because I feel that it gives leaders a false sense of security by convincing them that they possess power to bestow upon others. While you might have the authority to force *compliance*, it is not within your power to force *commitment*. Remember the violinist from Chapter 10's Music Paradigm experience, who said to the tightly controlling conductor, "If you're just going to tell me how to perform, then you'll get that and nothing more."

What if you were to treat the very talented people working for you as volunteers who have options about where they choose to donate their time? Because in good times—and even in bad times—your *best* employees do. I have worked with both for-profit and nonprofit organizations for years, because I feel that there is so much that I and they can learn from each other. Broadly speaking, corporations had been far ahead of nonprofit organizations in terms of financial acumen and measurability of outcomes valued by shareholders (aka donors and contributors in the not-for-profit world) for years. That situation has changed; as the level of philanthropic giving and government aid has declined over the years, nonprofits have been forced to make tough, fact-based choices on how to allocate funds from a diminishing pool of resources.

On the other hand, nonprofits were far superior to corporations in giving their employees a sense of mission and meaning in their daily jobs. The employment contract of the past, which promised that *we will take care of you and you take care of the company*, gave way to a free-agency mind-set on the part of employees when companies pulled back on benefits and perceived job security for life. Now, in order to

recruit the best and capture their intellectual capital, companies need to give those top-tier candidates a reason to choose
that firm, and provide reasons as to why potential employees
should share their mindshare and commitment to that
particular company. You can see this for yourself across the
corporate landscape, in the shift that has occurred from
"we stand for adding value and profit to our shareholders" to
"we are a company focused on the sustainability of the environment" (and hopefully make a profit from this push to go
green).

We each have our own power and can choose freely how
we use it. The team leader's job, therefore, is to create the
fertile environment and clarify the landscape so that everyone
knows what is important. Set the stage for the team's success,
and make effective functioning a priority. People can then
make their own decisions—from compliance to commitment,
from forced effort to discretionary effort—based on the best
possible information that you can give them. This is about
leaving a leadership legacy and being a role model for what
great management looks like in their organization. I am
encountering more and more executives whose desire to leave
a lasting impression on the company isn't based on achieving
an outstanding execution of a particular strategic initiative,
or making a merger bring the expected value to the company.
Rather, they are truly concerned about raising the bar for the
quality of leader that their company produces. And one of the
most critical roles for the leader of the future is—and will
continue to be—as a change agent.

One of the most profound ways that you can impact the
success of a critical change initiative (and truly, what business
initiative today doesn't involve some significant amount of
modification in human behavior?) is by crafting and communicating a compelling case for transformation. It may be
business-related and sweeping across the entire organization,
or it might specifically concern the need to drive the changes
we have been talking about throughout this book: greater
creativity and collaboration among the team, living up to the
team's new guiding principles, and focusing their efforts to
make the team vision for success a reality. These need to be
treated as part of a critical change initiative, and you need to be
the chief agent for and the champion of this transformation.

Leaders need to make change so very compelling that their team members will actually *choose* it for themselves. If a manager doesn't believe in his or her heart that it is the absolute right thing for the team and the business, then they won't be able to convince others of this fact. They must be able to communicate this message authentically over and over again until they feel they can't say it anymore; until they feel there must not be a single person in their organization who doesn't know it. And they say it twice as often when there are setbacks and hard times. This is the antithesis of the leader whose idea of change is simply giving everyone their own personal copy of *Who Moved My Cheese?* That is leadership at its worst—abdicating responsibility for communicating a compelling case for change.

As an agent for change, you need to create a persuasive picture of what the brighter future holds; and just as clear a picture of the current reality and what will happen if these critical improvements don't occur. Remember cognitive dissonance—the psychological principle that states that the human mind can't hold two equally clear pictures at the same time? Imagine a rubber band stretched tight between these two points: the future and the current reality. If the future picture is compelling enough, then it will pull that current reality forward. But the pull to stay the same and not move is also very strong.

So what is the leader to do? Communicate—constantly, consistently, convincingly. I see a significant push in corporate America to ramp up leaders' skills in the area of executive presence and large audience presentations (think town hall–type meetings), and I've seen this need reflected in my own consulting practice. A high-tech company recently hired me to help all of the managers—from the senior leaders to the first-line supervisors—prepare to effectively communicate a critical change throughout the organization. And it was going to be a pretty hard message.

As an interesting and I think very telling side note, there were several in the executive suite (led by the CEO) who couldn't understand why they even needed to undergo this training, especially when funds were so tight. Hadn't they already talked about the new strategic direction in the company newsletter, and again in the town-hall meeting last week? Why couldn't the employees figure out what they needed to know from those? What was taking them so long to get with the program? Change happens; get over it. And it's a sad but true fact that this company is not alone in this type of thinking. Amazingly, these leaders likely had been talking about this transformation for months—gathering data, understanding the options and the implications, and preparing for the change (and the personal impact on *them*). Yet they wanted employees to *get it* within a week or two of first hearing about it. How is that even possible? Yet I would bet you have had this same thing happen to you; or perhaps even you expected it of others at one time or another.

One of the most important pieces of these working sessions was to ensure that everyone heard the same message and then be able to put it into their own words. But first, they had to believe in it themselves. Through our discussions with senior management leading up to the kickoff of the workshops, these executives came to realize how important the managers' active participation in executing the change actually was, and decided to make this training mandatory. Now all we had to do was help the managers who attended believe the truth of this message of change, and help them to become advocates.

We had specifically selected someone within the ranks—a respected, straight-shooting, mid-level manager—to deliver the company message about the change. We had helped him to create this presentation with all the critical components there (Remember HBDI's Whole Brain® optimal flow from Chapter 18?):

- *Yellow*—The future picture of success for the company, as clear as we knew it at this time, and why this was the best alternative from all of the other options that were considered.
- *Blue*—The straight facts about the current situation, both from an internal and an external/competitive perspective. The new measures for success going forward, the targets the company needed to hit, and how these were determined.
- *Red*—The importance of the manager's role, since studies show that employees are far more trusting of what their immediate boss says when the company is in

a heightened state of change. How this was going to impact the performance objectives for their team that they were in the process of creating. What we were doing to equip them to effectively communicate this message, including this training. (Note: While you normally would make time for Q&A in this Red section, we had designed a different approach for this particular training session.)

- *Green*—What we specifically needed management to do to help effectively communicate this message to all employees and gain their commitment to make the needed changes. The specific timeline of events that would occur after this training, and the various roles and accountabilities for executing this action plan. This included a communication plan that laid out all the ways in which the company would be reinforcing the manager's message. During this session, each manager would create their own team- or department-specific communication plan, with key messages, vehicles, and timing. (Remember what I said in Chapter 9: In a time of change, however much you are communicating, multiply it by 100 and you are still not communicating enough.)

A component that critically enhanced the effectiveness of this presentation was our decision to distribute a handout to the managers. They were to use this to capture the key points that they would want to use in communicating the message to their employees. We gave them a three-by-five card and a pencil as well, and asked them to write down questions—either ones that *they* had, or that they thought *their employees* would have. This was a wonderful way to create a safe, yet thought-provoking environment. We were purposely allowing them anonymity to ask the really tough questions; and we thought this would give them a chance to see how this one manager (who made the presentation) would answer them. Not only did we answer them real-time, we also captured all of the questions and concerns (along with an effective way of responding) in an FAQ that we provided to all of the managers after all of the training sessions were completed. That way, even if there was a

222

question raised in one session that wasn't raised in another, every manager would be prepared to answer it.

Word began to spread to each of the successive training sessions about the discussions that were taking place. Managers seemed to be much more engaged with each class, and the questions got harder. By the time the final session was completed, the group was much better equipped to deal with the employees' questions and their reactions. They left with both a theoretical understanding of why people resist change and a practical understanding of how to overcome that resistance. No longer was this some amorphous change initiative; they saw concretely and clearly how it needed to be incorporated into their team's performance objectives, and how to engage those on their team in accomplishing them.

Sometimes it's necessary to open your mind to new approaches and techniques that you might not have originally considered when planning for team building. I hope that the following two stories about communication will spark your creativity the next time you have a critical change initiative that needs everyone's commitment to execute. Both involve collages; yes, that's right—*collages*. The first time I used this approach ... well, it was not my idea, it was the plant manager's. In fact, I was very much opposed to it. My mind was narrow; I simply could not imagine 150 manufacturing plant employees in one big room with magazines, scissors, and glue—all for the purpose of creating a common picture of the plant's success going forward. This plant had been experiencing significant productivity and quality problems that were hurting their competitiveness and profitability. The managers had participated in a change management session the day before (similar to the one above) to help them create their own message about the need for the change, and to prepare themselves for the tough questions that their employees were *definitely* going to have.

So here we are in this big room, with everyone seated in cross-functional teams, and I am on the stage up front explaining what they will be doing for the next 90 minutes. I ask them to think about and jot down their thoughts to these questions: "What are you most hopeful about with the new operating model? What is your picture of success?" Over the next 30 minutes, they were to share what they wrote down and together create a collage; literally, a *picture* of what they thought success looks like. I wouldn't have believed it, but after a few minutes of relative quiet and a couple of nervous laughs, the mood of the room suddenly changed. It got loud . . . really loud. All of these voices were raised in animated discussion of the topic, and then I saw someone borrow a magazine from the table to their left, trading the one they didn't need anymore. There were scissors cutting away, others holding down pictures while someone else glued it.

This was *not* what I expected; and I was even more astonished by what happened next. *My intention*—and what I *told them* to do—was for each table to appoint a representative to bring their table's collage up front, and tell the large group what it meant. I thought that having only one person speak would help to keep the process moving. Well, the table that volunteered to go first followed the rules, but the next table had a different idea. They brought all 10 tablemates up front, because, after all, it was *everyone's* collage! After that, every table made it a team effort, and they were exactly right. There was cheering as each team made its way up to the front of the room and told the story of their collage. When we debriefed about what the group had learned, they had clearly gotten it— the reasons for the changes in the plant operating model, how we needed to pull together to make the new plant priorities work, and how this could mean a great opportunity for all of us to shine. I was convinced; this *was* a great idea.

Only a couple of months after this uplifting session, I received a call from a company's sales organization. They were looking for a unique way to kick off their new fiscal year and ensure alignment of strategies across the various subteams. After several planning discussions, I found myself saying something I wouldn't have expected. "Trust me, this will work. I wouldn't have believed it either a few months ago, but I've seen with my own eyes how impactful this can be. Yes, that's right; I said . . . *collages*." While the tool was the same, the purpose and approach were different. It was not to communicate a change this time, but rather to provoke a different dialogue. The groups were to create a collage that represented their particular team's role in reaching the overall vision for success in the coming year, as set forth by the leader in his opening remarks.

As each group summarized what the various pictures on their poster meant for their role and strategies, a heightened sense of interest became palpable within the overall group, much more than a typical PowerPoint deck would evoke. Because they were using pictures to communicate their perspectives, others felt safer to explore more fully their meaning. Thus, they were not giving a simple left-brain interpretation of their strategy, but the underlying meaning and purpose behind it. What we really wanted was to break down silos, and have each department undergo a sense of understanding, ownership, and commitment about what the others were trying to accomplish. Based on all the comments shared during these collage debriefs and at the end of the day, we all succeeded.

Sometimes everyone, even the facilitator, needs to break free from conventional wisdom and take a risk. The leader has a vital role to play in shifting the culture away from fear and blame for failure to one that embraces risk-taking, learning, and continuous improvement. But large-scale, firmwide change can be hard . . . very hard. I know this firsthand. I was working with a company that was driving hard for increased innovation throughout the organization. The CEO asked me and two others from inside the organization to help him find the answer to a critically important question: "Why are people in this organization afraid to take risks, when no one has ever gotten fired for a risk they took?" It was especially perplexing to him because he had consistently and overtly made clear that he wanted people to take risks, and very few people were ever terminated from the company for any reason. It was a very intriguing problem, and we went straight to work to provide him with an answer.

The three of us gathered in an office and began to map out what we saw as the symptoms of the problem. I remember vividly as we each jumped up to the whiteboard to jot down our ideas—sometimes all staying huddled there to add on to each other's thoughts as we captured data points to explain the problem, noted examples to prove a point, or drew diagrams to illustrate what we were thinking. Mike finally said, "I think I have it. People don't take risks because they are afraid of being shunned!" And Jonathan and I immediately knew what he meant.

This strongly patriarchal company rewarded employee loyalty with very few terminations. However, there *was* a punishment in place that some employees might have potentially seen as *worse* than being fired. You could still be a part of the company, and yet not really *belong* anymore; not be *seen* by others. You knew it had happened to someone at this firm when they received a memo that explained a *restructuring*. On the surface, this new role might not appear to be such a bad thing; but for those in the know, it was an obvious demotion even if it wasn't accompanied by a pay cut. I described it as "being moved to the back page of the organization chart—where no one can see you." In fact, it was catastrophic to a long-term employee whose complete sense of belonging and identity was wrapped up in this company. It is true, as the CEO had said, that no one was fired, but this person's light had been snuffed out, and everyone could see the shadows that were left behind. No one wanted to join them on the back of that page. Even if you imagine yourself to be a leader who is driving creativity, innovation, and risk-taking throughout your team, department, or company, what barriers might be unseen to you, but known to others? And what's your plan for discovering and eradicating these?

So, how will your people benefit by adopting a new creative mind-set and embracing the changes that you are advocating? There are, in fact, amazing discoveries made every day about the way our brains function. An article in *HR Magazine* shared the latest findings of recent neuroscience research, which is conducted today using much more sophisticated equipment than scientists have ever had before. I am very happy to report that it shows that humans exhibit something called *brain plasticity* that allows us to constantly learn and change. Whereas the accepted wisdom used to be that our brains were hardwired very early in life, scientists are now aware that "the brain of a 71-year-old is the same as the brain of a 17-year-old in its ability to make new connections. Unfortunately, most people stop learning meaningful new concepts around age 30, and the brain's ability to learn begins to shrink."

This is incredibly exciting for a number of reasons. From a creativity standpoint, as long as you continue to learn and think in new ways, your brain will continue to accommodate this new learning. We don't have to keep doing the things we have always done. Which leads to my second point: this can be a very compelling message for those who are reluctant to change. It's good for you ... and will keep you (or at least *your brain*) young! I think the English cardinal, John Henry Newman, captured it so well when he wrote:

> To live is to change, and to be perfect is to have changed often.

You might be saying to yourself about now, "Well, I have one or two people who need to get their head examined ... because I think they are missing out on that plasticity." And you may be right. It *is* the leader's role to shore up the team and the change effort when the going gets hard. It is *also* the leader's job to take drastic action and hold people accountable if they can't get on board and support the changes that need to happen. If the leader has created a compelling case for change and provided the tools and support that's needed—and can look themselves in the eye and say they have done all they can to help this person make the change—then it is time to let them leave with dignity. After all, everyone wants to get up in the morning and do a good job; and most people don't come to work looking for ways to mess themselves or others up. So eventually, you simply have to release them into the world to find the place where they can shine the brightest.

It is equally important to send the message to others on your team as well that refusing to make the change is *not* an acceptable alternative. Be sure to spend your limited and valuable time and mindshare on those who can and will accept the change; not the ones who need to get off the bus because they don't like the new direction in which it is going. Leadership is about knowing how to distinguish from these two alternatives, and about finding an attainable middle ground.

> The pessimist complains about the wind; the optimist expects it to change; the realist adjusts the sails.
> — William Arthur Ward

Chapter Twenty-One

The End of the Day

What is life? It is the flash of a firefly in the night. It is the breath of a buffalo in the wintertime. It is the little shadow which runs across the grass and loses itself in the sunset.

These were the last words of Crowfoot, the great Blackfoot warrior and orator; and they are as true today as when he breathed his last breath in 1890. We are only on this earth for a relatively short time; no one knows which day may be their last. I have a passion for helping people to find joy and fulfillment in their professional and personal lives, and I truly mean it when I say to them, "Life is too short not to do everything you possibly can to enjoy the life you have now."

My hope is that you will take these words as a call to action—for you to be the light you want to see in the world. As I write this book, I feel a tremendous sense of urgency to help individuals and team leaders to take a look around—at their teammates, co-workers, colleagues, and significant others. What is going on right before you that you have not noticed before? Do you believe you are the only one who wants to find greater meaning and purpose in your daily moments and your life's work? The odds are that you aren't alone. But you must take the risk of believing that it is possible to make a difference, and that you do have it within you to cause a change, even if it is as small a change as that caused by the proverbial wing of a butterfly. For as Mahatma Gandhi once said, "We must become the change we want to see." You might be the spark that takes hold throughout your organization.

What is one thing that inspired or intrigued you from this book, and what are you going to do about it? These bullets (along with the handy chapter references) will remind you of the various stops on our journey and some of the most important tools and techniques you read about, all for the improvement of your team's effectiveness.

- ***Was it the belief that we all have creativity within us? (Chapter 2)*** Did you identify with this new definition of creativity—"To be original . . . to do something no one else would think of." If so, then take a risk and find your unique creativity—writing, painting, developing a new process, or discovering problems and opportunities that others didn't know existed. Remember something that made you special as a child. Look for those creative sparks throughout your day, then do something with them.

- ***What about that new role of leadership? (Chapter 3)*** Do you like the idea of no longer relying on command and control, but instead truly leading through inspiration and collaboration? If so, then look at your current behaviors and determine which are helping you to achieve your vision for leadership through engagement, and which are holding you back. Start small—and stick with it.

- ***Do you think there is untapped talent and unspoken knowledge on your team? (Chapter 4)*** If you do, then have your team members take the HBDI to help you to learn more about each other's strengths and areas of potential development. Then discover ways to use these talents to the team's advantage. You just might find that along the way, you have improved the creative thinking ability and communications effectiveness on your team.

- **How would you currently rate the level of trust on your team? (Chapter 5)**   Not what you might hope for? Consider suggesting a get-to-know-you-better warm-up exercise at your next team meeting—ask about a hidden talent, a first job, where team members grew up. Or have a group milestones dinner and go a level deeper by sharing a significant person or event in your life, and the impact that it (or they) has had on you. Take time to recognize the ways people contribute to the work of the team. Learn from each other using feed forward. Step out of your comfort zone and invite the newest, least-connected team member to join you for lunch.

- **Is conflict on your team a source of creative abrasion? (Chapter 6)**   How diverse is the thinking on your team? How are you capitalizing on those different perspectives to address critical team challenges? Begin with the mindset that conflict is natural, expected, and yes, even desired. Acknowledge and discuss the conflict that everyone knows is currently occurring. Keep the team's focus and energy on the real competition—the one in the marketplace. Deal with that ferocious firefly. Eliminate trustbusters like sarcastic humor. Consider taking your team through "The Jungle Escape." Find a way to reconnect with those who are distant, disengaged, or just plain dismal.

- **How much of your team's energy is wasted with irrelevant, personality-based infighting? (Chapter 7)**   In that last high-conflict one-on-one situation, did you ask yourself, "Why would a reasonable, rational, and decent person act like this?" Use what you learned from the individual HBDIs to see how much of the team conflict is simply a failure to communicate. As a leader, what kind of example are you setting? Let the optimal flow and coaching from others help you to resolve it. Remember, don't be ruled by the tyranny of the "or"; seek out the third way. Learn about a day in your co-worker's life.

- **Do you know what the vision for team success is, and how you will know when you get there?**

(Chapter 8)   As a team, dedicate time to focus on the future. Create a common understanding of the critical role that the group plays in the overall company's success. Make sure everyone sees how each role contributes and is interconnected and interdependent. Break down those silos that keep you from working collaboratively. Understand the barriers and challenges facing the team.

- *How do you turn this vision picture into a concrete plan? (Chapter 9)*   Determine tangible, clear measures for success. Focus on the critical few. Make those tough strategic decisions—not only what you *will* do, but just as importantly what you *won't* do. Engage your critical stakeholders. Monitor and course correct. Celebrate your successes.

- *What would it take to make this the best team you were ever a part of? (Chapter 10)*   Ask people to share their prior team experiences, and use these inspirational stories as the foundation for designing the four to six guiding principles for how this team will work together. After you create them, live up to them and expect everyone else on the team to do the same.

- *Is your team meeting the most exciting time of the week? (Chapter 11)*   No? What would it take to make it so? Don't give in to the common thinking that all meetings are bad and ineffective, because that doesn't have to be the case if you commit to doing the hard work that will make it better. Find out what people expect and want from these meetings, and then redesign the agenda to deliver that. Create an environment for fully engaged participation by all team members, and permit nothing less. Don't allow a select few to dominate (especially the team leader). Spice up your meetings with variety—in the location, the topics, the process, and at least in the seating! Start using a timer. You may laugh, but I—and my clients—swear that it works.

- *Does your team have really productive discussions that end with clear decisions, actions, and accountabilities? (Chapter 12)*   Start today by figuring out which items on the meeting agenda require a decision to be made, construct a clear and explicit decision-making process, and understand the rationale for the path chosen. Create conflict norms that will ensure that all voices are effectively heard. Send information out in advance to promote informed participation. Balance inquiry and advocacy. Keep a curious mind-set. Flip chart *Who? What?* and *By When?* Ask who needs to know what you all just decided and figure out how to communicate with them effectively. Remember WIIFM.

- ***Is the team leader keeping too tight a lid on the jar? (Chapter 13)*** If you are this team leader, then you can directly impact this *if* you think making a change is important enough and you commit to doing what it takes. Beware any dominating behavior in team meetings. Share your opinion last. Let small, breakout groups discuss controversial or sensitive topics before a large group debrief. Learn how to manage yourself and lead the team effectively through high-conflict situations and bring a discussion to closure, with full commitment from all team members to fully implement the final decision.

- ***Do your team members hold themselves accountable for living up to their commitments? (Chapter 14)*** If you don't have a common picture of what great personal accountability looks like, then start there and create one as a team. Make sure that you delegate and follow up effectively. Celebrate the right behaviors in the right way for each person on the team. Use team meetings as a showcase for members to uphold their commitments to each other and to you. Conduct an accountability assessment as a team, pick a few areas to improve upon, and then do it. Remember: "We give ourselves credit for our intentions; but hold others accountable for their results." Learn . . . then coach.

- ***What is your team doing to spark creativity in addressing the critical problems and opportunities it sees? (Chapter 15)*** Set aside time for creative problem solving. Pick problems about which people feel passionately. Be specific with the problem; it really will release more creative juices than leaving it wide open. Make it safe to make a suggestion. Get familiar with the creative problem-solving process I shared with you. Heck, use your creativity to improve upon it and make it your own!

- *Are there tools and techniques that your team should become familiar with and use on a regular basis? (Chapter 16)* Get each person to bring one creativity toy to the next problem-solving session. Try out the mind-mapping tool if you are left-brain oriented; or let the right-brainers give the brain-writing technique a chance. Use the impact/effort grid to aid your next decision; it is an easy and inventive way to ensure the entire team's collaboration on solving a specific problem. Employ a decision matrix for those tougher, more complex choices.

- *When was the last time your team got out of the office for a creative excursion? (Chapter 17)* Ask each person to bring one suggestion for an expedition to your next meeting. Go with an open mind, and come back with new ideas. Debrief what you learned and how you can apply it. Make it fun . . . make it happen.

- *Which department, division, or business unit does your team have the greatest conflict with? (Chapter 18)* And what kind of impact does this conflict have on your business results and theirs? Bring the leaders of the two groups together so that you begin on the same page. Find out what they are held accountable for and how your team can proactively help them to achieve their goals and vice versa. You both might be surprised by what you discover. Then make sure you both make good on your commitments.

- *Do you see the spark of creativity going on around you, perhaps that others aren't seeing . . . yet? (Chapter 19)* Be on the lookout for good things going on around you. I always have believed that you find what you look for. I know there are synchronous fireflies in your backyard waiting to be discovered by you. Call them best practices if you prefer; but look for them, share them with your team, adapt them to help all of you to excel.

- ***Do you like being the changer better than being the changee? (Chapter 20)*** Think about how many change initiatives you currently have underway. Be sure that the purpose of each, as well as how it supports the larger organizational strategy, is clear. (Remember the rain cloud metaphor?) Communicate your compelling change message over and over, using a variety of vehicles. Use the optimal flow to create it. Go out on a limb—try the collage exercise for one of your most difficult change initiatives.

Answering the above questions will help to light a fire under yourself and your team, and become the light you want to see in the world. Take the first step on the path to change, and simply start where you are. Your life and the life of your team can be different because of the actions you take. Pull out a sheet of paper. Write down just one thing from the list above that you really want to do—not what you think you *should* do, but something you *want* to do. Put your creativity to work to figure out how to get it done. Put a due date on it. Share it with one other person that you trust. Hold yourself accountable for achieving it. If you are the leader of a team, be the role model of someone you would want to follow. When you feel the positive reinforcement that one action causes, you will want to do it again. Start a movement—make it happen!

I am an avid believer in the power of paying it forward. You can recapture a lost dream and make a difference in the world. I have seen the wondrous things that occur when one unselfishly gives to another without thought of how or when repayment will be made. I am sure you have found this to be true on at least one, if not multiple occasions in your own personal experience. When you give to others, you receive so much more in return. My hope is that you have found something worthy of remembering from this book, and that you will pass it on to another . . . like the spark of the firefly which magically illuminates a dark night.

Index

BusinessWeek, 224
Buy-in, for decision making, 138

C
Caring, in conflict resolution, 64
Catmull, Ed, 22, 228–229
Celebrating success, 101
Center for Creative Leadership, 20
Change:
 creating compelling case for, 234–235
 directing, 232–233
 leaders as agents of, 234–235
 resistance to, 231–232
Chemiluminescence, 171
Closure, in decision making, 143
Coca-Cola, 59, 104, 232
Cognitive dissonance, 15, 235
Collaboration, 20–21
Collaborative innovation, 20–22
Collages, 238–240
Collins, Jim, 27
Commitment, compliance vs., 233
Common purpose, 77–91
 and force field analysis, 89–91
 strategic planning for, 79–91
 vision for, 77–79, 86–91
Common vision, 77–79
Communication:
 of decision making results, 144–145
 difficulties in, 103
 effective listening, 152, 153
 by leaders, 234–240
 of opinions, 150, 152
 optimal flow technique for, 67–68, 216–218
 in passionate debates, 152–155
 preferred styles of, 65–68
 at team meetings, 149
 of transformation initiatives, 234–235
Communication matrix, 99–101
Competition, external, 162

Compliance, commitment vs., 233
Conceptual Age, 19–20
Conflict:
 acknowledging, 54
 as creative abrasion, 51–61
 discomfort in dealing with, 129
 hidden, 54
 interteam, *see* Interteam conflict
 from lack of guiding principles, 107–108
 and productivity, 53
Conflict norms, 133–136
Conflict resolution, 63–73
 and communication preferences, 65–68
 "A Day in the Life" exercise for, 70–71
 guidelines for, 71–73
 holistic view in, 64
 between leader and subordinate, 68–70
 optimal flow for communication in, 67–68
 in team setting, 70–71
Consultative decision making, 138
Contributions, recognition of, 44–46
Copeland, Jonathan, 222–223
Correct questions, 158
Cortisol, 174
Creative abrasion, 51–61
 creating environment for, 52–53
 and disengagement, 58–61
 HBDI User Guide for creating, 66–68
 and individuals who won't share, 55–57
 mindset for, 52–54
 and sarcasm, 57–58
Creative brain trust, 228–229
Creativity, 4–5, 9–15
 as continuum, 11–12
 designating time for, 224–225

differing views of, 10
everyday, 172
loss of, 10–11
rediscovering, 11, 14–15.
  See also Sparking creativity
strengths as indicators of, 14
Creativity tools. *See*
  Brainstorming,
  Brainwriting, Excursions,
  Mindmapping
Critical processes, cross-
  departmental, 211–215
Crowfoot, 243
Crucial Conversations (Kerry
  Patterson), 64
Cultural differences, conflict
  norms and, 136
Customers:
  inspiration for innovation
  from, 227–228
  and vision development,
  88–89

D
Dashboard, 97
"A Day in the Life" exercise,
  70–71
Deadlines, for delegated tasks,
  160
Debates, handling, 152–155
Decision making, 129–145
  accountability in, 165–166
  after passionate debates,
  154–155
  agreed-upon process for, 137
  closure in, 143
  communicating results of,
  144–145
  creating conflict norms for,
  133–136
  implementation of, 142–144
  leader as role model in,
  133
  leader's role in, 140–141
  levels of, 138–140
  outside of team, 142–143
  planning based on, 143–144
  preconceived, 140–141

preliminary information for,
  141
rule of 3 for, 141–142
safe environment for, 132–133
stakeholders in, 144
suggested process for, 131
for team decisions, 165–166
Vroom-Yetton model for,
  137–140
wide variety of ideas for,
  140
Decision Matrix, 191, 194–198
Delegation, 159–165
  and allocation of resources/
  support, 159
  explaining rationale behind,
  159
  and progress-tracking
  procedures, 160–165
Differences, trying to eliminate,
  27
Disengagement, 58–61
Diversity:
  on teams, 53–54
  of team strengths, *see*
  Uniqueness
  in thinking, 51
The Diversity Game, 31
Dominating leaders, 109–111,
  148–155
  abandonment of legitimate
  role vs., 148
  avoiding role of, 149
  as dysfunctional, 148
  feedback for, 148–149
  and handling of debates,
  152–155
  signs of, 148
  and tendency to defer to
  leaders, 149–152
Drucker, Peter, 19

E
Edison, Thomas, 10
Effective listening, 152, 153
Einstein, Albert, 25
Emerson, Ralph Waldo, 37
Emotional intelligence, 21